QUEUE

High School Reading Comprehension

Teacher Edition

by Jonathan D. Kantrowitz and Sarah M. Williams
Edited by Patricia F. Braccio

Item Code QWK 7891 · Copyright © 2011 Queue, Inc.

Queue, Inc. · 80 Hathaway Drive, Stratford, CT 06615
(800) 232-2224 · Fax: (800) 775-2729 · www.qworkbooks.com

TABLE OF CONTENTS

TEACHER'S INTRODUCTION

Reading and writing are essential skills. A person who can understand what she or he has read possesses a key for learning in any field. Writing is a primary form of communication in our society and in today's world. An ability to communicate well is important in many life settings, including school, all fields of work, and home. Those individuals who are able to communicate clearly can participate and contribute to life in a rich and fulfilling way.

Test preparation is a matter of great importance in high school. The ability to perform well on tests is directly related to students' reading and writing skills. Students need to develop and refine such skills as reading critically, constructing informed opinions, organizing thoughts, communicating opinions appropriately for a specific audience, and using standard English grammar and vocabulary correctly.

This reading comprehension workbook is designed to give high school students the opportunity to read short passages of fiction, nonfiction, plays, and poetry; to reflect on what they have read; and then to respond to questions. The book is a sampler of some of the finest works of literature, as well as some of the world's most renowned dramatic and poetic pieces. Hopefully, the practice offered in this workbook will contribute to improving student performance. However, another hoped-for result of using this high school reading comprehension workbook—especially for those students who have not yet developed an appreciation for literature and good writing—is that students would be exposed to many writings in which imaginative expression, aesthetic form, universality of ideas, and permanence are characteristic features.

In introducing this workbook to your classes, clearly define each type of reading. Then, after your students have used the book for a while, it might be helpful to analyze which form, if any, is causing them difficulty. In this Teacher's Edition, the appropriate reading, critical-thinking, and literary analysis skills for each individual passage are listed at the end of the passages. This list may also help to identify areas where students will need more practice.

The questions following the reading passages are of two types: multiple-choice and open-ended. The multiple-choice questions require direct feedback of information given in the passage and, in some cases, application of the reasoning skills of thought and analysis. The choice for most answers should be clear-cut. However, most wrong choices will include references to the passage. Students who do not read the passage carefully and/or do not fully comprehend it—but just look to match words in the answer with words in the passage—will be most likely to choose a wrong answer.

The open-ended questions give students the chance to express their understanding of a passage and, in some instances, also present an invitation for creative writing. These questions ask students to think about what they have read and then to write one or more paragraphs that show insight into the reading selection. In many cases, students are being asked to employ terminology and concepts specific to reading comprehension to analyze a particular piece. This process works to reinforce these ideas and asks students to fully express their understanding of more conceptual-type information that they may be less comfortable with.

The combination of good teaching and lots of practice will help students to improve the effectiveness of their writing. A body of criteria to use in evaluating your students' writing is presented in the Writing Tasks Scoring Rubric (below). Keep in mind that many other rubrics can help you do this.

READING COMPREHENSION SKILLS

Reading Fiction

Analyzing Conflict, Plot, and Setting
Analyzing Characters
Analyzing Point of View
Analyzing Irony
Interpreting the Theme and Main Idea
Distinguishing Among Different Genres of Fiction

Reading Poetry

Analyzing Figurative Language
Analyzing Sound Devices and Rhythm
Analyzing Diction: Connotation and Denotation
Analyzing Paradox, Pun, and Oxymoron
Distinguishing Among Different Genres of Poetry

Reading Nonfiction

Analyzing Text Structure and Organization
Interpreting Text Features
Evaluating Validity, Credibility, and Reliability of Text
Analyzing Persuasion and Propaganda Techniques
Distinguishing Among Different Genres of Nonfiction

Critical Thinking

Using Prior Knowledge
Summarizing and Paraphrasing Information
Distinguishing Fact and Opinion
Analyzing Cause and Effect
Analyzing Problem and Solution
Making Inferences
Drawing Conclusions
Making Generalizations
Comparing and Contrasting

Literary Analysis

Analyzing the Author's Purpose
Recognizing the Author's Bias and Beliefs
Evaluating the Author's Craft
Evaluating the Author's Style
Evaluating the Quality of the Literature
Interpreting References from Culture and the Past
Examining Cultures and Historical Periods in Literature
Examining Literature from Several Critical Perspectives
Analyzing Development of Tone and Mood

Writing Tasks Scoring Rubric

Score of 1
- There is no good beginning or ending to the writing.
- The writing does not speak to the topic in a clear and organized way.
- There are numerous errors in usage.
- There are incomplete sentences and/or poor sentence structure.
- There are numerous errors in spelling, punctuation and capitalization.

Score of 2
- The writer fails to employ a good opening or closing to the piece.
- The writing drifts off focus.
- It lacks transitions between ideas.
- It does not contain well-developed descriptions or elaboration.
- It contains numerous and serious errors in usage, structure and mechanics.

Score of 3
- The writing exhibits some problems with organization.
- There is some connection between ideas.
- There may be repetition of ideas or lack of details.
- Sentences are all very similar in structure.
- There are still some errors in usage, syntax and mechanics.

Score of 4
- The organization is improving but still loosely connected.
- There is still some difficulty with developing details.
- There are still errors, but they usually do not interfere with the intended meaning of the author.

Score of 5
- The writing is generally well developed.
- Ideas are presented and organized logically.
- Different sentence patterns are used.
- There are very few errors.

Score of 6
- The writing is well developed and coherent.
- Ideas are presented in a logical manner.
- Transitions help the flow of the writing.
- Different types of sentence patterns are used.
- The writing contains details and good descriptions.
- There is only the occasional error.

Going Beyond the Text: Tips for Teachers

Don't limit yourself to just what is in the text. Here are a few suggestions on how you might use ideas from the text in planning additional lessons.

Teachers might use some of the writing tasks as first drafts. Students might work to revise or to improve some aspects of what they each have written. Students' responses could serve also to identify needed lessons in editing to correct common errors of spelling, punctuation or syntax. Another lesson might be to help students to use different pre-writing strategies to help them to organize their ideas before they write.

Some of the written work might be read or shared with the class to show how specific individuals responded differently to the same information.

Poems are just another form of writing. They tell stories, share feelings, and create word pictures. Similar activities to those in the text can be done using other poems. Moreover, students can learn about the different ways poems are written. They can be encouraged to write their own poems. Some of the stories or themes in the book may be used as ideas for original poems.

Any passage in the book—fiction, nonfiction, drama, or poetry—can form the basis for a class discussion. Some passages may also be appropriate for dramatization.

Themes or texts included in the themes might spark further reading or research by students. Encourage your students to become experts on a topic. Challenge them to put their reading and writing skills to work.

TO THE STUDENTS

In this workbook, you will read many fiction passages, as well as some nonfiction, poetry, and plays. You will then answer multiple-choice and open-ended questions about what you have read.

As you read and answer the questions, please remember:

- You may refer back to the text as often as you like.

- Read each question very carefully and choose the **best** answer.

- Indicate the correct multiple-choice answers directly in this workbook. Circle or underline the correct answer.

- Write your open-ended responses directly on the lines provided. If you need more space, use a separate piece of paper to complete your answer.

Here are some guidelines to remember when writing your open-ended answers:

- Organize your ideas and express them clearly.

- Correctly organize and separate your paragraphs.

- Support your ideas with examples when necessary.

- Make your writing interesting and enjoyable to read.

- Check your spelling and use of grammar and punctuation.

- Your answers should be accurate and complete.

THE GIFT OF THE MAGI

by O. Henry

One dollar and eighty-seven cents. That was all. And sixty cents of it was in pennies. Pennies saved one and two at a time by bulldozing the grocer and the vegetable man and the butcher until one's cheeks burned with the silent imputation of parsimony that such close dealing implied. Three times Della counted it. One dollar and eighty-seven cents. And the next day would be Christmas.

There was clearly nothing to do but flop down on the shabby little couch and howl. So Della did it. Which instigates the moral reflection that life is made up of sobs, sniffles, and smiles, with sniffles predominating.

While the mistress of the home is gradually subsiding from the first stage to the second, take a look at the home. A furnished flat at $8 per week. It did not exactly beggar description, but it certainly had that word on the lookout for the mendicancy squad.

In the vestibule below was a letter-box into which no letter would go, and an electric button from which no mortal finger could coax a ring. Also appertaining thereunto was a card bearing the name "Mr. James Dillingham Young."

The "Dillingham" had been flung to the breeze during a former period of prosperity when its possessor was being paid $30 per week. Now, when the income was shrunk to $20, though, they were thinking seriously of contracting to a modest and unassuming D. But whenever Mr. James Dillingham Young came home and reached his flat above he was called "Jim" and greatly hugged by Mrs. James Dillingham Young, already introduced to you as Della. Which is all very good.

Della finished her cry and attended to her cheeks with the powder rag. She stood by the window and looked out dully at a gray cat walking a gray fence in a gray backyard. Tomorrow would be Christmas Day, and she had only $1.87 with which to buy Jim a present. She had been saving every penny she could for months, with this result. Twenty dollars a week doesn't go far. Expenses had been greater than she had calculated. They always are. Only $1.87 to buy a present for Jim. Her Jim. Many a happy hour she had spent planning for something nice for him. Something fine and rare and sterling—something just a little bit near to being worthy of the honor of being owned by Jim.

There was a pier glass between the windows of the room. Perhaps you have seen a pier glass in an $8 flat. A very thin and very agile person may, by observing his reflection in a rapid sequence of longitudinal strips, obtain a fairly accurate conception of his looks. Della, being slender, had mastered the art.

Suddenly she whirled from the window and stood before the glass. Her eyes were shining brilliantly, but her face had lost its color within twenty seconds. Rapidly she pulled down her hair and let it fall to its full length.

Now, there were two possessions of the James Dillingham Youngs in which they both took a mighty pride. One was Jim's gold watch that had been his father's and his grandfather's. The other was Della's hair. Had the queen of Sheba lived in the flat across the airshaft, Della would have let her hair hang out the window some day to dry just to depreciate Her Majesty's jewels and gifts. Had King Solomon been the janitor, with all his treasures piled up in the basement, Jim would have pulled out his watch every time he passed, just to see him pluck at his beard from envy.

So now Della's beautiful hair fell about her rippling and shining like a cascade of brown waters. It reached below her knee and made itself almost a garment for her. And then she did it up again nervously and quickly. Once she faltered for a minute and stood still while a tear or two splashed on the worn red carpet.

On went her old brown jacket; on went her old brown hat. With a whirl of skirts and with the brilliant sparkle still in her eyes, she fluttered out the door and down the stairs to the street.

Where she stopped the sign read: "Mme. Sofronie. Hair Goods of All Kinds." One flight up Della ran, and collected herself, panting. Madame, large, too white, chilly, hardly looked the "Sofronie."

"Will you buy my hair?" asked Della.

"I buy hair," said Madame. "Take yer hat off and let's have a sight at the looks of it."

Down rippled the brown cascade.

"Twenty dollars," said Madame, lifting the mass with a practiced hand.

"Give it to me quick," said Della.

Oh, and the next two hours tripped by on rosy wings. Forget the hashed metaphor. She was ransacking the stores for Jim's present.

She found it at last. It surely had been made for Jim and no one else. There was no other like it in any of the stores, and she had turned all of them inside out. It was a platinum fob chain simple and chaste in design, properly proclaiming its value by substance alone and not by meretricious ornamentation—as all good things should do. It was even worthy of The Watch. As soon as she saw it she knew that it must be Jim's. It was like him. Quietness and value—the description applied to both. Twenty-one dollars they took from her for it, and she hurried home with the 87 cents.

With that chain on his watch Jim might be properly anxious about the time in any company. Grand as the watch was, he sometimes looked at it on the sly on account of the old leather strap that he used in place of a chain.

When Della reached home her intoxication gave way a little to prudence and reason. She got out her curling irons and lighted the gas and went to work repairing the ravages made by generosity added to love. Which is always a tremendous task, dear friends—a mammoth task.

Within forty minutes her head was covered with tiny, close-lying curls that made her look wonderfully like a truant schoolboy. She looked at her reflection in the mirror long, carefully, and critically.

"If Jim doesn't kill me," she said to herself, "before he takes a second look at me, he'll say I look like a Coney Island chorus girl. But what could I do—oh! what could I do with a dollar and eighty-seven cents?"

At 7 o'clock the coffee was made and the frying-pan was on the back of the stove hot and ready to cook the chops.

Jim was never late. Della doubled the fob chain in her hand and sat on the corner of the table near the door that he always entered. Then she heard his step on the stair away down on the first flight, and she turned white for just a moment. She had a habit of saying a little silent prayer about the simplest everyday things, and now she whispered: "Please God, make him think I am still pretty."

The door opened and Jim stepped in and closed it. He looked thin and very serious. Poor fellow, he was only twenty-two—and to be burdened with a family! He needed a new overcoat and he was without gloves.

Jim stopped inside the door, as immovable as a setter at the scent of quail.

His eyes were fixed upon Della, and there was an expression in them that she could not read, and it terrified her. It was not anger, nor surprise, nor disapproval, nor horror, nor any of the sentiments that she had been prepared for. He simply stared at her fixedly with that peculiar expression on his face.

Della wriggled off the table and went for him.

"Jim, darling," she cried, "don't look at me that way. I had my hair cut off and sold because I couldn't have lived through Christmas without giving you a present. It'll grow out again—you won't mind, will you? I just had to do it. My hair grows awfully fast. Say 'Merry Christmas!' Jim, and let's be happy. You don't know what a nice—what a beautiful, nice gift I've got for you."

"You've cut off your hair?" asked Jim, laboriously, as if he had not arrived at that patent fact yet even after the hardest mental labor.

"Cut it off and sold it," said Della. "Don't you like me just as well, anyhow? I'm me without my hair, ain't I?"

Jim looked about the room curiously.

"You say your hair is gone?" he said, with an air almost of idiocy.

"You needn't look for it," said Della. "It's sold, I tell you—sold and gone, too. It's Christmas Eve, boy. Be good to me, for it went for you. Maybe the hairs of my head were numbered," she went on with sudden serious sweetness, "but nobody could ever count my love for you. Shall I put the chops on, Jim?"

Out of his trance Jim seemed quickly to wake. He enfolded his Della. For ten seconds let us regard with discreet scrutiny some inconsequential object in the other direction. Eight dollars a week or a million

a year—what is the difference? A mathematician or a wit would give you the wrong answer. The magi brought valuable gifts, but that was not among them. This dark assertion will be illuminated later on.

Jim drew a package from his overcoat pocket and threw it upon the table.

"Don't make any mistake, Dell," he said, "about me. I don't think there's anything in the way of a haircut or a shave or a shampoo that could make me like my girl any less. But if you'll unwrap that package you may see why you had me going a while at first."

White fingers and nimble tore at the string and paper. And then an ecstatic scream of joy; and then, alas! a quick feminine change to hysterical tears and wails, necessitating the immediate employment of all the comforting powers of the lord of the flat.

For there lay The Combs—the set of combs, side and back, that Della had worshipped long in a Broadway window. Beautiful combs, pure tortoise shell, with jeweled rims—just the shade to wear in the beautiful vanished hair. They were expensive combs, she knew, and her heart had simply craved and yearned over them without the least hope of possession. And now, they were hers, but the tresses that should have adorned the coveted adornments were gone.

But she hugged them to her bosom, and at length she was able to look up with dim eyes and a smile and say: "My hair grows so fast, Jim!"

And then Della leaped up like a little singed cat and cried, "Oh, oh!"

Jim had not yet seen his beautiful present. She held it out to him eagerly upon her open palm. The dull precious metal seemed to flash with a reflection of her bright and ardent spirit.

3

"Isn't it a dandy, Jim? I hunted all over town to find it. You'll have to look at the time a hundred times a day now. Give me your watch. I want to see how it looks on it."

Instead of obeying, Jim tumbled down on the couch and put his hands under the back of his head and smiled.

"Dell," said he, "let's put our Christmas presents away and keep 'em a while. They're too nice to use just at present. I sold the watch to get the money to buy your combs. And now suppose you put the chops on."

The magi, as you know, were wise men—wonderfully wise men—who brought gifts to the Babe in the manger. They invented the art of giving Christmas presents. Being wise, their gifts were no doubt wise ones, possibly bearing the privilege of exchange in case of duplication. And here I have lamely related to you the uneventful chronicle of two foolish children in a flat who most unwisely sacrificed for each other the greatest treasures of their house. But in a last word to the wise of these days let it be said that of all who give gifts these two were the wisest. Of all who give and receive gifts, such as they are wisest. Everywhere they are wisest. They are the magi.

 POINT OF VIEW refers to who is actually telling the story. The "who" is often called the **narrator** of the story. Most stories are told in one of the following points of view:

✳ **First Person**: The author tells the story from one of the characters' points of view. The character can either be a major or minor character. It is characterized by the use of first person (I, We), and the audience only sees the thoughts of that one character.

✳ **Third Person Limited**: The author tells the story from the point of view of a narrator who can read the thoughts and emotions of just one character; therefore, the author better knows and makes judgments about this character. The narrator follows that character throughout the story but does not know about the thoughts and emotions of the other characters.

✳ **Third Person Omniscient:** The author tells the story from the point of view of a narrator who can read the minds and thoughts of all the characters. This narrator can comment and interpret all characters in the story and is said to be "all knowing."

✳ **Objective:** This narrator merely "records" what can be heard or seen in a story. This narrator cannot get into the thoughts of any character.

1. From which point of view is the story written?
   a. first person
   b. *third person limited*
   c. third person omniscient
   d. objective

4

Determining a **NARRATOR/AUTHOR'S BIAS** requires you to recognize the **narrator/author's opinion or belief** on an issue. In order to do this, you must carefully look to separate fact from opinion as well as to pay attention to specific details and words in the text.

In fiction, it may be helpful to identify when the narrator/author is speaking by drawing a circle around those places in the text. You may then begin to understand an author's bias or beliefs by analyzing those particular passages.

In nonfiction, you must carefully look at who wrote and published the material, identify specific word choices that illustrate emotion, consider how the information compares or contrasts to what you already know, and be aware of faulty logic or persuasive techniques.

2. According to the narrator, which type of moments mostly make up life?

   a. happy moments
   b. terribly sad moments
   c. somewhat sad moments
   d. angry moments

TONE is the attitude of the author or narrator towards the subject on which he or she is writing. This may even include the way the narrator feels towards the reader or himself/herself.

In our spoken language, tone is determined by the inflections we use in our voice. However, in literature we have to look for clues to determine tone. Tone is established by the following components of a piece of writing: word choice (diction); arrangement of words (syntax); detail selection; imagery; and figurative language.

Very similar to tone is the **MOOD** of a story. Mood refers to the way the audience is made to feel while reading the text and is created in the same way that tone is established.

3. Which of the following **best** describes the tone of the story as the narrator portrays Della in the first four paragraphs?

   a. somewhat comic
   b. extremely sad
   c. somewhat angry
   d. mostly happy

To infer means to conclude based on evidence or personal experience. For example, if a girl blows out candles and opens presents, it may be inferred that it is her birthday. Whenever you understand something that is only hinted at in the text, you are making an inference. Inferring also relates to the following processes:

* **Drawing Conclusions**: Drawing conclusions is using written or visual cues to figure out something that is not directly stated.

* **Making and Analyzing Predictions**: Predicting involves figuring out what will happen next based on evidence in the story. Later you should compare and contrast those predictions with what actually happens in the text.

* **Making Generalizations**: A generalization is a broad statement about a particular subject made based on a number of facts or observations about the subject.

4. The narrator mentions that Della wanted to buy Jim "something fine and rare and sterling—something just a little bit near to being worthy of the honor of being owned by Jim." From this quote, what can be inferred?

   a. Della considers herself equal to Jim.
   b. Jim treats Della like a queen.
   c. ***Della is subservient to Jim.***
   d. Jim wants to make Della happy.

5. What is the most likely climax of the story?

   a. Della cuts off all of her hair for $20.
   b. ***Jim arrives home and presents the combs.***
   c. Jim reveals he sold his watch for money.
   d. Della cries because she only has $1.87.

6. Right after Jim mentions that he sold his watch he says, "And now suppose you put the chops on." What is the most likely reason that he says this?

   a. He is angry that Della cut her hair.
   b. He is upset that he sold his watch.
   c. He is sad that he can't use his gift.
   d. ***He doesn't want Della to be upset.***

Irony is the difference between what is expected of something (or how something actually appears) and what actually is (the reality of something); irony is divided into three categories:

❋ **Situational Irony**: This is when what the audience expects to occur does not actually occur. This type of irony includes things such as surprise endings to books or stories.

❋ **Dramatic Irony**: This is when the audience knows more than a character in a story. It is often used in plays.

Example: The audience knows that someone is hiding in the room with a certain character but that character doesn't know; this is dramatic irony.

❋ **Verbal Irony**: This is when the opposite of what is said is true or the opposite of what is said is meant. Sarcasm is one form of verbal irony.

Example: Someone walks out into a cold, rainy day and says, "Ah, it's a beautiful day," and the listener understands that the speaker probably means the opposite.

7. What type of irony is found in the final paragraph when Jim says, "They're too nice to use just at present"?

    a. situational irony
    b. dramatic irony
    c. verbal irony
    d. no irony

7

Figurative language refers to the use of figures of speech. When you use a figure of speech, you are saying one thing by saying another. While some experts have named as many as 250 figures of speech, the main ones are listed below:

✳ **Simile**: This is a comparison between two unlike things using *like*, *as*, *than*, *similar to*, *resembles*, or *seems*.

    Example: She is like the sun.

✳ **Metaphor**: This is a comparison between two unlike things by saying that one thing "is" something else.

    Example: She was a rock.

✳ **Personification**: This gives human characteristics to abstract ideas or objects.

    Example: The tree limbs reached out and grabbed for me.

✳ **Hyperbole**: This is an exaggeration of the truth.

    Example: I could eat a whole cow.

8. The narrator comments that "Della's beautiful hair fell about her rippling and shining like a cascade of brown waters." Which figure of speech is used in this statement?

    a. hyperbole
    b. metaphor
    c. simile
    d. imagery

9. Describe the setting's effect on the overall story. How would you describe the couple's apartment? How does the apartment add to the overall effect of the story? Use specific details from the text to support your answer.

One possible answer:

The story most likely takes place in New York (with mention of Broadway and Coney Island) in the early 1900s (judging from technology, clothing, and value of dollar). The couple's apartment is rundown and shabby. The narrator mentions that the couple has a broken letter-box and electric doorbell. In addition, the narrator uses a pun when he says "It did not exactly beggar description, but it certainly had that word on the lookout for the mendicancy squad." The word, "beggar," in this case is first used in the sense of exceeding the limits, resources, or capabilities being described; however, later it refers to the idea of actually being impoverished and needing money. This description adds to the story; the gifts appear even more extravagant for the couple because they have so very little, further emphasizing the irony that neither of them, in the end, can actually use these extravagant gifts.

10. What would you say is the major conflict in the story? How is this conflict resolved at the end of the story? Use specific details to support your point.

One possible answer:

The major conflict in this story is the human person vs. himself or herself. The conflict is introduced when Della doesn't feel that she has enough money to buy Jim a worthy gift for Christmas. She has been saving for so long and still only has $1.87. The story builds to the climax when Jim arrives home and Della wonders whether or not Jim will love the gift despite the sacrifice she has had to make to get it. This conflict resolves itself as both characters realize the sacrifice the other has had to make. Both Della and Jim are happy at the end of the story. Jim mentions that they should "put our Christmas presents away and keep 'em a while" and then recommends that they start dinner. He is not focused on the gift but rather on the love of his wife. While Della had been worried at the beginning about how to afford a worthy gift, she learned that the true value has no ties to money at all; both she and Jim love the gifts not for the monetary price but for the loving sacrifice each was willing to make for the other.

9

Diction is the author's word choice when writing. In order to analyze diction, a word's denotation and connotation must be considered. Denotation is the actual dictionary definition of the word. Connotation includes all of the associations implied by a word in addition to its literal meaning.

For example, although *odor* and *scent* both are defined as a smell (the denotative meaning), we normally associated *odor* with a negative smell and *scent* with a positive smell (the connotative meaning).

11. O. Henry writes, "She stood by the window and looked out dully at a gray cat walking a gray fence in a gray backyard." What effect does the repetition of the word, "gray," have on the short story? What is the connotation of the word, "gray"? Why does the author use this word repeatedly at this point in the text? Use specific evidence from the text to support your answer.

The word, "gray," emphasizes the depressing world in which Della lives. The color gray often connotes gloom, darkness, and sadness. Della feels all of these at this point in the story. She has just finished crying because she doesn't have enough money to buy Jim a nice present. The emphasis on "gray" helps to show that Della feels surrounded by hopelessness at this point in the story.

12. Within the story, the author alludes to King Solomon and the Queen of Sheba. The Queen of Sheba was known to be beautiful, intelligent, and very rich. King Solomon was said to exceed all kings in riches and in wisdom. At one point the Queen of Sheba tested King Solomon's wisdom and, when he succeeded, she showered him in gifts. How do these allusions add to the development of the story? Use specific evidence from the text to support your answer.

One possible answer:

Both the allusions help to illustrate the value of the couple's most prized possessions. The narrator mentions that if both the Queen of Sheba and King Solomon lived in the building, Jim and Della would flaunt their possessions. Della would hang her hair out the window to dry "just to depreciate Her Majesty's jewels and gifts." In addition, Jim would pull out his watch when passing King Solomon "just to see him pluck at his beard from envy." The narrator notes that even in the presence of high royalty, Della and Jim would still hold their prized possessions in higher esteem than anything the king or queen could own. Because the audience understands the value of these possessions to Della and Jim, their sacrifice of these possessions for love later in the story is even more powerful, helping to build the overall theme.

13. What is ironic about this short story? What type of irony is it? How does it add to the main idea (theme) in the passage?

This passage contains situational irony. The audience expects that Jim will love the new chain for his watch that Della buys him for Christmas or maybe even be upset with Dell for sacrificing her beautiful hair. However, neither of these situations occurs. Rather the audience is surprised that Jim has sold his prized possession to buy Dell a Christmas present that she can no longer use. The story ends with neither of the two being able to the use other's gift, something the audience doesn't expect in this tale; however, it adds to the theme of love and sacrifice. While each person has given up something very valuable and received something unusable, both of them are still very happy at the end. It is really not about the gifts at all, but rather about the fact that each was willing to sacrifice something for the love of the other.

14. At the end of the story, the narrator first calls the couple "foolish children . . . who most unwisely sacrificed for each other the greatest treasures of their house." The narrator then says that "of all who give gifts these two were the wisest." How does your opinion of the couple compare and/or contrast with the author's opinion? Use specific evidence from the text to support your opinion of the couple.

Students may agree that Jim and Della are foolish children because they don't realize in the beginning that sacrificing for each other and loving each other is more important than the cost of any gift. Their love for each other is gift enough; therefore, there was no need to sell their prized possessions. Students may also note that both the characters are like children in the fact that they are very simplistic. Other students may disagree with the narrator's first statement, saying that the couple had to sacrifice the most important material items to truly reveal the most important treasure of the house — their love.

Students may also react differently to the narrator's second comment. While thinking Jim and Della to be fools, some students may still believe that while giving away the prized possessions was unnecessary, the reasons they did these things makes them very wise. Others may argue that the two are not wise because they cannot use the gifts for which they had sacrificed so much.

15. Evaluate "The Gift of the Magi." What qualities does it have that make it effective or ineffective for you as a reader? Give specific examples from the story to support your reasons for your evaluation.

Students who appreciate the story may value the ironic twist of the story or value the message that love is the most important gift. Another important feature is the narrator who has a strong presence in the short story. Students may comment on the narrator's values, insights, and somewhat comical commentary ("here I have lamely related to you"). Some students may appreciate the story more than others because they bring some prior knowledge of the biblical allusions, helping them to better understand the comparison being made between the couple and the Magi.

Question 1	Analyzing Point of View
Question 2	Recognizing Author's Bias/Beliefs
Question 3	Analyzing Tone/Mood
Question 4	Drawing Conclusions
Question 5	Analyzing Conflict, Plot, and Setting
Question 6	Drawing Conclusions
Question 7	Analyzing Irony
Question 8	Analyzing Figurative Language
Question 9	Analyzing Conflict, Plot, and Setting
Question 10	Analyzing Conflict, Plot, and Setting
Question 11	Analyzing Diction
Question 12	Interpreting References from Culture/Past
Question 13	Analyzing Irony
Question 14	Comparison/Contrast
Question 15	Evaluating the Quality of Literature

"THE BELLS"

by Edgar Allen Poe

I

Hear the sledges with the bells—   1
Silver bells!
What a world of merriment their melody foretells!
How they tinkle, tinkle, tinkle,
In the icy air of night!   5
While the stars that oversprinkle
All the heavens, seem to twinkle
With a crystalline delight;
Keeping time, time, time,
In a sort of Runic rhyme,   10
To the tintinnabulation that so musically wells
From the bells, bells, bells, bells,
Bells, bells, bells—
From the jingling and the tinkling of the bells.

II

Hear the mellow wedding bells,   15
Golden bells!
What a world of happiness their harmony foretells!
Through the balmy air of night
How they ring out their delight!
From the molten-golden notes,   20
And all in tune,
What a liquid ditty floats
To the turtle-dove that listens, while she gloats
On the moon!
Oh, from out the sounding cells,   25
What a gush of euphony voluminously wells!
How it swells!
How it dwells
On the Future! how it tells
Of the rapture that impels   30
To the swinging and the ringing
Of the bells, bells, bells,
Of the bells, bells, bells, bells,
Bells, bells, bells—
To the rhyming and the chiming of the bells!   35

14

III

Hear the loud alarum bells—
Brazen bells!
What a tale of terror, now, their turbulency tells!
In the startled ear of night
How they scream out their affright!   40
Too much horrified to speak,
They can only shriek, shriek,
Out of tune,
In a clamorous appealing to the mercy of the fire,
In a mad expostulation with the deaf and frantic fire,   45
Leaping higher, higher, higher,
With a desperate desire,
And a resolute endeavor,
Now—now to sit or never,
By the side of the pale-faced moon.   50
Oh, the bells, bells, bells!
What a tale their terror tells
Of Despair!
How they clang, and clash, and roar!
What a horror they outpour   55
On the bosom of the palpitating air!
Yet the ear it fully knows,
By the twanging,
And the clanging,
How the danger ebbs and flows: 60
Yet the ear distinctly tells,
In the jangling,
And the wrangling,
How the danger sinks and swells,
By the sinking or the swelling in the anger of the bells—   65
Of the bells—
Of the bells, bells, bells, bells,
Bells, bells, bells—
In the clamor and the clangor of the bells!

IV

Hear the tolling of the bells—   70
Iron Bells!
What a world of solemn thought their monody compels!
In the silence of the night,
How we shiver with affright
At the melancholy menace of their tone!   75
For every sound that floats
From the rust within their throats

15

Is a groan.
And the people—ah, the people—
They that dwell up in the steeple,   80
All Alone
And who, tolling, tolling, tolling,
In that muffled monotone,
Feel a glory in so rolling
On the human heart a stone—   85
They are neither man nor woman—
They are neither brute nor human—
They are Ghouls:
And their king it is who tolls;
And he rolls, rolls, rolls,   90
Rolls
A paean from the bells!
And his merry bosom swells
With the paean of the bells!
And he dances, and he yells;   95
Keeping time, time, time,
In a sort of Runic rhyme,
To the paean of the bells—
Of the bells:
Keeping time, time, time,   100
In a sort of Runic rhyme,
To the throbbing of the bells—
Of the bells, bells, bells—
To the sobbing of the bells;
Keeping time, time, time,   105
As he knells, knells, knells,
In a happy Runic rhyme,
To the rolling of the bells—
Of the bells, bells, bells:
To the tolling of the bells,   110
Of the bells, bells, bells, bells—
Bells, bells, bells—
To the moaning and the groaning of the bells

16

Authors often use language to create a certain rhythm or music to their writing. The sounds and rhythm often contribute to the overall meaning of the piece. Below are some of the sound devices authors use to create an effect within their writing:

* **Rhythm**: the recurring flow of strong and weak beats in a line

* **Rhyme**: another way writers add a musical quality to writing; the repetition of a vowel and following consonant sounds usually at the end of a word

* **Refrain**: a repeated line or group of lines usually coming in a similar place in each stanza of a poem

* **Alliteration**: the repetition of consonant sounds at close intervals at the beginning of words or first accented syllables

    Example: "The angels, not **h**alf so **h**appy in **h**eaven"

* **Assonance**: the repetition of vowel sounds at close intervals within words.

    Example: "And so, all the n**i**ght-t**i**de, **I** l**i**e down by the s**i**de."

* **Consonance**: the repetition of consonant sounds at close intervals at the end of words or last accented syllables.

    Example: I we**nt** to bu**nt** but could**n't**.

* **Onomatopoeia**: using words that mimic their meaning with their sound

    Example: buzz, snap, clatter

1. Line 54 is an example of

    a. rhyme.
    b. assonance.
    c. consonance.
    d. onomatopoeia.

2. Line 20 is an example of

    a. alliteration.
    b. assonance.
    c. onomatopoeia.
    d. personification.

3. Line 38 is an example of

    a. alliteration.
    b. assonance.
    c. onomatopoeia.
    d. rhythm.

4. Lines 40–41 are an example of

   a. alliteration.
   b. assonance.
   c. onomatopoeia.
   d. personification.

5. Besides alliteration, the words, "sinking" and "swelling," are also examples of

   a. onomatopoeia.
   b. personification.
   c. consonance.
   d. rhyme.

6. The final stanza most likely deals with

   a. sleeping.
   b. heartbreak.
   c. death.
   d. loneliness.

7. Choose one of the examples from questions 1–3 and explain what effect the literary device in the example has on that point in the poem.

Students may choose Line 54: "How they clang, and clash, and roar!" By imitating the harsh cacophony of the bells as they announce the fire, through onomatopoeia Poe captures the confusion and urgency of the moment. Just as the words are harsh to the ears, the bell's announcement is disconcerting to the soul: Poe notes "How the danger sinks and swells, / By the sinking or the swelling in the anger of the bells." The actual sound of the bells helps to accentuate the terrifying moments.

Students may also choose Line 20: "From the molten-golden notes." This assonance of the long "o" sound helps to accentuate the serious tone of the wedding, perhaps foreshadowing the dark tone that comes with stanzas 3 and 4. This deeper, more serious sound contrasts with the quick, shorter "i" sound found in stanza 1. While the wedding is still a happy, harmonious moment, the second stanza lacks the youthful play of the first stanza, providing a transition between the lighter and darker moments of the poem.

Lastly, students may choose Line 38: "What a tale of terror, now, their turbulency tells." Similar to the effect of Line 54, the alliteration used with the "t" sound creates a hard sound as piercing as the bells Poe is describing. The "t" sound lacks the softness found in

18

the second stanza, reminding readers that the poem has taken a turn to a much harsher, brazen bell. The "t" sound is very poignant, similar to the harsh sound of the bells warning the public of the fire.

8. What changes in tone do you notice between stanzas? Use specific details from the text, including the refrain and connotation of certain words, to illustrate how the tone changes throughout the poem.

One possible Answer:

The poem starts off with a very innocent tone. Along with the more playful sounds in Stanza I as mentioned above, the words themselves present happiness and innocence. "Twinkle," "sprinkle," "tinkling," and "jingling" are often associated with childhood, being present in holiday and childhood songs (such as "Jingle Bells" or "Twinkle, Twinkle Little Star"). Onomatopoeic words such as "tintinnabulation" also have a whimsical connotation. Positive words such as "merriment," "melody", and "musically" also develop the harmonious and pleasurable tone of the first stanza.

The second stanza also has some of the contentment of the first stanza but takes on a much more serious tone. This is established immediately in the first line with the word "mellow," connoting a much more mature tone from the tinkling bells of Stanza I. This is reinforced when looking at the change in the refrain between Stanza I and II: the bells go from "jingling and tinkling" to "rhyming and chiming." While the words still show happiness and accord (further reinforced by words in the stanza such as "harmony" and "euphony"), the words have a more adult connotation. In addition, the "silver" bells have now changed to "golden" bells; golden is often associated with age more so than silver. As mentioned earlier, the change to the longer vowel sounds in Stanza 2 creates the content, yet calm tone.

The third stanza brings a sharp change in tone. The tone is much more brash, indicated by the change to "Brazen bells" in the second line. While Stanza II emphasizes the euphony of the bells, Stanza III stresses a dissonance with violent and harsh words such as "clash," "clang," "roar," "loud," "wrangling," "danger," and "shriek." In addition, the refrain once again changes; moving the bells from "rhyme" and "chime" to "clamor" and "clangor." At one point, Poe uses personification to illustrate the urgency and desperation of the bells: "In a clamorous appealing to the mercy of the fire, / In a mad expostulation with the deaf and frantic fire." Ironically, no matter how loud the bells are, the deaf fire will not concede. All

19

this, along with the harsher consonant sounds repeated through the stanza, helps to create the terrifyingly urgent tone.

The fourth stanza loses the urgency of the third stanza and changes to a more despondent tone. This is first established with the change to the cold tolling of the iron bell. Other words such as "solemn," "melancholy," "silence," "shiver," "monody" (poem in which a speaker mourns another's death), "sobbing," and "throbbing" create the gloom of impending death.

In the final refrain, the bells are now "moaning" and "groaning," insinuating old age and death; this is reinforced as the bells now let the sound flow "from the rust within their throats." The only words with a positive connotation come as the king of the Ghouls dances and yells merrily while the bells seem to exalt him. The changing tone throughout the poem leads the reader from childish youth to impending death.

9. How does the strong rhythm and rhyme help to add to effect to the poem? Use specific details from the text to support your answer.

The poem depends on sound to emphasize its point of the different bells, further emphasizing the change in tone between stanzas. The poem starts off with a fairly strong rhythm, mirroring the happier topics of sleigh riding and marriage; however, as the poem progresses to the final stanza, the rhythm becomes more chaotic. This accentuates the terrifying end of the poem as the king of the Ghouls dances and yells, contributing to the fright of the people. In addition, the rhyme also becomes less organized as the poem progresses. While Poe uses a variety of rhyming words at the beginning of the poem, his last stanza has 15 lines ending with the word, "bells." Not only does this emphasize the bells, but it also detracts from the craft of rhyming. At this point, the poem is so emotionally charged that only one word will do—bells. Poe creates a more chaotic rhythm and rhyme as the poem progresses by also creating an irregular stanza length; each stanza is longer than the previous, making it more difficult to hold a consistent rhyme and rhythm.

An **AUTHOR'S STYLE** refers to the way an author presents information whether in a story, an essay, or a speech. Many times an author will use the same style throughout multiple pieces of literature.

Determining an author's style includes looking at the author's diction, syntax (grammatical arrangement), tone, literary devices (including figurative language and sound devices), and details. In order to **evaluate an author's style**, you must determine how well these elements combine to achieve the author's desired effect.

10. Evaluate Poe's style. How effective is his style in conveying his ideas?

Students must first identify Poe's main idea. Some students may find that Poe is merely showing the passing of the seasons of life: youth, young adulthood, adulthood, and old age. Those students may appreciate the author's change in tone between stanzas created through both diction and sound devices. Others may add to this idea by saying that the bells represent some consistency in the passing of time, although the bells themselves show signs of aging. These students may note the repetition of the word, "bells," throughout the poem, helping to create the consistent presence of the bells through all phases of life.

Students may also comment on the syntax, including punctuation, within the poem. Poe consistently uses the exclamation point throughout the four stanzas. Some may feel it captures the excitement of the bells while others may feel it is inappropriate in certain places. Poe uses multiple exclamatory sentences, e.g., " What a world of solemn thought their monody compels!" Students may have differing opinions about how effective this is.

Most students will note that Poe's wide use of rhythm, rhyme, and sound devices effectively communicate the sounds of the bells in the different stanzas.

FROM *GREAT EXPECTATIONS*

by Charles Dickens

My sister, Mrs. Joe Gargery, was more than twenty years older than I, and had established a great reputation with herself and the neighbors because she had brought me up "by hand." Having at that time to find out for myself what the expression meant, and knowing her to have a hard and heavy hand, and to be much in the habit of laying it upon her husband as well as upon me, I supposed that Joe Gargery and I were both brought up by hand.

She was not a good-looking woman, my sister; and I had a general impression that she must have made Joe Gargery marry her by hand. Joe was a fair man, with curls of flaxen hair on each side of his smooth face, and with eyes of such a very undecided blue that they seemed to have somehow got mixed with their own whites. He was a mild, good-natured, sweet-tempered, easy-going, foolish, dear fellow—a sort of Hercules in strength, and also in weakness.

My sister, Mrs. Joe, with black hair and eyes, had such a prevailing redness of skin that I sometimes used to wonder whether it was possible she washed herself with a nutmeg-grater instead of soap. She was tall and bony, and almost always wore a coarse apron, fastened over her figure behind with two loops, and having a square impregnable bib in front, that was stuck full of pins and needles.

She made it a powerful merit in herself, and a strong reproach against Joe, that she wore this apron so much. Though I really see no reason why she should have worn it at all: or why, if she did wear it at all, she should not have taken it off, every day of her life.

Joe's forge adjoined our house, which was a wooden house, as many of the dwellings in our country were—most of them, at that time. When I ran home from the churchyard, the forge was shut up, and Joe was sitting alone in the kitchen. Joe and I being fellow-sufferers, and having confidences as such, Joe imparted a confidence to me, the moment I raised the latch of the door and peeped in at him opposite to it, sitting in the chimney corner.

"Mrs. Joe has been out a dozen times, looking for you, Pip. And she's out now, making it a baker's dozen."

"Is she?"

"Yes, Pip," said Joe; "and what's worse, she's got Tickler with her."

At this dismal intelligence, I twisted the only button on my waistcoat round and round, and looked in great depression at the fire. Tickler was a wax-ended piece of cane, worn smooth by collision with my tickled frame.

"She sot down," said Joe, "and she got up, and she made a grab at Tickler, and she Ram-paged out. That's what she did," said Joe, slowly clearing the fire between the lower bars with the poker, and looking at it: "she Ram-paged out, Pip."

"Has she been gone long, Joe?" I always treated him as a larger species of child, and as no more than my equal.

"Well," said Joe, glancing up at the Dutch clock, "she's been on the Ram-page, this last spell, about five minutes, Pip. She's a-coming! Get behind the door, old chap, and have the jack-towel betwixt you."

I took the advice. My sister, Mrs. Joe, throwing the door wide open, and finding an obstruction behind it, immediately divined the cause, and applied Tickler to its further investigation. She concluded by throwing me—I often served as a connubial missile—at Joe, who, glad to get hold of me on any terms, passed me on into the chimney and quietly fenced me up there with his great leg.

"Where have you been, you young monkey?" said Mrs. Joe, stamping her foot. "Tell me directly what you've been doing to wear me away with fret and fright and worrit, or I'd have you out of that corner if you was fifty Pips, and he was five hundred Gargerys."

1. What does Pip mean when he says that he and Joe have been raised "by hand"?

   a. Mrs. Joe physically abused them.
   b. Mrs. Joe frequently hugged them.
   c. Mrs. Joe frequently applauded them.
   d. Mrs. Joe raised them by herself.

2. When Mrs. Joe says, "I'd have you out of that corner if you was fifty Pips, and he was five hundred Gargerys," she is using

   a. personification.
   b. allusion.
   c. simile.
   d. hyperbole.

3. When Mrs. Joe Gargery complained that "she wore this apron so much," she is really complaining that she

   a. doesn't have any other clothes to wear.
   b. needs to wash her dirty apron.
   c. has to do too much work.
   d. wants a new apron to wear.

4. The story is written in

   a. first person.
   b. third person limited.
   c. third person omniscient.
   d. objective.

5. The narrator, Pip, can **best** be described as

   a. serious.
   b. mean.
   c. naïve.
   d. humorous.

 <#>

An author has to decide how to address each **CHARACTER** in the story. If the author chooses to make a character's personality or outlook significantly change throughout the story, the character is considered a **dynamic** character. However, if the character basically stays the same throughout the text, the character is said to be **static**.

If the character only has one or two major characteristics developed throughout the story, that character is a **flat** character; someone easily summed up in a few sentences. However, if the character is fully developed—you get to see multiple sides of a character and really get to know him or her—then the character is said to be **round**.

6. If Mrs. Joe Gargery continued to treat Pip the way she did throughout the novel without much more being revealed about her, what type of character would she be?

   a. flat, static character
   b. round, static character
   c. flat, dynamic character
   d. round, dynamic character

7. Explain the irony of the Tickler. What type of irony is it and how does it add to the overall effect of the passage?

The Tickler refers to the piece of cane that Mrs. Joe uses to beat Pip. The irony comes with the name. A "tickle" is thought of as something that does not hurt but rather makes someone laugh or giggle. Tickling is often a sort of play between children or between adults and children. Therefore, this is situational irony because the audience would not expect that something with such a name associated with play might be used to punish and hurt Pip. This adds to the overall effect of the passage by reminding the audience that, while the neighbors applaud Mrs. Joe for raising Pip "by hand," the actual way she treats Pip is quite cruel. The audience recognizes that being beaten by the Tickler is probably the closest Pip will ever get to engaging in any kind of play with his sister. This is further emphasized as Pip describes that the cane has been worn smooth by his "tickled frame."

Authors use both **DIRECT AND INDIRECT CHARACTERIZATION** to help us get to know the characters in a story, as well as to develop our attitudes toward the characters.

✱ **Direct Characterization:** Author comes right out and tells the audience the character's traits; sometimes another character may do this for the author.

✱ **Indirect Characterization:** Author shows the audience the character's traits in five different ways:

- through the character's looks or the way she or he dresses

- through the character's actions

- through the character's thoughts

- through the character's spoken words

- through the comments of other characters in the story

8. How would you describe Mr. Joe Gargery? Find examples of both direct and indirect characterization to support your response.

One possible answer:

Joe Gargery could be described as protective and loving. At one point Pip, the narrator, directly says that he was "good-natured, sweet-tempered, [and] easy-going." In addition, this is emphasized through indirect characterization. Joe warns Pip that Mrs. Joe Gargery has the Tickler and that Pip should prepare himself (what Joe's character says). This is further emphasized when Joe catches Pip after Mrs. Joe Gargery throws him across the room and when he places his leg in the way of any further abuse (actions).

9. In paragraph 2, Pip describes Joe as a "sort of Hercules in strength, and also in weakness." Hercules was a physically strong mythological hero who was often either helped or hindered by female gods. What literary device does Dickens use by referring to Hercules? Explain why he chooses this mythological hero to describe Joe using support from the text to support your answer.

Dickens uses an allusion to Hercules to illustrate Joe's strengths and weaknesses. Like Hercules, Joe is a physically strong character shown when Pip describes that Joe fences him in with his "great leg." He has many qualities—"mild, good-natured, sweet-tempered"—that Pip admires. However, like Hercules, Joe is also at the mercy of others, particularly Mrs. Joe. Pip calls Joe "foolish," perhaps referring to his inability to stand up to Mrs. Joe's anger and dominance. He can only react to Mrs. Joe rather than to take control of the situation, similar to the way Hercules can only react to the will of the female gods rather than to take control of his own fate.

10. Compare and contrast the relationship Pip has with Mr. Joe Gargery with the relationship he has with Mrs. Joe Gargery. Use evidence from the text to support your answer.

One possible answer:

While both Mr. Joe Gargery and Mrs. Joe Gargery are older than Pip and, therefore, initially presented as parental figures for Pip, they take vastly different approaches to this responsibility. Pip's relationship with Mrs. Joe Gargery is one of fear and submission whereas Pip's relationship with Mr. Joe Gargery is one of friendship and protection; the relationships are shown in the way Pip treats each of them as well as in the way each of them treats Pip.

The way Pip chooses to address Mr. and Mrs. Joe Gargery illustrates the vast differences in his relationship with each of them. Throughout the passage, Pip refers to his sister as Mrs. Joe or Mrs. Joe Gargery. Nowhere in the passage does he give his sister's first name; this is a sign of the formal and rigid relationship he has with his sister. In contrast, Pip refers to Mr. Joe Gargery simply as Joe throughout the passage. He leaves off the formal "Mr.," indicating the friendly nature of his relationship with Joe. Later in the passage he even says that he treated Joe as "as a larger species of child, and as no more than my equal."

The differences in relationships are also seen in the ways Mr. and Mrs. Joe Gargery treat Pip. Not only does Joe warn Pip about Mrs. Joe's rampage the way one friend would protect another against some threat, he also refers to Pip as "old chap," a friendly term of endearment. This starkly contrasts with Mrs. Joe's first acknowledgement of Pip as "young monkey" after she storms in the house. Whereas Joe thinks of Pip as a friend, Mrs. Joe thinks of him as almost a pet she has the unfortunate task of caring for and punishing. This is emphasized as she hits Pip before even finding out why he has arrived home late; only after she has thrown and hit him does she ask where he has been.

Question 1	Making Inferences
Question 2	Analyzing Figurative Language
Question 3	Making Inferences
Question 4	Analyzing Point of View
Question 5	Analyzing Point of View/Development of Tone
Question 6	Analyzing Character
Question 7	Analyzing Irony
Question 8	Analyzing Character
Question 9	Interpreting References from Culture/Past
Question 10	Comparing and Contrasting

27

AN INQUIRY INTO THE CAUSES AND EFFECTS OF THE VARIOLÆ VACCINÆ, OR COW-POX

by Edward Jenner

The deviation of man from the state in which he was originally placed by nature seems to have proved to him a prolific source of diseases. From the love of splendor, from the indulgences of luxury, and from his fondness for amusement he has familiarized himself with a great number of animals, which may not originally have been intended for his associates.

The wolf, disarmed of ferocity, is now pillowed in the lady's lap. The cat, the little tiger of our island, whose natural home is the forest, is equally domesticated and caressed. The cow, the hog, the sheep, and the horse, are all, for a variety of purposes, brought under his care and dominion.

There is a disease to which the horse, from his state of domestication, is frequently subject. The farriers have called it *the grease*. It is an inflammation and swelling in the heel, from which issues matter possessing properties of a very peculiar kind, which seems capable of generating a disease in the human body (after it has undergone the modification which I shall presently speak of), which bears so strong a resemblance to the smallpox that I think it highly probable it may be the source of the disease.

In this dairy country a great number of cows are kept, and the office of milking is performed indiscriminately by men and maid servants. One of the former having been appointed to apply dressings to the heels of a horse affected with the grease, and not paying due attention to cleanliness, incautiously bears his part in milking the cows, with some particles of the infectious matter adhering to his fingers. When this is the case, it commonly happens that a disease is communicated to the cows, and from the cows to the dairymaids, which spreads through the farm until the most of the cattle and domestics feel its unpleasant consequences. This disease has obtained the name of the cowpox. It appears on the nipples of the cows in the form of irregular pustules. At their first appearance they are commonly of a palish blue, or rather of a color somewhat approaching to livid, and are surrounded by an erysipelatous inflammation. These pustules, unless a timely remedy be applied, frequently degenerate into phagedenic ulcers, which prove extremely troublesome. The animals become indisposed, and the secretion of milk is much lessened. Inflamed spots now begin to appear on different parts of the hands of the domestics employed in milking, and sometimes on the wrists, which quickly run on to suppuration, first assuming the appearance of the small vesications produced by a burn. Most commonly they appear about the joints of the fingers and at their extremities; but whatever parts are affected, if the situation will admit, these superficial suppurations put on a circular form, with their edges more elevated than their center, and of a color distantly approaching to blue. Absorption takes place, and tumors appear in each axilla. The system becomes affected—the pulse is quickened; and shiverings, succeeded by heat, with general lassitude and pains about the loins and limbs, with vomiting, come on. The head is painful, and the patient is now and then even affected with delirium. These symptoms, varying in their degrees of violence, generally continue from one day to three or four, leaving ulcerated sores about the hands, which, from the sensibility of the parts, are very troublesome, and commonly heal slowly, frequently becoming phagedenic, like those from whence they sprung. The lips, nostrils, eyelids, and other parts of the body are sometimes affected with sores; but these evidently arise from their being heedlessly rubbed or scratched with the patient's infected fingers. No eruptions on the skin have followed the decline of the feverish symptoms in any instance that has come under my inspection, one only excepted, and in this case a very few appeared on the arms: they were very minute, of a vivid red color, and soon died away without advancing to maturation; so that I cannot determine whether they had any connection with the preceding symptoms.

Thus the disease makes its progress from the horse to the nipple of the cow, and from the cow to the human subject.

Morbid matter of various kinds, when absorbed into the system, may produce effects in some degree similar; but what renders the cow-pox virus so extremely singular is that the person who has been thus affected is forever after secure from the infection of the small-pox; neither exposure to the variolous effluvia, nor the insertion of the matter into the skin, producing this distemper.

To determine an **AUTHOR'S PURPOSE** means to decide what the author wants to accomplish in the text. In general, an author's purpose usually falls into one or more of the following categories: to express emotions; to inform; to give an opinion; or to persuade. However, these can be broken down into more specific purposes such as to entertain, analyze, evaluate, define, criticize, draw comparisons, reflect, or predict effects.

To determine purpose you must look at the material presented as well as the way it is arranged and expressed. For example, in writing about the first year of high school, if a person's purpose is to express emotions, he may write about his personal emotions during his first year. However, if his purpose is to inform, he may include information that may be useful to a first-year high school student. If the author's purpose is to persuade, he may recommend courses of action to be most successful in the first year of high school.

---

1. What is the purpose of this piece?

   a. inform
   b. give an opinion
   c. persuade
   d. entertain

2. Which genre of nonfiction is this piece?

   a. biography
   b. autobiography
   c. essay
   d. personal narrative

29

Analyzing **CAUSE AND EFFECT** requires a person to analyze relationships between events in a text. Many causes may contribute to a single effect, or one cause may have multiple effects.

❋ **Cause** refers to the reasons why something occurs; to determine cause, ask, "Why did this happen?"

❋ **Effect** refers to the outcome of an action or event; to determine effect ask, "What happened because of this?"

Many times, relationships are more complicated; for example, a chain reaction may occur: "I forgot my homework in my locker so I didn't complete math homework. I didn't complete my math homework so I received a detention. I received a detention, so I was grounded by my parents."

3. Which does the author cite as a direct cause of the cowpox?

 a. the dressing of the horse heels
 b. the horse
 c. smallpox
 d. the grease

4. Which is **not** an effect of the cowpox disease presented in this piece?

 a. less secretion of milk
 b. inflammation of the heel
 c. blue, ulcerous sores
 d. immunity to smallpox

5. Which of these is a conclusion that Jenner draws in the essay?

 a. Cowpox is the source of smallpox.
 b. Humans need to better care for their animals.
 c. Cowpox is not a painful disease for people.
 d. Cowpox symptoms come after a fever.

6. The tone of this piece is

 a. lighthearted.
 b. enthusiastic.
 c. foreboding.
 d. clinical.

7. From this passage, it can be inferred that Jenner believes that men and maid servants

 a. are easily infected with diseases.
 b. infect all animals on the farm.
 c. are sometimes careless with their work.
 d. shouldn't work with horses and cows.

8. Identify one fact and one opinion from the passage, explaining how you know which is which.

Students may choose from a variety of facts throughout the essay including the following: "The farriers have called it the grease"; "This disease has obtained the name of the cowpox"; ". . . the pulse is quickened; and shiverings, succeeded by heat, with general lassitude and pains about the loins and limbs."

No matter which facts students choose, they should recognize that they are facts because they tell things that are known to be true or things that really happened. Students may also mention that a fact is something that can be proven with evidence. For example, one could consult the farriers to see if they actually call the disease, "the grease," or one could observe someone who is suspected of having cowpox for the listed symptoms. Students should then identify opinions within the essay, such as "which bears so strong a resemblance to the smallpox that I think it highly probable it may be the source of the disease" and "From the love of splendor, from the indulgences of luxury, and from his fondness for amusement he has familiarized himself with a great number of animals."

Students should identify that an opinion is someone's beliefs, thoughts, or feelings. An opinion is often identified because it can be argued. For example, another person may disagree with Jenner's interpretation as to why humans have surrounded themselves with animals.   They may cite nutritional needs as one example instead. Students may also note that opinions are often included in seemingly factual statements. For example, Jenner notes "the office of milking is performed indiscriminately by men and maid servants. One of the former having been appointed to apply dressings to the heels of a horse affected with the grease, and not paying due attention to cleanliness, incautiously bears his part in milking the cows." While it may be fact that men and maid servants milk the cows, the way in which it is done (indiscriminately, incautiously) is Jenner's opinion.

31

9. Analyze cause and effect as it is presented in this piece. Is there a single cause with multiple effects? Are there multiple causes with a single effect? Is there a chain reaction? Determine which type of cause and effect is presented. Use specific evidence from the text to support your answer.

The type of cause and effect presented in this essay most clearly resembles a chain reaction. According to Jenner, human desire causes us to domesticate animals. The effect of this domestication is that animals develop certain diseases such as the grease to which we expose ourselves. This disease, along with our own carelessness, then causes other animals, such as cows, to become infected with cowpox. Jenner mentions a number of effects of this disease on both humans and cows including blue, ulcerous sores. While the effects of cowpox seem quite unpleasant, the exposure to cowpox causes one to become immune from smallpox.

When we tap into what we know or have experienced, this is known as **"ACTIVATING" PRIOR KNOWLEDGE**. As the words suggest, this requires us to act, or **do** something before, during, and after reading a new story or learning new material. One way to act is through the **KWL System**.

✳ **K**: What do I **know** about the topic of the story or new material? Have I studied this topic before? What experiences have I had in my personal life that relate to the topic?

This should be done before reading or studying the new material. Quickly review the material—including titles, headings, and illustrations—to gain an idea about the story or new material.

✳ **W**: What do I **want to know**? What do I wonder about in terms of the topic? What is interesting to me about this topic? What questions from my own experiences might be answered or elaborated on in this new material? What confuses me about this topic?

This should also be done before reading or studying new material. In addition, new questions may be added during the reading or learning process.

✳ **L**: What have I **learned**? What new information do I now know? How does this relate to the information or experiences I've already had with the topic? How does this support what I already know or have experienced about the topic? How does this raise new questions or affect my point of view of the topic?

This should take place after you have read a story or been introduced to new material. This process allows you to think about whether or not the new material has reaffirmed, developed, changed or influenced your thinking about a topic.

10. At the beginning of the piece, Jenner notes the following:

The deviation of man from the state in which he was originally placed by nature seems to have proved to him a prolific source of diseases. From the love of splendor, from the indulgences of luxury, and from his fondness for amusement he has familiarized himself with a great number of animals, which may not originally have been intended for his associates.

Analyze the cause and effect relationship in these lines. What is Jenner saying about the nature of human beings? What prior knowledge (movies, news stories, books, personal experiences) either supports or rejects what Jenner is saying?

The author suggests that man's selfishness and desire for indulgences has actually hurt him. Because man has deviated from what Jenner claims to be a natural state (one where man does not tame another animal), both he and the animals have been negatively impacted through the spread of disease. Jenner believes that man's nature is to want more extravagance, even to the point of his own detriment.

This idea has been ever present in society. Students may recall how man's desire to cross oceans to explore new territory (something nature perhaps didn't plan for) ultimately led to the deaths of many men as different groups of people exposed each other to different diseases. Keeping up on more current events, students may also bring up the idea of mad-cow disease. Desiring to keep things cheap for the public and to make more money, many people used unhealthy and unnatural cattle feed and this ultimately led to the spread of the disease in Europe in the early late 1980s and early 1990s. Mad-cow disease eventually developed into a human form of the disease — Creutzfeldt-Jakob disease. Students may also comment more generally on examples from their personal lives, movies they've seen, or books they've read in which human greed has led to negative effects for mankind.

Question 1	Analyzing Author's Purpose
Question 2	Distinguishing Genres of Nonfiction
Question 3	Analyzing Cause and Effect
Question 4	Analyzing Cause and Effect
Question 5	Drawing Conclusions
Question 6	Analyzing Development of Tone and Mood
Question 7	Making Inferences
Question 8	Distinguishing Fact and Opinion
Question 9	Analyzing Cause and Effect
Question 10	Using Prior Knowledge

33

On Women's Right to Vote

by Susan B. Anthony

Friends and Fellow Citizens:—I stand before you tonight under indictment for the alleged crime of having voted at the last presidential election, without having a lawful right to vote. It shall be my work this evening to prove to you that in thus voting, I not only committed no crime, but, instead, simply exercised my *citizen's rights,* guaranteed to me and all United States citizens by the National Constitution, beyond the power of any State to deny.

The preamble of the Federal Constitution says:

> We, the people of the United States, in order to form a more perfect union, establish justice, insure *domestic* tranquility, provide for the common defense, promote the general welfare, and secure the blessings of liberty to ourselves and our posterity, do ordain and establish this Constitution for the United States of America.

It was we, the people; not we, the white male citizens; nor yet we, the male citizens; but we, the whole people, who formed the Union. And we formed it, not to give the blessings of liberty, but to secure them; not to the half of ourselves and the half of our posterity, but to the whole people—women as well as men. And it is a downright mockery to talk to women of their enjoyment of the blessings of liberty while they are denied the use of the only means of securing them provided by this democratic-republican government—the ballot.

For any State to make sex a qualification that must ever result in the disfranchisement of one entire half of the people is to pass a bill of attainder, or an *ex post facto* law, and is therefore a violation of the supreme law of the land. By it the blessings of liberty are forever withheld from women and their female posterity. To them this government has no just powers derived from the consent of the governed. To them this government is not a democracy. It is not a republic. It is an odious aristocracy; a hateful oligarchy of sex; the most hateful aristocracy ever established on the face of the globe; an oligarchy of wealth, where the rich govern the poor. An oligarchy of learning, where the educated govern the ignorant, or even an oligarchy of race, where the Saxon rules the African, might be endured; but this oligarchy of sex, which makes father, brothers, husband, sons, the oligarchs over the mother and sisters, the wife and daughters of every household—which ordains all men sovereigns, all women subjects, carries dissension, discord and rebellion into every home of the nation.

Webster, Worcester and Bouvier all define a citizen to be a person in the United States, entitled to vote and hold office.

The only question left to be settled now is: Are women persons? And I hardly believe any of our opponents will have the hardihood to say they are not. Being persons, then, women are citizens; and no State has a right to make any law, or to enforce any old law, that shall abridge their privileges or immunities. Hence, every discrimination against women in the constitutions and laws of the several States is today null and void, precisely as in every one against Negroes.

1. What is Susan B. Anthony's purpose?

    a. to inform the public on the Constitution
    b. to inform the public of the charges against her
    c. to persuade that women have the right to vote
    d. to persuade that women are people, too

2. When Susan B. Anthony says that her rights are "guaranteed to me and all United States citizens by the National Constitution, beyond the power of any State to deny" Susan B. Anthony means that

    a. state law reigns over national law.
    b. national law reigns over state law.
    c. state and national law work together.
    d. neither law allows women to vote.

3. Susan B. Anthony feels she has the right to vote because she is a

    a. woman.
    b. Saxon.
    c. person.
    d. citizen.

4. When Susan B. Anthony says that the union was formed "not to give the blessings of liberty, but to secure them," she suggests that the Union

    a. gives people freedom.
    b. sets people free from slavery.
    c. protects people's freedom.
    d. protects itself from invaders.

5. Why does Susan B. Anthony feel that an oligarchy of sex is the worst kind?

    a. It affects every single home.
    b. It makes people want to rebel.
    c. It makes people unhappy.
    d. It allows men to rule women.

6. Susan B. Anthony compares women's situation with the

    a. Anglo Saxon's situation.
    b. Negro's situation.
    c. National Constitution.
    d. men's situation.

7. Which type of nonfiction is this?

    a. essay
    b. speech
    c. biography
    d. autobiography

35

8. How does Susan B. Anthony use language to help make her point? Consider her diction and, specifically, the connotation of certain words that she uses.

One possible answer:

Susan B. Anthony uses language to show her disgust for the way the local governments have excluded women from voting yet still declare the government a democracy. She uses words such as "odious," "hateful" (twice), "dissension," "discord," and "rebellion" all within the same paragraph to convey her anger towards the injustice. All of these words are emotionally charged, specifically addressing the type of oligarchy that she feels exists. Her choice to use the word, "oligarchy," is equally as powerful. An oligarchy is a government of the few. This sharply contrasts with the democratic government of the people that the United States citizens embrace. Knowingly, she plays off this pride when she says that, by not letting women vote, the government is denying the democracy the nation holds so dear. Earlier in the speech she repeatedly mentions that the government is only serving <u>half</u> the people as opposed to the <u>whole</u> people, again conveying her thought that the United States is not the complete democracy it claims to be.

9. How does your prior knowledge help add to your comprehension of the speech? What personal experiences, stories, or movies does the speech bring to mind and why?

Students may be reminded of personal experiences of discrimination. They may cite certain instances of racial or sexual discrimination when they felt their rights were being violated. Other students may be reminded of the plight of African Americans and other groups who have had to fight for equal rights over the years, citing movies and books that they have read or seen. Students should then comment about how their own experiences and knowledge add to their comprehension. Some students may better understand the anger that Anthony sometimes expresses in the speech. Others will be able to better identify with her argument that people living in the United States are citizens with the same rights as everyone else. Furthermore, students may better understand the courage and strength of Susan B. Anthony, recognizing from personal experiences, books, and movies that those who speak out against injustice are often criticized and even punished for doing so.

10. Susan B. Anthony uses a combination of facts and opinions to make her point. Find examples of both fact and opinion in this speech. Analyze how the facts and opinions work together to make her point.

Students may find a number of facts, including "I stand before you tonight under indictment for the alleged crime of having voted at the last presidential election, without having a lawful right to vote"; "Webster, Worcester and Bouvier all define a citizen to be a person in the United States, entitled to vote and hold office."; or when she quotes the Preamble to the Constitution. Students may note that she uses these facts to build her argument throughout the text. For example, immediately after she states the fact that she is charged for having voted at the last election, she returns with her opinion that she "committed no crime, but, instead, simply exercised my citizen's rights." In addition, after citing the words of the Preamble to the Constitution she returns with her strong opinion that "it is a downright mockery to talk to women of their enjoyment of the blessings of liberty while they are denied the use of the only means of securing them provided by this democratic-republican government—the ballot." Even though the Constitution presents one opinion of the way government should be run, she brings it into the speech by factually citing what the Constitution says. Finally, she factually states the definition she found in a dictionary for the word, "citizen," to support her opinion that since women are people in the United States, they are citizens and deserve the right to vote. Anthony carefully states each fact before expressing her opinion to the audience.

The following are different ways of **APPROACH**.

Logos: This is an appeal based on logic or reason. It includes factual data and statistics, quotations, historical analogies, citations from experts and authorities, informed opinions.

Pathos: This is an appeal based on emotion. It includes emotionally-loaded words, vivid descriptions, emotional tone, figurative language, emotional stories or examples.

Ethos: This is an appeal based on character of the speaker. It includes appropriate language, a fair-minded presentation, respect towards the audience, appropriate use of support, and accurate information.

To **persuade** someone is to call someone to action; it is to try to convince someone to do something or act in a certain way. Three main appeals are used to persuade:

Propaganda refers to the deliberate attempt to influence a mass audience to act or think a certain way. Usually the term is associated with an intent to deceive. In promoting certain causes, sometimes people use the following propaganda techniques:

Loaded Words: This is using words with a strong connotation. This technique is also known as using "slanted words" because the speaker or writer will choose words for their persuasive emotional charge.

Glittering Generalities: These present a specific type of loaded words; comments using glittering generalities are vague and have a positive connotation. For example, words like "strength," "democracy", and "freedom" all carry a positive connotation.

Bandwagon: The speaker persuades people to do something by suggesting that everyone else is following a certain trend.

Plain-Folks Appeal: The speaker tries to present himself/herself as one of the crowd, therefore seeming to have the same interests and desires as the audience.

Snob Appeal: The speaker tries to present himself/herself as one of the beautiful, wealthy, or special people.

Appeal to Human Needs/Desire: The speaker claims that acting a certain way will meet a basic need. All human beings need food, drink, clothing, and shelter to survive. In addition, we also have such emotional needs as to be loved and cared for, to have meaningful work, and to have self-worth.

Appeal to Fears: The speaker tries to say that, if the audience doesn't act a certain way, something they fear will occur.

Testimonial: The speaker uses an association with a famous person to sell an idea or product.

Slogans: The speaker uses a catchy phrase that is often repeated and easily remembered.

Repetition: The speaker repeatedly restates an idea or phrase.

Powerful Images: The speaker uses certain pictures to make the audience feel a certain way. For example, sunshine and rainbows tend to make people happy.

Card Stacking: False statements, false calculations, and false information is presented to deceive the listener.

11. What persuasive techniques does Susan B. Anthony incorporate into her speech? Does she use any propaganda in her speech? If so, when? Use specific examples from the text to support your answer.

Anthony uses logos, pathos, and ethos within her speech to convince the audience that women have the right to vote. She uses logos when she cites both the preamble to the federal Constitution and the definition of the word, "citizen." Knowing that her audience recognizes the federal Constitution as the highest law of the land, she builds a basis for her logical argument by including it. With the definition of a citizen, Anthony not only builds logos but also ethos. She does not just mention one dictionary but the editors of three dictionaries: Webster, Worcester and Bouvier. This builds her credibility as a speaker; the audience perceives her to be a researcher who cross-references reputable sources as distinct from one who takes the definition of one unknown source. She uses both the Constitution and the dictionary to come to her logical point. If dictionaries define citizens as those who live in the United States and the Constitution says that citizens have a right to "secure the blessings of liberty to ourselves and our posterity," then women have the right to vote in order to ensure their liberty, since they live in the United States. She further establishes herself as a credible speaker when she claims that "any State to make sex a qualification that must ever result in the disfranchisement of one entire half of the people is to pass a bill of attainder." Again referring to the federal Constitution, she builds pathos as she offers another reason why disallowing women the right to vote is illegal and ethos by using correct terminology, illustrating her knowledge of the law.

In addition to logos and ethos, she builds pathos. As noted earlier, using such words as "hateful oligarchy," Anthony solicits an emotional response from the audience; the listeners do not want to consider America as a government of a few. She associates voting with liberty and dramatically emphasizes the real crime by commenting that "the blessings of liberty are forever withheld from women." "Forever withheld" sharply contrasts with "blessings of liberty"; the audience asks, "How can we let this happen?" Also, she uses emotional examples as she claims that not allowing women to vote creates discord amongst sons, fathers, mothers, and daughters. Using logos, pathos, and ethos, Anthony convinces the audience of woman's right to vote.

39

While developing her argument, Anthony does use propaganda. She plays off the audience's fears; if woman are not allowed to vote, our government is an oligarchy not a democracy. She also uses glittering generalities. She associates voting with such vague yet noble beliefs as liberty and posterity. In addition, she quickly associates herself with her audience beginning her address carefully with "Friends and Fellow Citizens." Not only does she identify herself as a citizen (which is a major part of her later argument), but she puts herself on the same level as her audience in her plain-folks appeal. Towards the end of her speech she recognizes that the only thing left to argue is whether or not women are persons. She uses a bandwagon approach, saying, "And I hardly believe any of our opponents will have the hardihood to say they are not." She makes it sound as if no one would dare to really ask that question. Overall, Susan B. Anthony uses a combination of propaganda and persuasive tools to make her point.

THE LAST CLASS: THE STORY OF A LITTLE ALSATIAN

by Alphonse Daudet

I was very late for school that morning, and I was terribly afraid of being scolded, especially as Monsieur Hamel had told us that he should examine us on participles, and I did not know the first thing about them. For a moment I thought of staying away from school and wandering about the fields. It was such a warm, lovely day. I could hear the blackbirds whistling on the edge of the wood, and in the Rippert field, behind the sawmill, the Prussians going through their drill. All that was much more tempting to me than the rules concerning participles; but I had the strength to resist, and I ran as fast as I could to school.

As I passed the mayor's office, I saw that there were people gathered about the little board on which notices were posted. For two years all our bad news had come from that board—battles lost, conscriptions, orders from headquarters; and I thought without stopping:

"What can it be now?"

Then, as I ran across the square, Wachter the blacksmith, who stood there with his apprentice, reading the placard, called out to me:

"Don't hurry so, my boy; you'll get to your school soon enough!"

I thought that he was making fun of me, and I ran into Monsieur Hamel's little yard all out of breath.

Usually, at the beginning of school, there was a great uproar which could be heard in the street, desks opening and closing, lessons repeated aloud in unison, with our ears stuffed in order to learn quicker, and the teacher's stout ruler beating on the desk:

"A little more quiet!"

I counted on all this noise to reach my bench unnoticed; but as it happened, that day everything was quiet, like a Sunday morning. Through the open window I saw my comrades already in their places, and Monsieur Hamel walking back and forth with the terrible iron ruler under his arm. I had to open the door and enter, in the midst of that perfect silence. You can imagine whether I blushed and whether I was afraid!

But no! Monsieur Hamel looked at me with no sign of anger and said very gently:

"Go at once to your seat, my little Frantz; we were going to begin without you."

I stepped over the bench and sat down at once at my desk. Not until then, when I had partly recovered from my fright, did I notice that our teacher had on his handsome blue coat, his plaited ruff, and the black silk embroidered breeches, which he wore only on days of inspection or of distribution of prizes. Moreover, there was something extraordinary, something solemn about the whole class. But what surprised me most was to see at the back of the room, on the benches which were usually empty, some people from the village sitting, as silent as we were: old Hauser with his three-cornered hat, the ex-mayor, the ex-postman, and others besides. They all seemed depressed; and Hauser had brought an old spelling-book with gnawed edges, which he held wide-open on his knee, with his great spectacles askew.

While I was wondering at all this, Monsieur Hamel had mounted his platform, and in the same gentle and serious voice with which he had welcomed me, he said to us:

"My children, this is the last time that I shall teach you. Orders have come from Berlin to teach nothing but German in the schools of Alsace and Lorraine. The new teacher arrives tomorrow. This is the last class in French, so I beg you to be very attentive."

Those few words overwhelmed me. Ah! The villains! That was what they had posted at the mayor's office.

My last class in French!

And I barely knew how to write! So I should never learn! I must stop short where I was! How angry I was with myself because of the time I had wasted, the lessons I had missed, running about after nests, or sliding on the Saar! My books, which only a moment before I thought so tiresome, so heavy to carry—my grammar, my sacred history—seemed to me now like old friends, from whom I should be terribly grieved to part. And it was the same about Monsieur Hamel. The thought that he was going away, that I should never see him again, made me forget the punishments, the blows with the ruler.

Poor man! It was in honor of that last lesson that he had put on his fine Sunday clothes; and I understood now why those old fellows from the village were sitting at the end of the room. It seemed to mean that they regretted not having come oftener to the school. It was also a way of thanking our teacher for his forty years of faithful service, and of paying their respects to the fatherland which was vanishing.

I was at that point in my reflections, when I heard my name called. It was my turn to recite. What would I not have given to be able to say from beginning to end that famous rule about participles, in a loud, distinct voice, without a slip! But I got mixed up at the first words, and I stood there swaying against my bench, with a full heart, afraid to raise my head. I heard Monsieur Hamel speaking to me:

"I will not scold you, my little Frantz; you must be punished enough; that is the way it goes; every day we say to ourselves: 'Pshaw! I have time enough. I will learn tomorrow.' And then you see what happens. Ah! it has been the great misfortune of our Alsace always to postpone its lessons until tomorrow. Now those people are entitled to say to us: 'What! You claim to be French, and you can neither speak nor write your language!' In all this, my poor Frantz, you are not the guiltiest one. We all have our fair share of reproaches to address to ourselves."

"Your parents have not been careful enough to see that you were educated. They preferred to send you to work in the fields or in the factories, in order to have a few more sous. And have I nothing to reproach myself for? Have I not often made you water my garden instead of studying? And when I wanted to go fishing for trout, have I ever hesitated to dismiss you?"

Then, passing from one thing to another, Monsieur Hamel began to talk to us about the French language, saying that it was the most beautiful language in the world, the most clear, the most substantial; that we must always retain it among ourselves, and never forget it, because when a people falls into servitude, "so long as it clings to its language, it is as if it held the key to its prison." Then he took the grammar and read us our lesson. I was amazed to see how readily I understood. Everything that he said seemed so easy to me, so easy. I believed, too, that I had never listened so closely, and that he, for his part, had never been so patient with his explanations. One would have said that, before going away, the poor man desired to give us all his knowledge, to force it all into our heads at a single blow.

When the lesson was at an end, we passed to writing. For that day Monsieur Hamel had prepared some entirely new examples, on which was written in a fine, round hand: "France, Alsace, France,

42

Alsace." They were like little flags, waving all about the class, hanging from the rods of our desks. You should have seen how hard we all worked and how silent it was! Nothing could be heard save the grinding of the pens over the paper. At one time some cock-chafers flew in; but no one paid any attention to them, not even the little fellows who were struggling with their straight lines, with a will and conscientious application, as if even the lines were French. On the roof of the schoolhouse, pigeons cooed in low tones, and I said to myself as I listened to them:

"I wonder if they are going to compel them to sing in German too!"

From time to time, when I raised my eyes from my paper. I saw Monsieur Hamel sitting motionless in his chair and staring at the objects about him as if he wished to carry away in his glance the whole of his little schoolhouse. Think of it! For forty years he had been there in the same place, with his yard in front of him and his class just as it was! But the benches and desks were polished and rubbed by use; the walnuts in the yard had grown, and the hop-vine which he himself had planted now festooned the windows even to the roof. What a heart-rending thing it must have been for that poor man to leave all those things, and to hear his sister walking back and forth in the room overhead, packing their trunks! For they were to go away the next day—to leave the province forever.

However, he had the courage to keep the class to the end. After the writing, we had the lesson in history; then the little ones sang all together the *ba, be, bi, bo, bu.* Yonder, at the back of the room, old Hauser had put on his spectacles, and, holding his spelling-book in both hands, he spelled out the letters with them. I could see that he too was applying himself. His voice shook with emotion, and it was so funny to hear him, that we all longed to laugh and to cry. Ah! I shall remember that last class.

Suddenly the church clock struck twelve, then the Angelus rang. At the same moment, the bugles of the Prussians returning from drill blared under our windows. Monsieur Hamel rose, pale as death, from his chair. Never had he seemed to me so tall.

"My friends," he said, "my friends, I— I—"

But something suffocated him. He could not finish the sentence.

Thereupon he turned to the blackboard, took a piece of chalk, and, bearing on with all his might, he wrote in the largest letters he could:

"VIVE LA FRANCE!"

Then he stood there, with his head resting against the wall, and without speaking, he motioned to us with his hand:

"That is all; go."

43

1. In what point of view is the story written?

   a. first person
   b. third person limited
   c. third person omniscient
   d. objective

2. What has caused the teacher to have to give up his teaching position?

   a. The town decided that he is not a good teacher.
   b. He has reached the age when he must retire.
   c. Alsace has been taken over by Prussia.
   d. His sister has gotten into trouble and must leave.

3. What important piece of information given in the exposition does **not** directly help the development of the short story later?

   a. Prussians were going through their drill.
   b. The narrator did not want to go to school.
   c. People were gathered around the notice board.
   d. It was a warm and lovely day in the town.

4. Which of the following answers **best** represents the climax of the story?

   a. The boy sees the townspeople sitting in the back of the room.
   b. The teacher writes "Vive La France!" on the blackboard.
   c. The teacher gives his speech after the narrator recites incorrectly.
   d. The teacher explains to students that this will be his last lesson.

5. Which of the following does **not** represent a change in Monsieur Hamel on his last day?

   a. He carries his iron ruler with him.
   b. He is calm when the narrator is late.
   c. He is more patient with students.
   d. He wears his fancy jacket and pants.

6. The teacher says, "They preferred to send you to work in the fields or in the factories, in order to have a few more sous." The word, "sous," most likely refers to which of the following?

   a. moment of time
   b. money
   c. privileges
   d. experiences

44

7. After hearing the bugles of the Prussians, why can't Monsier Hamel finish his sentence?

  a. He is scared of the Prussians.
  b. He is choking on something.
  c. *He is heartbroken about leaving*.
  d. He has nothing else to say.

8. Why does Old Hauser join in with the little ones when they recite their lesson?

  a. He wants them to be louder when they recite their lessons.
  b. He never learned how to speak French when he was a boy.
  c. He wants to correct their mistakes as they recite their lessons.
  d. *He realizes the importance of the French language and culture*.

9. How does the narrator's attitude toward the lesson and the teacher at the beginning of the short story compare and/or contrast to your prior knowledge about school? How does this aid your comprehension of the boy's feelings as he arrives at school? Be sure to use specific evidence from the text and your prior knowledge to support your opinion.

Students may identify with the narrator's lack of enthusiasm, tardiness, or lack of preparation for the day's lesson. Some students may even express fear of some teachers. However, others may see learning as a rewarding, fun experience and, therefore, comment how this student reminds them of their peers. Any answer may help to build the idea that the boy doesn't appreciate or even understand the opportunity he has been given to learn French; he does not understand why it is so important to learn the language until it's too late. Be sure that students use both specific evidence from the text and their own prior knowledge (movies, books, or personal experiences) to clarify the way the boy is feeling at the beginning of this passage. This will help students to recognize the significance of the change in the boy's opinion later in the passage.

10. Would you consider the narrator to be a dynamic or static character? Support your answer using evidence from the text.

One possible answer:

The narrator is a dynamic character because he learns the importance of learning his native language. In a larger sense, he finds a sense of patriotism toward both his teacher and his culture only when it almost too late. In the beginning of the story the boy dreads going to class, commenting that he would rather enjoy the wonderful day outside than learn about participles. However, after finding out that this is his teacher's last day and his last day to learn French, he works hard to understand the material and hardly even notices as birds find their way into the classroom. He mentions that his books have suddenly become "old friends" instead of burdens. He also comments that the new samples that his instructor created seem like little flags, further emphasizing his own newfound patriotism toward his language and culture. This character who once saw his instructor as heartless and rigid is now able to empathize with his instructor, imagining the instructor's heartache as he listens to his sister packing up their belongings in the room above the school.

11. Alphonse Daudet's short story was translated from French to English. In some translations it is called "The Last Lesson" as opposed to "The Last Class." Consider the differences in denotation and connotation between the words, "class" and "lesson." Which do you feel is the better title? Use specific details from the text to support your answer.

While "class" and "lesson" are related terms, they are quite different in what they infer. A person may say "I'm going to class" or "I'm going to my lesson"; however, there are slight differences in meaning. "Class" refers more to an actual academic grouping, not necessarily directly suggesting that any learning or teaching is actually taking place. In contrast, "lesson" insinuates something that either needs to be taught or needs to be learned. In this sense, "The Last Lesson" serves as a much better title for what actually happens in the short story. When first reading the title, readers assume the title refers to the teacher's last lesson in the sense that it is the last day that he will teach. However, upon further examination, "lesson" could also be referring to the last piece of wisdom that the students learn from the teacher: "Every day we say to ourselves: 'Pshaw! I have time enough. I will learn tomorrow.'

And then you see what happens. Ah! it has been the great misfortune of our Alsace always to postpone its lessons until tomorrow." Some students may make the connection that the boy is not the only person to learn the final lesson. The old men in the village are sitting in the back of the room and the teacher changes his demeanor on this final day by saying, "We all have our fair share of reproaches to address to ourselves." The instructor realizes that putting things off until tomorrow has put the province in this position with Prussia and caused him to lose his job. In addition, the student, on his final day with his instructor, finally learns the importance of the lessons he had been dreading.

12. The story took place in 1870–1871, soon after the Franco-Prussian War had ended. The Germans overwhelmingly defeated the French and took control of places such as Alsace. What does the teacher mean when he says, "so long as it clings to its language, it is as if it held the key to its prison." Paraphrase this sentence in your own words and then explain the teacher's meaning within the context of the story. Use specific details from the passage to support your answer.

One possible answer:

The teacher means that, if a community holds onto its language, then no matter who tries to take over the community will still have the means to set itself free from an oppressor. This is particularly important in this short story because the students will now have to learn their lessons in German; they are at risk of losing their culture and language, thereby being "imprisoned" by the culture of the new ruling party. The teacher mentions that people will not take the town seriously when it says it's French if the people of the town cannot even speak the language. The instructor tries to emphasize to the students and to those adults in the back of the classroom that as long as they know and understand their own culture (which includes their language), they will have the ability to practice their culture and more importantly, the desire to practice it freely. This desire, this patriotism, is what the teacher wants to emphasize as the key to freedom. Therefore, Monsieur Hamel spends his last class trying to instill the value of the French language into his students, saying it is the most beautiful language in the world, and being more patient than usual in teaching the lessons. The danger is that, if people do not know their own culture, they lose the ability and the desire to practice it.

13. Predict what will happen next. How will the town be the same or how will it be different? How will the narrator be the same or different? How will the teacher be the same or different? Use specific details from the passage to support your answer.

Students may think that all the characters will be changed forever. Although the narrator will have to learn his lessons in German, he may be inspired by his instructor's final lesson to pursue learning more about his French language and culture on his own. Certainly the boy's attitude has changed as he works hard during this final French lesson from this teacher and finally realizes its importance: "How angry I was with myself because of the time I had wasted, the lessons I had missed, running about after nests, or sliding on the Saar!" Optimistically, the students, along with the adults in the town, will embrace their French culture, thereby weakening the power of German influence. Some hope is given in the fact that Old Hauser repeats the lessons with the children. Hopefully the community will no longer put things off until tomorrow. This lesson perhaps will change the teacher forever as well; he also realizes he has also put off teaching the culture and language so important to the students, often allowing them to water his garden instead of studying. Monsieur Hamel's renewed sense of purpose may make him a better teacher.

However, other students may feel that it is too late for the community. Some may feel that some of the older citizens coming to the lesson suggests that they don't feel as comfortable with the language as they should. Some will point out that at the beginning the man tells the narrator not to hurry because he will get to school "soon enough." In addition, while the students may have worked hard on the last day, they still have not mastered the material in time. While the community may avoid putting things off in the future, giving themselves up to the German language and culture will be inevitable.

14. What do you see as the major theme of this short story? Support your answer with specific evidence from the text, considering how the point of view, characterization, and plot development all help to create this theme.

One possible answer:

The theme of this story is the value of embracing the opportunities and duties presented each day rather than putting them off. All the elements of the story, including point of view, characterization, and plot development all support this theme.

The first person point of view and characterization help the audience to identify with the narrator as he has his epiphany. The audience first identifies with the narrator; most people have had the experience of not wanting to go to school or feeling unprepared. However, as the narrator learns the importance of taking advantage of opportunities, the audience learns the lesson with him, perhaps remembering a time when an opportunity passed. By making the narrator a dynamic character, the theme is developed. Other characters within the text seem to learn the same lesson including the teacher, the other students, and even the older citizens.

The climax of the story also coincides with the theme of the story. As the narrator prepares for punishment when he cannot recite the lesson correctly, he is instead surprised by the instructor's patience and comments: "I will not scold you, my little Frantz; you must be punished enough; that is the way it goes." The teacher continues by saying they have all put off opportunities and duties and will have to face up to it. It is at this point in the story when the narrator switches from being fearful of his teacher to truly understanding the opportunity that the teacher is presenting to him.

15. Evaluate "The Last Class." What qualities does it have that make it effective or ineffective for you as a reader? Give specific examples from the story to support your reasons for your evaluation.

Students who favorably evaluate the story might, for example, point out that the characters are believable because of their real emotions and desires; the conflict is intriguing and the plot well developed; the theme is appropriate to the setting and historical period and well-supported by all parts of the short story. Students may comment on the timelessness of the story even though it comes from the 1800s. Students should use specific examples from the text to support their evaluations.

"I Wandered Lonely As a Cloud"

by William Wordsworth

I wandered lonely as a cloud	1
That floats on high o'er vales and hills,	
When all at once I saw a crowd,	
A host, of golden daffodils;	
Beside the lake, beneath the trees,	5
Fluttering and dancing in the breeze.	
Continuous as the stars that shine	
And twinkle on the milky way,	
They stretched in never-ending line	
Along the margin of a bay:	10
Ten thousand saw I at a glance,	
Tossing their heads in sprightly dance.	
The waves beside them danced; but they	
Out-did the sparkling waves in glee:	
A poet could not but be gay,	15
In such a jocund company:	
I gazed—and gazed—but little thought	
What wealth the show to me had brought:	
For oft, when on my couch I lie	
In vacant or in pensive mood,	20
They flash upon that inward eye	
Which is the bliss of solitude;	
And then my heart with pleasure fills,	
And dances with the daffodils.	

1. Line 1 of this poem contains which of the following poetic devices?

    a. metaphor
    b. hyperbole
    c. *simile*
    d. personification

2. Line 6 of this poem contains which of the following poetic devices?

    a. metaphor
    b. hyperbole
    c. simile
    d. *personification*

3. Lines 9–10 of this poem contain which of the following poetic devices?

    a. metaphor
    b. *hyperbole*
    c. simile
    d. personification

4. What is the overall tone of this poem?

    a. sad
    b. regretful
    c. *jovial*
    d. frenzied

5. The narrator of this poem is most likely speaking

    a. while standing in the field years later.
    b. as the moment happens in the field.
    c. *while sitting somewhere else years later.*
    d. after the narrator has already died.

6. How does the strong beat or rhythm add to the overall effect of the poem? Be sure to use specific evidence from the text to support your answer.

One possible answer:

The author includes a very consistent beat throughout the entire poem that is enhanced by the ababcc rhyme scheme. This consistency helps to achieve two effects. The reader actually feels nature's rhythm as it is alluded to in the poem. Wordsworth writes about the daffodils, "Ten thousand saw I at a glance/ tossing their heads in sprightly dance." Not only are the daffodils dancing, but in Line 13 the waves are also described as dancing. The dancing beat helps the reader to experience the moment that the narrator recalls. The consistency also helps to build the lasting effect of the moment on the narrator. Just as he continues to remember the moment long after experiencing it ("And then my heart with pleasure fills/ And dances with the daffodils"), the consistent beat also stays with the reader; essentially the audience has now experienced the effect of the lasting memory.

7. Paraphrase lines 19–22. What exactly is the author saying here?

One possible answer:
The following is a paraphrase of the lines:

"Many times when I am relaxing on the couch and reflecting or thinking about things, I remember the daffodils. I see them in my memory, the most heavenly place of seclusion."

The narrator tries to get the audience to see the positive and lasting impact the moment in the field has had on him. Even though he may be in his residence in the crowded city, he still feels the presence and exhilaration of that day. Literally, he is alone with his thoughts; however, rather than feeling lonely, he feels fulfilled with the memory of the daffodils' company.

53

8. What effect does the repetition on Line 17 have on the overall effect of the poem? What is the connotation of the word, "gazed"? How does punctuation also play a role in this effect?

The word, "gaze," insinuates an intense staring. Normally the word is associated with looking at something out of the ordinary or something that provokes a strong curiosity or amazement—either good or bad—within the reader. Most of the time "gaze" also suggests a longer period of staring. The repetition of this word emphasizes an even longer period of watching, a period when the narrator has a chance to drink in his surroundings, not knowing at the time "What wealth the show to me had brought." While some people may not even notice the daffodils as they walk—certainly not feeling curious or amazed—this narrator recognizes the power of the moment and is rewarded with the lasting memory. The dashes also add to the line by extending the length and depth of the narrator's gaze.

9. What is a major theme of this poem? Use specific examples from the text to show how the theme is developed.

One possible answer:

A major theme of this poem is nature's ability to fulfill the soul. This theme is developed through figurative language and rhythm.

The theme's development begins in the first lines of the poem. When the poem begins, the narrator feels alone: "I wandered lonely as a cloud." Although he immediately identifies his connection with nature by using this simile, he also emphasizes through words such as "wandered" and "lonely" how lost he felt when he first arrived on the scene of daffodils.

Figurative language also develops the effect the daffodils have on the narrator. The narrator describes the overwhelming scene before him, comparing the daffodils to the magnitude of the shining stars by using a simile. He continues to show his connection by personifying the daffodils; the dancing daffodils now have something distinctly human about them, further connecting them to the narrator. This scene of the daffodils changes the narrator's mood as he notes, "A poet could not help but be gay,/in such a jocund

company." At this point, the narrator no longer feels as if he is wandering alone.

Rhythm also helps to develop the connection between man and nature. As noted in

Question 6, the strong beat throughout the text stays with the reader in the same way that

the memory of the daffodils has stayed with the narrator. At the end of the poem the

narrator actually cherishes his solitude, referring to his memory as the "bliss of solitude."

While the narrator may be physically alone, he will never be lonely because of the

connection he has made with nature.

10. Evaluate Wordsworth's "I Wandered Lonely As A Cloud." What qualities does it have that make it effective or ineffective for you as a reader? Give specific examples from the poem to support your reasons for your evaluation.

Students may acknowledge the quality that the rhythm and rhyme add to the poem and the

development of the theme. They may appreciate the timelessness of the message or amount

of figurative language in such a brief poem. While some students may appreciate the poem,

others may criticize the poem for seeming a bit cliché; for example, dancing flowers may

seem too commonplace. However, students may need to be reminded that the poem was

written toward the beginning of the Romantic period (approximately 1798-1837) in which

such descriptions were not clichés. In either case, students should provide specific support

from the text to support their evaluations.

Question 1	Analyzing Figurative Language
Question 2	Analyzing Figurative Language
Question 3	Analyzing Figurative Language
Question 4	Analyzing Development of Tone/Mood
Question 5	Making Inferences
Question 6	Analyzing Sound Devices and Rhythm
Question 7	Summarizing and Paraphrasing Info
Question 8	Analyzing Diction/Evaluating Style
Question 9	Interpreting Theme and Main Idea
Question 10	Evaluating the Quality of Literature

"How the Case Stands" from *How the Other Half Lives*

by Jacob A. Riis

What, then, are the bald facts with which we have to deal in New York?

I. That we have a tremendous, ever swelling crowd of wage-earners which it is our business to house decently.

II. That it is not housed decently.

III. That it must be so housed *here* for the present, and for a long time to come, all schemes of suburban relief being as yet utopian, impracticable.

IV. That it pays high enough rents to entitle it to be so housed, as a right.

V. That nothing but our own slothfulness is in the way of so housing it, since "the condition of the tenants is in advance of the condition of the houses which they occupy" (Report of Tenement-house Commission).

VI. That the security of the one no less than of the other half demands, on sanitary, moral, and economic grounds, that it be decently housed.

VII. That it will pay to do it. As an investment, I mean, and in hard cash. This I shall immediately proceed to prove.

VIII. That the tenement has come to stay, and must itself be the solution of the problem with which it confronts us.

This is the fact from which we cannot get away, however we may deplore it. Doubtless the best would be to get rid of it altogether; but as we cannot, all argument on that score may at this time be dismissed as idle. The practical question is what to do with the tenement. I watched a Mott Street landlord, the owner of a row of barracks that have made no end of trouble for the health authorities for twenty years, solve that question for himself the other day. His way was to give the wretched pile a coat of paint, and put a gorgeous tin cornice on with the year 1890 in letters a yard long. From where I stood watching the operation, I looked down upon the same dirty crowds camping on the roof, foremost among them an Italian mother with two stark-naked children who had apparently never made the acquaintance of a wash-tub. That was a landlord's way, and will not get us out of the mire.

The "flat" is another way that does not solve the problem. Rather, it extends it. The flat is not a model, though it is a modern, tenement. It gets rid of some of the nuisances of the low tenement, and of the worst of them, the overcrowding—if it gets rid of them at all—at a cost that takes it at once out of the catalogue of "homes for the poor," while imposing some of the evils from which they suffer upon those who ought to escape from them.

There are three effective ways of dealing with the tenements in New York:

I. By law.

II. By remodeling and making the most out of the old houses.

III. By building new, model tenements.

Private enterprise—conscience, to put it in the category of duties, where it belongs—must do the lion's share under these last two heads. Of what the law has effected I have spoken already. The drastic measures adopted in Paris, in Glasgow, and in London are not practicable here on anything like as large a scale. Still it can, under strong pressure of public opinion, rid us of the worst plague-spots. The Mulberry Street Bend will go the way of the Five Points when all the red tape that binds the hands of municipal effort has been unwound. Prizes were offered in public competition, some years ago, for the best plans of modern tenement-houses. It may be that we shall see the day when the building of model tenements will be encouraged by subsidies in the way of a rebate of taxes. Meanwhile the arrest and summary punishment of landlords, or their agents, who persistently violate law and decency, will have a salutary effect. If a few of the wealthy absentee landlords, who are the worst offenders, could be got within the jurisdiction of the city, and by arrest be compelled to employ proper overseers, it would be a proud day for New York. To remedy the overcrowding, with which the night inspections of the sanitary police cannot keep step, tenements may eventually have to be licensed, as now the lodging-houses, to hold so many tenants, and no more; or the State may have to bring down the rents that cause the crowding, by assuming the right to regulate them as it regulates the fares on the elevated roads. I throw out the suggestion, knowing quite well that it is open to attack. It emanated originally from one of the brightest minds that have had to struggle officially with this tenement-house question in the last ten years. In any event, to succeed, reform by law must aim at making it unprofitable to own a bad tenement. At best, it is apt to travel at a snail's pace, while the enemy it pursues is putting the best foot foremost.

In this matter of profit the law ought to have its strongest ally in the landlord himself, though the reverse is the case. This condition of things I believe to rest on a monstrous error. It cannot be that tenement property that is worth preserving at all can continue to yield larger returns, if allowed to run down, than if properly cared for and kept in good repair. The point must be reached, and soon, where the cost of repairs, necessary with a house full of the lowest, most ignorant tenants, must overbalance the saving of the first few years of neglect; for this class is everywhere the most destructive, as well as the poorest

paying. I have the experience of owners, who have found this out to their cost, to back me up in the assertion, even if it were not the statement of a plain business fact that proves itself. I do not include tenement property that is deliberately allowed to fall into decay because at some future time the ground will be valuable for business or other purposes. There is unfortunately enough of that kind in New York, often leasehold property owned by wealthy estates or soulless corporations that oppose all their great influence to the efforts of the law in behalf of their tenants.

There is abundant evidence, on the other hand, that it can be made to pay to improve and make the most of the worst tenement property, even in the most wretched locality. The example set by Miss Ellen Collins in her Water Street houses will always stand as a decisive answer to all doubts on this point. It is quite ten years since she bought three old tenements at the corner of Water and Roosevelt Streets, then as now one of the lowest localities in the city. Since then she has leased three more adjoining her purchase, and so much of Water Street has at all events been purified. Her first effort was to let in the light in the hallways, and with the darkness disappeared, as if by magic, the heaps of refuse that used to be piled up beside the sinks. A few of the most refractory tenants disappeared with them, but a very considerable proportion stayed, conforming readily to the new rules, and are there yet. It should here be stated that Miss Collins's tenants are distinctly of the poorest. Her purpose was to experiment with this class, and her experiment has been more than satisfactory. Her plan was, as she puts it herself, fair play between tenant and landlord. To this end the rents were put as low as consistent with the idea of a business investment that must return a reasonable interest to be successful. The houses were thoroughly refitted with

57

proper plumbing. A competent janitor was put in charge to see that the rules were observed by the tenants, when Miss Collins herself was not there. Of late years she has had to give very little time to personal superintendence, and the care-taker told me only the other day that very little was needed. The houses seemed to run themselves in the groove once laid down. Once the reputed haunt of thieves, they have become the most orderly in the neighborhood. Clothes are left hanging on the lines all night with impunity, and the pretty flower-beds in the yard where the children not only from the six houses, but of the whole block, play, skip, and swing, are undisturbed. The tenants, by the way, provide the flowers themselves in the spring, and take all the more pride in them because they are their own. The six houses contain forty-five families, and there "has never been any need of putting up a bill." As to the income from the property, Miss Collins said to me last August: "I have had six and even six and three-quarters per cent on the capital invested; on the whole, you may safely say five and a half per cent. This I regard as entirely satisfactory." It should be added that she has persistently refused to let the corner-store, now occupied by a butcher, as a saloon; or her income from it might have been considerably increased.

Miss Collins's experience is of value chiefly as showing what can be accomplished with the worst possible material, by the sort of personal interest in the poor that alone will meet their real needs. All the charity in the world, scattered with the most lavish hand, will not take its place. "Fair play" between landlord and tenant is the key, too long mislaid, that unlocks the door to success everywhere as it did for Miss Collins. She has not lacked imitators whose experience has been akin to her own. The case of Gotham Court has been already cited. On the other hand, instances are not wanting of landlords who have undertaken the task, but have tired of it or sold their property before it had been fully redeemed, with the result that it relapsed into its former bad condition faster than it had improved, and the tenants with it. I am inclined to think that such houses are liable to fall even below the average level. Backsliding in brick and mortar does not greatly differ from similar performances in flesh and blood.

1. Which method of organization does this author predominately use in this passage?

    a. cause and effect
    b. comparing and contrasting
    c. problem and solution
    d. definition

2. What is the purpose of the passage?

    a. to draw comparisons
    b. to reflect
    c. to predict effects
    d. to suggest solutions

3. Which does the author establish as the **main problem** in this passage?

   a. *what to do with the tenements*
   b. how to get rid of bad landlords
   c. how to paint the tenements
   d. what to do with bad tenants

4. The word, "bald," used in the first line of the passage, most nearly means lacking

   a. treads.
   b. *disguise.*
   c. hair.
   d. natural covering.

5. Which of the following statements would the author support?

   a. Painting the tenements would be a tremendous improvement.
   b. Building more flats would definitely help the housing problem.
   c. *Private landowners need to do more to remodel tenements*.
   d. Right now the landlord is the strongest ally in fixing tenements.

6. Why does the author cite evidence from the Report of Tenement-house Commission?

   a. *It helps to build logos.*
   b. It helps to build pathos.
   c. It makes his report longer.
   d. It appeals to human fears.

7. What does the author mean when he says, "The Mulberry Street Bend will go the way of the Five Points when all the red tape that binds the hands of municipal effort has been unwound"?

   a. The people of the municipal effort have been arrested.
   b. *Too many steps and rules are restricting the efforts.*
   c. Many people are overwhelmed by all the trash.
   d. People who live in the tenements feel trapped.

8. How does the author feel about his suggestions for law reform?

   a. They are guaranteed to work.
   b. *They are open to criticism.*
   c. No one can think of anything else.
   d. People will openly accept them.

9. "At best, it is apt to travel at a snail's pace, while the enemy it pursues is putting the best foot foremost." What does this statement illustrate about the author's beliefs?

   a. The landlords will do their best to fix the tenements.
   b. Instituting law reform will be a quick process.
   c. Both the law and landlords will fix the tenements.
   d. *Instituting law reform will be a slow process.*

10. What does the author mean at the end of the passage when he says, "Backsliding in brick and mortar does not greatly differ from similar performances in flesh and blood"?

    a. The housing will stay at an average level of quality for most tenements.
    b. The brick and mortar is not strong enough to be used to repair tenements.
    c.   A regression in housing is very similar to a regression in human behavior.
    d. The tenements will fall down because humans don't care to restore them.

Evaluating the **AUTHOR'S CRAFT** means to consider how well the author has chosen to put together the text to address the purpose of the piece. When evaluating the author's craft, a reader should consider how the author's point of view, foreshadowing, flashback, symbolism, irony, mood, and figurative language work together to create an effect or follow a purpose. In addition, part of the author's craft includes the way the writer uses logos, pathos, and ethos as well as organization to achieve a purpose.

11. Why does the author include the story of Miss Ellen Collins? Evaluate the effectiveness of the author's craft. Use specific evidence from the text to support your point.

One possible answer:

The story of Miss Ellen Collins builds logos and ethos within the text, helping to convince readers that the author's solutions may work. Early in the text the author makes it clear that the landlords are those who should be responsible for the turn-around needed: "Private enterprise—conscience, to put it in the category of duties, where it belongs—must do the lion's share under these last two heads." However, the author recognizes that landlords want to yield some kind of profit. The Collins' story illustrates how profit and sufficient living conditions can coexist. Miss Collins cleaned up the building area and kept the rent so that a satisfactory earning could be met. Because she has upheld the integrity of the building (by enforcing strict rules and not allowing a saloon to inhabit part of it), the neighbors have taken pride in their living space (leaving clothes on the line overnight and planting flowers). The story of Miss Collins shows that the author's suggestions of a "fair play" between tenant and landlord actually works, adding to his credibility (ethos) and building support for his solution (logos).

12. How does the author present his problems and solutions? What effect does this feature have on the overall passage? Use specific evidence from the text to support your point.

One possible answer:

The author uses Roman numeral lists to emphasize both the problems and solutions within the text. He presents a list of opinions in a very factual tone in the first set of Roman numerals. The list format allows readers to easily follow how he gets to the specific, stated problem with few questions about the reasoning he uses to get there. He begins with the broad topic of housing people decently and narrows down to a more specific aspect of housing—the tenements. His defined problem (How are we going to use the tenements to create more decent housing?) is answered in another set of Roman numerals later in the text. He lists his three-part plan; this clearly-defined resolution makes the author appear well organized and serious—two qualities he needs to convince his audience that his solution is the right one. The use of Roman numerals creates conciseness and clarity within the text, allowing the reader to focus more on the plan itself instead of the way it is presented.

> A **PROBLEM AND SOLUTION** text is one in which a problem is presented to the audience and one or more solutions follow. Many times the author will address possible arguments against his/her solution in order to strengthen his/her point. In addition, the author should use multiple examples that support his/her solution. To **analyze problems and solutions** means to determine the problems and analyze the possible solutions. In some cases, you may be asked to come up with your own solution to a problem while in other cases you may be determining the quality or practicality of solutions presented.

13. What does the author see as some of the things standing in the way of creating a working solution?

The author believes that the one thing standing in the way of his working solution is the greed and apathy of others. The author first mentions this idea in his first set of Roman numerals: "That nothing but our own slothfulness is in the way of so housing it, since 'the condition of the tenants is in advance of the condition of the houses which they occupy.'" Quoting a conclusion by the Report of Tenement-house Commission, he begins to address people's own apathy towards helping others who want to rise above their meager surroundings. This is further developed when the author addresses laws that may promote reform. However, he mentions that, without these laws, change will not occur. Landlords will continue on their course until lawmakers "aim at making it unprofitable to own a bad tenement."

The author even moves beyond the individual and addresses the large companies that purposefully allow tenement property "to fall into decay because at some future time the ground will be valuable for business or other purposes." He adds that in order to make a profit later they often "oppose all their great influence to the efforts of the law in behalf of their tenants."

All of these examples contrast sharply with the example of Miss Collins. She is able to restore her tenement because of her hard work enforcing stricter rules and remodeling the tenements. Most noteworthy, however, is that she "has persistently refused to let the corner-store, now occupied by a butcher, as a saloon; or her income from it might have been considerably increased." The solution has worked because she has not let her greed or her apathy get in the way as it has with others. The author even mentions those who attempted to imitate Miss Collins' admirable quest to fix the tenements; however, they "have undertaken the task, but have tired of it or sold their property before it had been fully redeemed, with the result that it relapsed into its former bad condition faster than it had improved, and the tenants with it." The author recognizes throughout the passage that both greed and apathy may stand in the way of his solution to the tenement problem.

PASSAGE 1: FROM *NATURE*

by Ralph Waldo Emerson

To go into solitude, a man needs to retire as much from his chamber as from society. I am not solitary whilst I read and write, though nobody is with me. But if a man would be alone, let him look at the stars. The rays that come from those heavenly worlds, will separate between him and what he touches. One might think the atmosphere was made transparent with this design, to give man, in the heavenly bodies, the perpetual presence of the sublime. Seen in the streets of cities, how great they are! If the stars should appear one night in a thousand years, how would men believe and adore; and preserve for many generations the remembrance of the city of God which had been shown! But every night come out these envoys of beauty, and light the universe with their admonishing smile.

The stars awaken a certain reverence, because though always present, they are inaccessible; but all natural objects make a kindred impression, when the mind is open to their influence. Nature never wears a mean appearance. Neither does the wisest man extort her secret, and lose his curiosity by finding out all her perfection. Nature never became a toy to a wise spirit. The flowers, the animals, the mountains, reflected the wisdom of his best hour, as much as they had delighted the simplicity of his childhood.

When we speak of nature in this manner, we have a distinct but most poetical sense in the mind. We mean the integrity of impression made by manifold natural objects. It is this which distinguishes the stick of timber of the wood-cutter, from the tree of the poet. The charming landscape which I saw this morning, is indubitably made up of some twenty or thirty farms. Miller owns this field, Locke that, and Manning the woodland beyond. But none of them owns the landscape. There is a property in the horizon which no man has but he whose eye can integrate all the parts, that is, the poet. This is the best part of these men's farms, yet to this their warranty-deeds give no title.

To speak truly, few adult persons can see nature. Most persons do not see the sun. At least they have a very superficial seeing. The sun illuminates only the eye of the man, but shines into the eye and the heart of the child. The lover of nature is he whose inward and outward senses are still truly adjusted to each other; who has retained the spirit of infancy even into the era of manhood. His intercourse with heaven and earth, becomes part of his daily food. In the presence of nature, a wild delight runs through the man, in spite of real sorrows. Nature says,—he is my creature, and maugre all his impertinent griefs, he shall be glad with me. Not the sun or the summer alone, but every hour and season yields its tribute of delight; for every hour and change corresponds to and authorizes a different state of the mind, from breathless noon to grimmest midnight. Nature is a setting that fits equally well a comic or a mourning piece. In good health, the air is a cordial of incredible virtue. Crossing a bare common, in snow puddles, at twilight, under a clouded sky, without having in my thoughts any occurrence of special good fortune, I have enjoyed a perfect exhilaration. I am glad to the brink of fear. In the woods too, a man casts off his years, as the snake his slough, and at what period soever of life, is always a child. In the woods, is perpetual youth. Within these plantations of God, a decorum and sanctity reign, a perennial festival is dressed, and the guest sees not how he should tire of them in a thousand years. In the woods, we return to reason and faith. There I feel that nothing can befall me in life,—no disgrace, no calamity, (leaving me my eyes,) which nature cannot repair. Standing on the bare ground,—my head bathed by the blithe air, and uplifted into infinite space,—all mean egotism vanishes. I become a transparent eyeball; I am nothing; I see all; the currents of the Universal Being circulate through me; I am part or particle of God. The name of the nearest friend sounds then foreign and accidental: to be brothers, to be acquaintances,— master or servant, is then a trifle and a disturbance. I am the lover of uncontained and immortal beauty. In the wilderness, I find something more dear and connate than in streets or villages. In the tranquil landscape, and especially in the distant line of the horizon, man beholds somewhat as beautiful as his own nature.

PASSAGE II:
"MY HEART LEAPS UP WHEN I BEHOLD"
by William Wordsworth

My heart leaps up when I behold   1
A rainbow in the sky:
So was it when my life began,
So is it now I am a man,
So be it when I shall grow old   5
Or let me die!
The Child is father of the Man:
And I could wish my days to be
Bound each to each by natural piety.

Passage I

1. In the first paragraph Emerson notes, "If the stars should appear one night in a thousand years, how would men believe and adore; and preserve for many generations the remembrance of the city of God which had been shown!" From this quote, the reader infers that Emerson believes man

   a.   doesn't enjoy spending time in nature.
   b.   loves watching and adoring the stars.
   c.   ***doesn't appreciate his daily surroundings.***
   d.   passes memories to other generations.

2. Using paragraph 3, Emerson feel that poets

   a.   ***understand the value of nature.***
   b.   need to acquire their own land.
   c.   now the best parts of the land to farm.
   d.   can see the horizon line better than others.

65

3. Emerson writes, "In the woods too, a man casts off his years, as the snake his slough, and at what period soever of life, is always a child." In order to make his point he uses

   a. consonance.
   b. simile.
   c. hyperbole.
   d. personification.

4. In the final paragraph, Emerson comments, "The lover of nature is he whose inward and outward senses are still truly adjusted to each other; who has retained the spirit of infancy even into the era of manhood. His intercourse with heaven and earth, becomes part of his daily food." This statement suggests that a person

   a. cannot survive without eating fruits and vegetables.
   b. must act childish in order to feel fulfilled.
   c. begins to need the relationship with nature.
   d. feels hungry after spending time in the city.

5. In the final paragraph Emerson writes, "Within these plantations of God, a decorum and sanctity reign, a perennial festival is dressed, and the guest sees not how he should tire of them in a thousand years." Who is the guest?

   a. nature
   b. God
   c. man
   d. the festival

Passage II

6. Line 1 of Wordsworth's poem contains an example of

   a. metaphor.
   b. simile.
   c. hyperbole.
   d. personification.

7. The word, "bound," in this poem is most synonymous with

   a. restrained.
   b. fastened.
   c. tied.
   d. united.

Passages I and II

8. How would you summarize Emerson's view of nature? Use specific details from the text to support your summary.

One possible answer:

Emerson is saying that a person's ability to make a sincere connection with nature is necessary to achieve a bond with a higher power. The passage begins with the example of the stars. Although the stars are out every night, most people do not recognize the sanctity within them. Rather the stars look down with an "admonishing smile," silently reprimanding those below who are unaware of them. Emerson asserts in his first lines that a person must leave not only society but also even his own chamber and the solitary pursuits of reading and writing to truly achieve a connection with a higher power. While farmers may spend their days with nature, Emerson recognizes that even they are not making a sincere connection, commenting that they do not realize "the best part of these men's farms, yet to this their warranty-deeds give no title."

Perhaps the strongest evidence about Emerson's feelings on nature comes when he describes himself standing on the bare ground: "I become a transparent eyeball; I am nothing; I see all; the current of the Universal Being circulate through me." Only after Emerson has removed himself from all aspects of society and communed with nature can he actually shed his own selfishness, allowing himself to experience the energy and purity of a higher understanding.

> **PARADOX** is a literary device in which a statement appears contradictory but actually reveals a kind of truth. For example, in Shakespeare's *Julius Caesar* he writes, "A coward dies many times before his death." At first glance it doesn't appear to be possible (How can a person die many times?); however, after some thought, Shakespeare's message becomes clear.

9. Find an example of a paradox either in Emerson's *Nature* or Wordsworth's "My Heart Leaps Up When I Behold." Discuss the meaning of the paradox and how it adds to the overall development of the piece. Be sure to use specific details from the text to support your answer.

Students have multiple examples to choose from. Students may comment on the paradox in Wordsworth's poem: " The Child is father of the Man." While the audience may first wonder how a child can be a father of someone older, the paradox develops the idea that a child's innocence (devoid of all pressures and responsibilities of an adult in society) allows him or her to sincerely appreciate such natural miracles as a rainbow. Wordsworth points out that adults should learn, or rather relearn, this important quality. Students may also comment on the religious overtones of the paradox: the capitalized word, Child, may represent Jesus, again developing the idea that people need to return to those natural things most basic and pure such as a rainbow.

Students may also choose one of Emerson's many paradoxes such as "I am not solitary whilst I read and write, though nobody is with me." Again, by definition most people would define solitary as having no one around. However, although Emerson may be physically alone, he is still surrounded by the thoughts of society (what he reads) and his reaction to society (what he writes). This is the beginning of Emerson's point in which he suggests that, in order to be truly solitary and therefore able to understand a higher Truth, he must escape to the haven of nature.

Another example from Emerson's book comes in the fourth paragraph when he says, "few adult persons can see nature." While it is obvious that adults can actually see nature, the reader quickly realizes that Emerson refers to actually understanding nature in its entirety. This paradox helps to develop an earlier point in which he says that "it is this which distinguishes the stick of timber of the wood-cutter, from the tree of the poet." The woodcutter cannot fully understand the importance or majesty of the tree. He only sees the tree as a means of profit. Similar to Wordsworth, this also establishes the point that children are more apt to truly experience nature than adults are. Finally, the paradox is a precursor for Emerson's climatic transformation in which he describes himself as a " transparent eyeball" that "sees all." Emerson has transcended the confines of adulthood to truly "see" nature for the holy and majestic thing that it is.

10. Compare and contrast Emerson's *Nature* with Wordsworth's "My Heart Leaps Up When I Behold." Consider how they compare and contrast in terms of ideas and style (literary devices, diction, tone, syntax, and detail).

While Ralph Waldo Emerson's Nature *and Wordsworth's "My Heart Leaps Up When I Behold" use different genres and different tones in their works, they both use the element of paradox to express the pure relationship with nature necessary to reach a higher existence.*

Wordsworth creates a more informal and simplistic tone through poetry while Emerson creates a formal and mature piece in his book. Poetry by nature is more concise. Rather than support his opinion by offering multiple examples, Wordsworth keeps his message simple and informal, spending six of his nine lines wishing to keep the sacred connection he has with nature. This author's personal reflection makes the audience feel as if it overhears words rather than being directly addressed. (Notice he uses first person singular throughout the poem.)

Emerson, however, uses prose to offer multiple scenarios that create a more formal address to the audience. Whereas Wordsworth only uses "I," Emerson speaks directly to his audience by using "We." He establishes the responsibility of keeping the sacred connection with nature as everyone's task by offering examples when men cannot see nature for what it is: Men do not appreciate the stars; woodcutters and other landowners do not see the beauty of the land; adults do not truly see nature.

In addition, the difference in tone is accentuated through each author's diction. Wordsworth's casual, simplistic tone is created mostly through his diction: he mostly uses single-syllable words, creating a piece that a wide audience, including children, can understand. Wordsworth captures that youth he hopes to hold with him all his life through his language. Emerson, on the other hand, offers a more complex vocabulary to develop his more formal tone. Words such as "indubitably," "calamity," "exhilaration," "admonishing," "impertinent," and "maugre" all create the formal, mature address to the audience.

While the authors present their ideas differently, they both use the power of the paradox to make the same message clear: One must approach nature with the purity of a child in order to truly appreciate the great opportunity nature gives us to unite with a higher power.

Both men use a paradox directly addressing the power that a child beholds. Wordsworth comments, "The Child is father of man" while Emerson notes, " few adult persons can see nature." Both of these are discussed above in question 9. In addition, both authors note that this innocent approach to nature is important to being able to fully experience nature's power. Wordsworth knows that "so it is now I am a man" because he is still able to internally feel nature's power as he sees a rainbow. Similarly, Emerson states, " In the woods too, a man casts off his years, as the snake his slough, and at what period soever of life, is always a child. In the woods, is perpetual youth." Both men feel that the youthful energy is not about age but rather a state of mind that allows them to feed off of the energy and knowledge that nature beholds; it becomes their "daily food."

Finally, both men feel that this energy allows them to connect with a more sacred power. Wordsworth's final word, "piety," connotes a religious devotion by which Wordsworth would like to be "bound." Emerson more directly states this connection, commenting " the currents of the Universal Being circulate through me; I am part or particle of God." Both men carry similar messages of nature's power.

Question 1	Making Inferences
Question 2	Recognizing the Author's Beliefs/Bias
Question 3	Analyzing Figurative Language
Question 4	Making Inferences
Question 5	Summarizing and Paraphrasing
Question 6	Analyzing Figurative Language
Question 7	Analyzing Diction
Question 8	Summarizing and Paraphrasing
Question 9	Analyzing Paradox
Question 10	Comparing and Contrasting

Her First Ball

by Katherine Mansfield

Exactly when the ball began Leila would have found it hard to say. Perhaps her first real partner was the cab. It did not matter that she shared the cab with the Sheridan girls and their brother. She sat back in her own little corner of it, and the bolster on which her hand rested felt like the sleeve of an unknown young man's dress suit; and away they bowled, past waltzing lamp-posts and houses and fences and trees.

"Have you really never been to a ball before, Leila? But, my child, how too weird—" cried the Sheridan girls.

"Our nearest neighbor was fifteen miles," said Leila softly, gently opening and shutting her fan.

Oh dear, how hard it was to be indifferent like the others! She tried not to smile too much; she tried not to care. But every single thing was so new and exciting . . . Meg's tuberoses, Jose's long loop of amber, Laura's little dark head, pushing above her white fur like a flower through snow. She would remember forever. It even gave her a pang to see her cousin Laurie throw away the wisps of tissue paper he pulled from the fastenings of his new gloves. She would like to have kept those wisps as a keepsake, as a remembrance. Laurie leaned forward and put his hand on Laura's knee.

"Look here, darling," he said. "The third and the ninth as usual. Twig?"

Oh, how marvelous to have a brother! In her excitement Leila felt that if there had been time, if it hadn't been impossible, she couldn't have helped crying because she was an only child, and no brother had ever said "Twig?" to her; no sister would ever say, as Meg said to Jose that moment, "I've never known your hair go up more successfully than it has tonight!"

But, of course, there was no time. They were at the drill hall already; there were cabs in front of them and cabs behind. The road was bright on either side with moving fan-like lights, and on the pavement gay couples seemed to float through the air; little satin shoes chased each other like birds.

"Hold on to me, Leila; you'll get lost," said Laura.

"Come on, girls, let's make a dash for it," said Laurie.

Leila put two fingers on Laura's pink velvet cloak, and they were somehow lifted past the big golden lantern, carried along the passage, and pushed into the little room marked "Ladies." Here the crowd was so great there was hardly space to take off their things; the noise was deafening. Two benches on either side were stacked high with wraps. Two old women in white aprons ran up and down tossing fresh armfuls. And everybody was pressing forward trying to get at the little dressing-table and mirror at the far end.

A great quivering jet of gas lighted the ladies' room. It couldn't wait; it was dancing already. When the door opened again and there came a burst of tuning from the drill hall, it leaped almost to the ceiling.

Dark girls, fair girls were patting their hair, tying ribbons again, tucking handkerchiefs down the fronts of their bodices, smoothing marble-white gloves. And because they were all laughing it seemed to Leila that they were all lovely.

"Aren't there any invisible hair-pins?" cried a voice. "How most extraordinary! I can't see a single invisible hair-pin."

"Powder my back, there's a darling," cried some one else.

"But I must have a needle and cotton. I've torn simply miles and miles of the frill," wailed a third.

71

Then, "Pass them along, pass them along!" The straw basket of programs was tossed from arm to arm. Darling little pink-and-silver programs, with pink pencils and fluffy tassels. Leila's fingers shook as she took one out of the basket. She wanted to ask some one, "Am I meant to have one too?" but she had just time to read: "Waltz 3. 'Two, Two in a Canoe.' Polka 4. 'Making the Feathers Fly,'" when Meg cried, "Ready, Leila?" and they pressed their way through the crush in the passage towards the big double doors of the drill hall.

Dancing had not begun yet, but the band had stopped tuning, and the noise was so great it seemed that when it did begin to play it would never be heard. Leila, pressing close to Meg, looking over Meg's shoulder, felt that even the little quivering colored flags strung across the ceiling were talking. She quite forgot to be shy; she forgot how in the middle of dressing she had sat down on the bed with one shoe off and one shoe on and begged her mother to ring up her cousins and say she couldn't go after all. And the rush of longing she had had to be sitting on the veranda of their forsaken up-country home, listening to the baby owls crying "More pork" in the moonlight, was changed to a rush of joy so sweet that it was hard to bear alone. She clutched her fan, and, gazing at the gleaming, golden floor, the azaleas, the lanterns, the stage at one end with its red carpet and gilt chairs and the band in a corner, she thought breathlessly, "How heavenly; how simply heavenly!"

All the girls stood grouped together at one side of the doors, the men at the other, and the chaperones in dark dresses, smiling rather foolishly, walked with little careful steps over the polished floor towards the stage.

"This is my little country cousin Leila. Be nice to her. Find her partners; she's under my wing," said Meg, going up to one girl after another.

Strange faces smiled at Leila—sweetly, vaguely. Strange voices answered, "Of course, my dear." But Leila felt the girls didn't really see her. They were looking towards the men. Why didn't the men begin? What were they waiting for? There they stood, smoothing their gloves, patting their glossy hair and smiling among themselves. Then, quite suddenly, as if they had only just made up their minds that that was what they had to do, the men came gliding over the parquet. There was a joyful flutter among the girls. A tall, fair man flew up to Meg, seized her programs, scribbled something; Meg passed him on to Leila. "May I have the pleasure?" He ducked and smiled. There came a dark man wearing an eyeglass, then cousin Laurie with a friend, and Laura with a little freckled fellow whose tie was crooked. Then quite an old man—fat, with a big bald patch on his head—took her programs and murmured, "Let me see, let me see!" And he was a long time comparing his programs, which looked black with names, with hers. It seemed to give him so much trouble that Leila was ashamed. "Oh, please don't bother," she said eagerly. But instead of replying the fat man wrote something, glanced at her again. "Do I remember this bright little face?" he said softly. "Is it known to me of yore?" At that moment the band began playing; the fat man disappeared. He was tossed away on a great wave of music that came flying over the gleaming floor, breaking the groups up into couples, scattering them, sending them spinning . . .

Leila had learned to dance at boarding school. Every Saturday afternoon the boarders were hurried off to a little corrugated iron mission hall where Miss Eccles (of London) held her "select" classes. But the difference between that dusty-smelling hall—with calico texts on the walls, the poor terrified little woman in a brown velvet toque with rabbit's ears thumping the cold piano, Miss Eccles poking the girls' feet with her long white wand—and this was so tremendous that Leila was sure if her partner didn't come and she had to listen to that marvelous music and to watch the others sliding, gliding over the golden floor, she would die at least, or faint, or lift her arms and fly out of one of those dark windows that showed the stars.

"Ours, I think—" Some one bowed, smiled, and offered her his arm; she hadn't to die after all. Someone's hand pressed her waist, and she floated away like a flower that is tossed into a pool.

"Quite a good floor, isn't it?" drawled a faint voice close to her ear.

"I think it's most beautifully slippery," said Leila.

"Pardon!" The faint voice sounded surprised. Leila said it again. And there was a tiny pause before the voice echoed, "Oh, quite!" and she was swung round again.

He steered so beautifully. That was the great difference between dancing with girls and men, Leila decided. Girls banged into each other, and stamped on each other's feet; the girl who was gentleman always clutched you so.

The azaleas were separate flowers no longer; they were pink and white flags streaming by.

"Were you at the Bells' last week?" the voice came again. It sounded tired. Leila wondered whether she ought to ask him if he would like to stop.

"No, this is my first dance," said she.

Her partner gave a little gasping laugh. "Oh, I say," he protested.

"Yes, it is really the first dance I've ever been to." Leila was most fervent. It was such a relief to be able to tell somebody.

"You see, I've lived in the country all my life up till now . . ."

At that moment the music stopped, and they went to sit on two chairs against the wall. Leila tucked her pink satin feet under and fanned herself, while she blissfully watched the other couples passing and disappearing through the swing doors.

"Enjoying yourself, Leila?" asked Jose, nodding her golden head.

Laura passed and gave her the faintest little wink; it made Leila wonder for a moment whether she was quite grown up after all. Certainly her partner did not say very much. He coughed, tucked his handkerchief away, pulled down his waistcoat, took a minute thread off his sleeve. But it didn't matter. Almost immediately the band started and her second partner seemed to spring from the ceiling.

"Floor's not bad," said the new voice. Did one always begin with the floor? And then, "Were you at the Neaves' on Tuesday?" And again Leila explained. Perhaps it was a little strange that her partners were not more interested. For it was thrilling. Her first ball! She was only at the beginning of everything. It seemed to her that she had never known what the night was like before. Up till now it had been dark, silent, beautiful very often—oh yes—but mournful somehow. Solemn. And now it would never be like that again—it had opened dazzling bright.

"Care for an ice?" said her partner. And they went through the swing doors, down the passage, to the supper room. Her cheeks burned, she was fearfully thirsty. How sweet the ices looked on little glass plates and how cold the frosted spoon was, iced too! And when they came back to the hall there was the fat man waiting for her by the door. It gave her quite a shock again to see how old he was; he ought to have

73

been on the stage with the fathers and mothers. And when Leila compared him with her other partners he looked shabby. His waistcoat was creased, there was a button off his glove, his coat looked as if it was dusty with French chalk.

"Come along, little lady," said the fat man. He scarcely troubled to clasp her, and they moved away so gently, it was more like walking than dancing. But he said not a word about the floor. "Your first dance, isn't it?" he murmured.

"How did you know?"

"Ah," said the fat man, "that's what it is to be old!" He wheezed faintly as he steered her past an awkward couple. "You see, I've been doing this kind of thing for the last thirty years."

"Thirty years?" cried Leila. Twelve years before she was born!

"It hardly bears thinking about, does it?" said the fat man gloomily. Leila looked at his bald head, and she felt quite sorry for him.

"I think it's marvelous to be still going on," she said kindly.

"Kind little lady," said the fat man, and he pressed her a little closer, and hummed a bar of the waltz. "Of course," he said, "you can't hope to last anything like as long as that. No-o," said the fat man, "long before that you'll be sitting up there on the stage, looking on, in your nice black velvet. And these pretty arms will have turned into little short fat ones, and you'll beat time with such a different kind of fan—a black bony one." The fat man seemed to shudder. "And you'll smile away like the poor old dears up there, and point to your daughter, and tell the elderly lady next to you how some dreadful man tried to kiss her at the club ball. And your heart will ache, ache"— the fat man squeezed her closer still, as if he really was sorry for that poor heart—

"because no one wants to kiss you now. And you'll say how unpleasant these polished floors are to walk on, how dangerous they are. Eh, Mademoiselle Twinkletoes?" said the fat man softly.

Leila gave a light little laugh, but she did not feel like laughing. Was it—could it all be true? It sounded terribly true. Was this first ball only the beginning of her last ball, after all? At that the music seemed to change; it sounded sad, sad; it rose upon a great sigh. Oh, how quickly things changed! Why didn't happiness last forever? Forever wasn't a bit too long.

"I want to stop," she said in a breathless voice. The fat man led her to the door.

"No," she said, "I won't go outside. I won't sit down. I'll just stand here, thank you." She leaned against the wall, tapping with her foot, pulling up her gloves and trying to smile. But deep inside her a little girl threw her pinafore over her head and sobbed. Why had he spoiled it all?

"I say, you know," said the fat man, "you mustn't take me seriously, little lady."

"As if I should!" said Leila, tossing her small dark head and sucking her underlip . . .

Again the couples paraded. The swing doors opened and shut. Now new music was given out by the bandmaster. But Leila didn't want to dance any more. She wanted to be home, or sitting on the veranda listening to those baby owls. When she looked through the dark windows at the stars, they had long beams like wings . . .

But presently a soft, melting, ravishing tune began, and a young man with curly hair bowed before her. She would have to dance, out of politeness, until she could find Meg. Very stiffly she walked into the middle; very haughtily she put her hand on his sleeve. But in one minute, in one turn, her feet glided, glided. The lights, the

74

azaleas, the dresses, the pink faces, the velvet chairs, all became one beautiful flying wheel. And when her next partner bumped her into the fat man and he said, "Pardon," she smiled at him more radiantly than ever. She didn't even recognize him again.

1. The text is which genre of fiction?

   a. novella
   b. novel
   c. short story
   d. drama

2. This story is written in

   a. first person.
   b. third person limited.
   c. third person omniscient.
   d. objective.

3. Which event **best** represents the climax in the story?

   a. when she is standing at the door upset
   b. when she arrives to the ladies room
   c. when she dances with her first partner
   d. when she doesn't recognize the old man

4. Leila could **best** be described as

   a. snobbish.
   b. sensitive.
   c. naïve.
   d. depressed.

5. The author describes Leila as she begins her first dance saying, "she floated away like a flower that is tossed into a pool." What effect does this create?

   a. It shows that Leila feels like she's drowning.
   b. It emphasizes the soft smoothness of the dance.
   c. It illustrates the loneliness she feels at the ball.
   d. It shows how excited she is to be at the ball.

6. "She clutched her fan, and, gazing at the gleaming, golden floor" is an example of

   a. alliteration.
   b. assonance.
   c. onomatopoeia.
   d. personification.

7. "A great quivering jet of gas lighted the ladies' room. It couldn't wait; it was dancing already." This passage contains an example of

   a. simile.
   b. metaphor.
   c. hyperbole.
   d. personification.

8. For what are the " darling little pink-and-silver programs, with pink pencils and fluffy tassels" used?

   a. to review and study the different dance moves
   b. to record the experiences from the evening
   c. to learn more about the people at the dance
   d. to reserve dances with specific men

9. Which of the following can be concluded from the first two dance partners' comments and Leila's thoughts while she is with them?

   a. It is their first dance as well.
   b. They have little interest in Leila.
   c. They are not very good dancers.
   d. They both enjoy Leila's company.

10. Which can be inferred when Leila is described as sucking her underlip?

    a. Leila has chapped lips.
    b. Leila is tired of talking.
    c. Leila is about to cry.
    d. Leila is very thirsty.

11. What is Leila mostly likely to do after her dance with the curly-haired young man?

    a. Leila will dance with the old man again.
    b. Leila will go home because she is upset.
    c. Leila will stay and continue to dance.
    d. Leila will sit outside and look at the stars.

12. Which generalization can be made from the short story?

    a. The women initiate most of the action at the ball.
    b. The men initiate most of the action at the ball.
    c. The chaperones control what happens at the ball.
    d. The band controls what happens at the ball.

13. Is Leila a static or dynamic character? Use evidence from the text to support your answer.

One possible answer:

While Leila may be experiencing new things at her first ball, her character remains unchanged from the beginning of the story to the end, making her a static character. In the beginning of the story, the narrator comments, "the azaleas were separate flowers no longer; they were pink and white flags streaming by," describing the elation Leila feels as she is dancing with her first partner. Even after the old man's comments disturb Leila, she still feels the euphoria and wonder of her first dance: "The lights, the azaleas, the dresses, the pink faces, the velvet chairs, all became one beautiful flying wheel." If her naïve outlook on the ball and its meaning had changed, she would perhaps have no longer seen it this way. The transient impact of the old man's comments is once again emphasized in the final line of the story when she bumps into the old man, smiles brightly, and doesn't even recognize him.

14. Evaluate the opening paragraph of the short story. What does the author do to make it effective or ineffective for you in terms of setting up the rest of the story? Be sure to use specific evidence from the text to support your answer.

One possible answer:

The opening paragraph is effective in this short story because it captures the excitement and wonder that characterizes Leila's first ball. The author opens the story by mentioning that Leila didn't even know when the ball began. This immediately identifies Leila's experience as some kind of dream or fantasy; in anticipation of her arrival at the ball, she imagines the taxi bolster is "like the sleeve of an unknown young man's dress suit." Just as the man in her daydream is unknown, the entire experience of the ball is foreign to her. The author is able to catch both her naiveté and excitement in this simile, providing a springboard for later events in the story. In particular, the idea of the extended arm comes up before her first dance. In her novice insecurity Leila's hopes are almost dashed as the first song begins to play and she still has no arm. However, just in time "someone bowed, smiled, and offered her his arm." The audience can make the connection that her fantasy from the cab has so far come to fruition.

11

Along with similes, the narrator also uses personification in her first paragraph to create excitement. With her childlike imagination Leila envisions dancing with this "unknown man" past "waltzing lampposts"; this personification once again emphasizes the almost Cinderella fantasy Leila seems to be living. The author continues to bring everything to life around Leila, commenting on the bathroom light's desire to dance later in the text. The naiveté and excitement in the first paragraph which is developed in subsequent paragraphs provide a sharp contrast with Leila's feelings after she talks to the old man and a reference point for Leila's return to elation after she begins dancing again.

"My Mistress' Eyes Are Nothing Like the Sun"

by William Shakespeare

My mistress' eyes are nothing like the sun;   1
Coral is far more red than her lip's red:
If snow be white, why then her breasts are dun;
If hair be wires, black wires grow on her head.
I have seen roses damasked, red and white,   5
But no such roses see I in her cheeks;
In some perfumes there is more delight
Than the breath with which my mistress reeks.
I love to hear her speak, yet well I know
Music hath a far more pleasing sound: 10
I grant I never saw a goddess go, —
My mistress, when she walks, treads on the ground:
　　And yet, by heaven, I think my love as rare
　　As any she belied with false compare.

1. This poem is an example of a(n)

    a. ballad.
    b. ode.
    c. sonnet.
    d. elegy.

2. The word, "treads," carries the connotation of

    a. tiptoeing.
    b. trampling.
    c. running.
    d. crawling.

3. The speaker believes that

    a. beauty is important.
    b. his mistress is beautiful.
    c. his mistress is special.
    d. his mistress is smart.

4. It can be concluded that the woman in the poem

    a. is not physically attractive.
    b. is smarter than most people.
    c. is as beautiful as a goddess.
    d. doesn't love the speaker.

5. The tone of this poem is

   a. angry.
   b. disgusted.
   c. concerned.
   d. content.

6. How does rhyme help to emphasize meaning in this poem? Use specific evidence from the text to support your answer.

   The rhyme scheme fits that of a typical Shakespearean sonnet: ababcdcdefefgg. The rhyme scheme helps draw attention to the two most important lines of the entire poem. While the reader may be thrown off by the first 12 lines, determining that the speaker does not like his mistress, the last two lines depart from the rhyme scheme of the rest of the poem in the form of a rhymed couplet, clarifying why the speaker says all of those seemingly cruel things. Even though his woman is not the most beautiful, the poet loves her just as much if not more than he would were she the most beautiful.

7. Explain how Shakespeare uses figurative language to create an effect in this poem. Be sure to use specific evidence from the text to support your answer.

   Shakespeare uses metaphors and similes to paint an unattractive, almost comic, picture of his mistress. He begins with "My mistress' eyes are nothing like the sun." Using this simile, the reader is immediately taken aback; many love poems compare a beautiful woman to the sun. However, Shakespeare establishes that his woman's eyes do not have a brilliant shine. He continues with the metaphor, "If hair be wires, black wires grow on her head." Again, wires, carrying the connotation of stiffness and stringiness, are a far departure from the soft, flowing hair usually associated with the beautiful female in love poems. Shakespeare's use of similes and metaphors immediately causes the reader to compare the description of the woman in the poem with the descriptions of women often found in love poems. This contrast between the two types of women ultimately helps Shakespeare to make his point in the final two lines.

8. How does this love poem compare or contrast to other love poems you've read or heard? Consider your prior knowledge of love poems, including those you've encountered in books, cards, movies, or even those you've written. Why does Shakespeare present his poem this way?

Students will most likely remember poems they've read in the past that glorify the beauty of women such as, "Shall I Compare Thee To a Summer's Day" (also by Shakespeare) or "She Dwelt Among Untrodden Ways." Students may also conjure images of movies they've seen in which a character has professed his love to another, while commenting on the woman's beauty. Students will note the sharp contrast between Shakespeare's poem and most poems about love. Some students may even note that the last two lines do not make up for what he has said about her.

In any event, Shakespeare creates this contrast to emphasize a a truer, purer love, one that is not about infatuation. This more spiritual love is emphasized in Shakespeare's poem when he includes "by heaven" in the last two lines. He insinuates that his love is a purer love than that of someone who may only be able to comment on the woman's outer beauty. Distinctly different from typical love poems in which woman are presented as perfect beings, Shakespeare's final two lines are even more moving: "While you are not perfect, I love you more than those who falsely compare their women's beauty to natural wonders of the earth."

Question 1   Distinguishing Genres of Poetry
Question 2   Analyzing Diction
Question 3   Recognizing Author's Beliefs
Question 4   Drawing Conclusions
Question 5   Analyzing Development of Tone
Question 6   Analyzing Sound Devices and Rhythm
Question 7   Analyzing Figurative Language
Question 8   Using Prior Knowledge

"DELIGHT IN DISORDER"

by Robert Herrick

A sweet disorder in the dress	1
Kindles in clothes a wantonness;	
A lawn about the shoulders thrown	
Into a fine distraction;	
An erring lace, which here and there	5
Enthrals the crimson stomacher;	
A cuff neglectful, and thereby	
Ribbons to flow confusedly;	
A winning wave, deserving note,	
In the tempestuous petticoat;	10
A careless shoe-string, in whose tie	
I see a wild civility;—	
Do more bewitch me, than when art	
Is too precise in every part.	

1. Line 8 contains an example of

   a. simile.
   b. metaphor.
   c. hyperbole.
   d. personification.

2. The word, "bewitch," in this poem most nearly means

   a. cast a spell.
   b. captivate.
   c. attract.
   d. beguile.

3. The tone of this poem is

   a. admiring.
   b. sarcastic.
   c. sentimental.
   d. cheery.

4. Which of the following generalizations can be made?

   a. The narrator loves all kinds of art.
   b. The narrator appreciates imprecision.
   c. The narrator likes dressing sloppily.
   d. The narrator loves the chaos in life.

5. "Deserving note" modifies

    a. winning.

    b. *wave.*

    c. tempestuous.

    d. petticoat.

6. Which genre of poetry is the poem?

    a. *sonnet*

    b. ballad

    c. ode

    d. elegy

 An **OXYMORON** is a figure of speech in which contradictory or opposite words are used conjointly for an effect. "Jumbo shrimp," "deafening silence," "alone together," and "original copy" are just some examples.

7. Find two examples of oxymoron in the poem. For each one, explain the oxymoron and how it helps the development of the poem.

One possible answer:

"Sweet disorder" is one example that comes immediately in the first line. The word, "disorder," generally has a negative connotation; therefore, pairing it with "sweet" seems contradictory. However, Herrick's point is that such slight imperfections in the way a person dresses actually arouses an attraction, a point he makes throughout the poem.

A second example comes in line 12 with "wild civility." "Civil" insinuates domestication, the exact opposite of "wild." This oxymoron defines Herrick's attraction; he doesn't want people to walk around undone, but he enjoys a flirtatious suggestion of this wilder side as presented in this case in the slight discrepancies of a woman's dress.

8. Explain how the rhyme in this poem helps to further the author's point.

The rhyme in this poem mirrors the slight yet powerful inconsistencies that Herrick admires in the woman's clothing throughout the poem. While the poem keeps a strong rhyme scheme of aabb throughout its entirety, the rhymes themselves are not perfect. Words such as "thrown" and "distraction" or "thereby" and "confusedly" are not perfect rhymes, similar to the way the woman's shoe string is not perfectly tied or the lawn about her shoulders is not perfectly placed. Herrick delights in the wild organization of the rhyme in the same way he delights in the "wild civility" of the woman.

9. What is the major theme of this poem? Use specific evidence from the text to support your answer.

One possible answer:

Throughout the poem Herrick develops the idea that truly captivating aesthetics result from the slight imperfections found within art. In this case, he notices the beauty of the women's slight discrepancies in dress: "neglectful cuff," "careless shoestring," "tempestuous petticoat," and "erring lace"; his use of personification in these examples suggests that these imperfections have a life, or vibrancy, in themselves. He further illustrates his delight in the disarray using words such as "kindles," "fine" distraction, "enthralls," and "winning" wave to develop his admiring tone. All of these words mirror Herrick's sentiments in the final lines of the poem: "Do more bewitch me, than when art / is too precise in every part." While many admire perfect rhyme in a poem or the perfect likeness of someone in a painting, the narrator appreciates the slight variances in art. This point is further emphasized through his rhyme and use of oxymoron.

Question 1	Analyzing Figurative Language
Question 2	Analyzing Diction
Question 3	Analyzing Development of Tone/Mood
Question 4	Making Generalizations
Question 5	Applying Appropriate Reading Strategies
Question 6	Distinguishing Genres of Poetry
Question 7	Analyzing Oxymoron
Question 8	Analyzing Sound Devices and Rhythm
Question 9	Interpreting the Theme and Main Idea

84

FROM "THE MOST DANGEROUS GAME"

by Richard Connell

He lifted the knocker, and it creaked up stiffly, as if it had never before been used. He let it fall, and it startled him with its booming loudness. He thought he heard steps within; the door remained closed. Again Rainsford lifted the heavy knocker, and let it fall. The door opened then—opened as suddenly as if it were on a spring—and Rainsford stood blinking in the river of glaring gold light that poured out. The first thing Rainsford's eyes discerned was the largest man Rainsford had ever seen—a gigantic creature, solidly made and black bearded to the waist. In his hand the man held a long-barrelled revolver, and he was pointing it straight at Rainsford's heart.

Out of the snarl of beard two small eyes regarded Rainsford.

"Don't be alarmed," said Rainsford, with a smile which he hoped was disarming. "I'm no robber. I fell off a yacht. My name is Sanger Rainsford of New York City."

The menacing look in the eyes did not change. The revolver pointing as rigidly as if the giant were a statue. He gave no sign that he understood Rainsford's words, or that he had even heard them. He was dressed in uniform—a black uniform trimmed with grey astrakhan.

"I'm Sanger Rainsford of New York," Rainsford began again. "I fell off a yacht. I am hungry."

The man's only answer was to raise with his thumb the hammer of his revolver. Then Rainsford saw the man's free hand go to his forehead in a military salute, and he saw him click his heels together and stand at attention. Another man was coming down the broad marble steps, an erect, slender man in evening clothes. He advanced to Rainsford and held out his hand.

In a cultivated voice marked by a slight accent that gave it added precision and deliberateness, he said, "It is a very great pleasure and honor to welcome Mr. Sanger Rainsford, the celebrated hunter, to my home."

Automatically Rainsford shook the man's hand.

"I've read your book about hunting snow leopards in Tibet, you see," explained the man. "I am General Zaroff."

Rainsford's first impression was that the man was singularly handsome; his second was that there was an original, almost bizarre quality about the general's face. He was a tall man past middle age, for his hair was a vivid white; but his thick eyebrows and pointed military moustache were as black as the night from which Rainsford had come. His eyes, too, were black and very bright. He had high cheekbones, a sharpcut nose, a spare, dark face—the face of a man used to giving orders, the face of an aristocrat. Turning to the giant in uniform, the general made a sign. The giant put away his pistol, saluted, withdrew.

"Ivan is an incredibly strong fellow," remarked the general, "but he has the misfortune to be deaf and dumb. A simple fellow, but, I'm afraid, like all his race, a bit of a savage."

"Is he Russian?"

"He is a Cossack," said the general, and his smile showed red lips and pointed teeth. "So am I."

"Come," he said, "we shouldn't be chatting here. We can talk later. Now you want clothes, food, rest. You shall have them. This is a most-restful spot."

Ivan had reappeared, and the general spoke to him with lips that moved but gave forth no sound.

"Follow Ivan, if you please, Mr. Rainsford," said the general. "I was about to have my dinner when you came. I'll wait for you. You'll find that my clothes will fit you, I think."

It was to a huge, beam-ceilinged bedroom with a canopied bed big enough for six men that Rainsford followed the silent giant. Ivan laid out an evening suit, and Rainsford, as he put it on, noticed that it came from a London tailor who ordinarily cut and sewed for none below the rank of duke.

The dining room to which Ivan conducted him was in many ways remarkable. There was a medieval magnificence about it; it suggested a baronial hall of feudal times with its oaken panels, its high ceiling, its vast refectory tables where twoscore men could sit down to eat. About the hall were mounted heads of many animals—lions, tigers, elephants, moose, bears; larger or more perfect specimens Rainsford had never seen. At the great table the general was sitting, alone.

"You'll have a cocktail, Mr. Rainsford," he suggested. The cocktail was surpassingly good; and, Rainsford noted, the table appointments were of the finest— the linen, the crystal, the silver, the china.

They were eating *borsch*, the rich, red soup with whipped cream so dear to Russian palates. Half apologetically General Zaroff said, "We do our best to preserve the amenities of civilization here. Please forgive any lapses. We are well off the beaten track, you know. Do you think the champagne has suffered from its long ocean trip?"

"Not in the least," declared Rainsford. He was finding the general a most thoughtful and affable host, a true cosmopolite. But there was one small trait of the general's that made Rainsford uncomfortable. Whenever he looked up from his plate he found the general studying him, appraising him narrowly.

"Perhaps," said General Zaroff, "you were surprised that I recognized your name. You see, I read all books on hunting published in English, French, and Russian. I have but one passion in my life, Mr. Rainsford, and it is the hunt."

"You have some wonderful heads here," said Rainsford as he ate a particularly well-cooked *filet mignon*. "That Cape buffalo is the largest I ever saw."

"Oh, that fellow. Yes, he was a monster."

"Did he charge you?"

"Hurled me against a tree," said the general. "Fractured my skull. But I got the brute."

"I've always thought," said Rainsford, "that the Cape buffalo is the most dangerous of all big game."

For a moment the general did not reply; he was smiling his curious red-lipped smile. Then he said slowly, "No. You are wrong, sir. The Cape buffalo is not the most dangerous big game." He sipped his wine. "Here in my preserve on this island," he said in the same slow tone, "I hunt more dangerous game."

Rainsford expressed his surprise. "Is there big game on this island?"

The general nodded. "The biggest."

"Really?"

"Oh, it isn't here naturally, of course. I have to stock the island."

"What have you imported, general?" Rainsford asked. "Tigers?"

The general smiled. "No," he said. "Hunting tigers ceased to interest me some years ago. I exhausted their possibilities, you see. No thrill left in tigers, no real danger. I live for danger, Mr. Rainsford."

The general took from his pocket a gold cigarette case and offered his guest a long black cigarette with a silver tip; it was perfumed and gave off a smell like incense.

"We will have some capital hunting, you and I," said the general. "I shall be most glad to have your society."

"But what game—" began Rainsford.

"I'll tell you," said the general. "You will be amused, I know. I think I may say, in all modesty, that I have done a rare thing. I have invented a new sensation. May I pour you another glass of port?"

"Thank you, general."

The general filled both glasses, and said, "God makes some men poets. Some He makes kings, some beggars. Me He made a hunter. My hand was made for the trigger, my father said. He was a very rich man with a quarter of a million acres in the Crimea, and he was an ardent sportsman. When I was only five years old he gave me a little gun, specially made in Moscow for me, to shoot sparrows with. When I shot some of his prize turkeys with it, he did not punish me; he complimented me on my marksmanship. I killed my first bear in the Caucasus when I was ten. My whole life has been one prolonged hunt. I went into the army—it was expected of noblemen's sons—and for a time commanded a division of Cossack cavalry, but my real interest was always the hunt. I have hunted every kind of game in every land. It would be impossible for me to tell you how many animals I have killed."

The general puffed at his cigarette.

"After the debacle in Russia I left the country, for it was imprudent for an officer of the Czar to stay there. Many noble Russians lost everything. I, luckily, had invested heavily in American securities, so I shall never have to open a tea-room in Monte Carlo or drive a taxi in Paris. Naturally, I continued to hunt—grizzlies in your Rockies, crocodiles in the Ganges, rhinoceroses in East Africa. It was in Africa that the Cape buffalo hit me and laid me up for six months. As soon as I recovered I started for the Amazon to hunt jaguars, for I had heard they were unusually cunning. They weren't." The Cossack sighed. "They were no match at all for a hunter with his wits about him, and a high-powered rifle. I was bitterly disappointed. I was lying in my tent with a splitting headache one night when a terrible thought pushed its way into my mind. Hunting was beginning to bore me! And hunting, remember, had been my life. I have heard that in America businessmen often go to pieces when they give up the business that has been their life."

"Yes, that's so," said Rainsford.

The general smiled. "I had no wish to go to pieces," he said. "I must do something. Now, mine is an analytical mind, Mr. Rainsford. Doubtless that is why I enjoy the problems of the chase."

"No doubt, General Zaroff."

"So," continued the general, "I asked myself why the hunt no longer fascinated me. You are much younger than I am, Mr. Rainsford, and have not hunted as much, but you perhaps can guess the answer."

"What was it?"

"Simply this: hunting had ceased to be what you call `a sporting proposition.' It had become too easy. I always got my quarry. Always. There is no greater bore than perfection."

The general lit a fresh cigarette.

"No animal had a chance with me any more. That is no boast; it is a mathematical certainty. The animal had nothing but his legs and his instinct. Instinct is no match for reason. When I thought of this it was a tragic moment for me, I can tell you."

Rainsford leaned across the table, absorbed in what his host was saying.

"It came to me as an inspiration what I must do," the general went on.

"And that was?"

The general smiled the quiet smile of one who has faced an obstacle and surmounted it with success. "I had to invent a new animal to hunt," he said.

"A new animal? You're joking." "Not at all," said the general. "I never joke about hunting. I needed a new animal. I found one. So I bought this island built this house, and here I do my hunting. The island is perfect for my purposes—there are jungles with a maze of traits in them, hills, swamps—"

"But the animal, General Zaroff?"

"Oh," said the general, "it supplies me with the most exciting hunting in the world. No other hunting compares with it for an instant. Every day I hunt, and I never grow bored now, for I have a quarry with which I can match my wits."

Rainsford's bewilderment showed in his face.

"I wanted the ideal animal to hunt," explained the general. "So I said, 'What are the attributes of an ideal quarry?' And the answer was, of course, 'It must have courage, cunning, and, above all, it must be able to reason.'"

"But no animal can reason," objected Rainsford.

"My dear fellow," said the general, "there is one that can.

1. The word, "creaked," is an example of

    a. personification.
    b. onomatopoeia.
    c. metaphor.
    d. consonance.

2. "'Don't be alarmed,' said Rainsford, with a smile which he hoped was disarming." In this statement, "disarming" most nearly means to

    a. lay down arms.
    b. render harmless.
    c. reduce armed forces.
    d. overcome suspicion.

3. "The revolver pointing as rigidly as if the giant were a statue." This simile from the text emphasizes Ivan's

    a. size.
    b. pasty features.
    c. stillness.
    d. meanness.

4. The narrator feels that General Zaroff

    a. is civilized.
    b. is a good hunter.
    c. has a magnificent place.
    d. has helpful servants.

5. It can be inferred that General Zaroff

    a. is a very high-class citizen.
    b. treats his employees well.
    c. has visitors almost weekly.
    d. loves hunting buffalo best.

6. Anticipation is built within the story by

    a. Ivan's presence throughout the story.
    b. the many animal heads on the wall.
    c. the general not naming the animal.
    d. the general smoking his cigarettes.

7. In what point of view is this story written? Explain how the story would be less effective if it had been written in a different point of view.

One possible answer:

The story is written in third person limited. Because of this, the reader hears Rainsford's thoughts but not anyone else's in the story. For example, at the beginning of the passage the reader knows that Rainsford looks at Ivan with a "smile which he hoped was disarming." Later the reader is able to overhear Rainsford's first impressions of the general and his place. The story would be much different if it had been written in third person omniscient. The entire anticipation and suspense of the passage would have been lost because the audience would know which animal the general had decided to hunt much earlier in the story. In third person limited, the audience may suspect early in the passage that the general wants to hunt humans; this suspicion turns to shock in the audience as more clues are given that this is the case. This development of sheer horror in the audience as both Rainsford and the audience figure it out would be missing if the audience had heard the general's thoughts right away.

8. How does Connell use indirect characterization to develop General Zaroff? Use specific evidence from the text to support your answer.

General Zaroff is depicted as a man who demands control, a trait developed in the passage through indirect characterization. The general is first defined by the way others react to him; for example, upon first seeing the general, Ivan salutes him. In addition, Rainsford immediately notes that "he had high cheekbones, a sharpcut nose, a spare, dark face — the face of a man used to giving orders, the face of an aristocrat." Zaroff's domineering demeanor is also developed by what he says. Rather than asking Rainsford if he would like a drink, he says, "You'll have a cocktail, Mr. Rainsford." He later comments, "We will have some capital hunting, you and I," again telling Rainsford what he will do as opposed to asking him. Through what the general says, the way he looks, and what others say about him, he is developed as a authoritarian character.

9. What is the new animal that General Zaroff hunts?   Predict which new animal General Zaroff will hunt, providing evidence from the text to support your prediction.

One possible answer:
Most students will say that the General Zaroff hunts humans. This is insinuated in a number of lines. The narrator notes, ". . . but there was one small trait of the general's that made Rainsford uncomfortable. Whenever he looked up from his plate he found the general studying him, appraising him narrowly." This comment, compounded by the general's comments that they will "have some capital hunting" leads the reader to be suspicious of the general. Later in the passage the reader's fears are affirmed when Zaroff notes that the perfect animal must have "courage, cunning, and, above all, it must be able to reason." While Rainsford objects, "no animal can reason" the reader is horribly aware of the general's intentions when he returns, "there is one that can." These all lead the reader to his conclusion.

10. How does the setting of the passage help to develop meaning? Use specific evidence from the text to support your answer.

The setting helps to establish General Zaroff as a successful hunter and civilized man. Rainsford first notices that "about the hall were mounted heads of many animals—lions, tigers, elephants, moose, bears; larger or more perfect specimens Rainsford had never seen." Zaroff's large display supports his comments later on in the passage when he mentions that he no longer feels challenged when hunting typical game. In addition, Zaroff's home establishes him as a well-to-do, civilized man. The narrator notes, "the dining room to which Ivan conducted him was in many ways remarkable. There was a medieval magnificence about it; it suggested a baronial hall of feudal times with its oaken panels, its high ceiling, its vast refectory tables where twoscore men could sit down to eat." In addition, the bedroom was to "a huge, beam-ceilinged bedroom with a canopied bed big enough for six men." The fine linens, china, and champagne during dinner develop the lavishness of the house even further. The very civilized surroundings contrast with the uncivilized, insinuated suggestion to hunt humans. However, some students may note that the animal heads on the wall did indicate a more savage side as well.

11. Would you describe General Zaroff as civilized or uncivilized? Use evidence from the text to support your answer.

Students may argue that Zaroff is not civilized. He vaguely calls himself a savage. He comments that Ivan, like all his race, is "a bit of a savage." In the lines that follow Zaroff associates himself with Ivan, saying they are both Cossack. In addition, the general is described as having pointed teeth, almost like that of a wild animal. Finally, students will cite the final, eerie lines of the passage in which it is inferred that the general is talking about hunting humans.

Other students may argue that Zaroff is civilized. They may cite his ability to read in three different languages, the fine house and food he surrounds himself with, and/or his treatment of guests such as Rainsford. They may argue that not enough evidence has been given in this passage to truly deem him uncivilized.

Question 1	Analyzing Figurative Language
Question 2	Analyzing Diction
Question 3	Analyzing Figurative Language
Question 4	Recognizing Author's Bias and Beliefs
Question 5	Making Inferences
Question 6	Analyzing Conflict, Plot, and Setting
Question 7	Analyzing Point of View
Question 8	Analyzing Character
Question 9	Analyzing Predictions
Question 10	Analyzing Conflict, Plot, and Setting
Question 11	Analyzing Character

"To Autumn"

by John Keats

Season of mists and mellow fruitfulness,   1
Close bosom-friend of the maturing sun;
Conspiring with him how to load and bless
With fruit the vines that round the thatch-eaves run;
To bend with apples the mossed cottage-trees,   5
And fill all fruit with ripeness to the core;
To swell the gourd, and plump the hazel shells
With a sweet kernel; to set budding more,
And still more, later flowers for the bees,
Until they think warm days will never cease,   10
For Summer has o'er-brimmed their clammy cell.

Who hath not seen thee oft amid thy store?
Sometimes whoever seeks abroad may find
Thee sitting careless on a granary floor,
Thy hair soft-lifted by the winnowing wind;   15
Or on a half-reaped furrow sound asleep,
Drowsed with the fume of poppies, while thy hook
Spares the next swath and all its twined flowers;
And sometimes like a gleaner thou dost keep
Steady thy laden head across a brook;   20
Or by a cider-press, with patient look,
Thou watchest the last oozings, hours by hours.

Where are the songs of Spring? Ay, where are they?
Think not of them, thou hast thy music too,—
While barred clouds bloom the soft-dying day,   25
And touch the stubble-plains with rosy hue;
Then in a wailful choir, the small gnats mourn
Among the river sallows, borne aloft
Or sinking as the light wind lives or dies;
And full-grown lambs loud bleat from hilly bourn;   30
Hedge-crickets sing; and now with treble soft
The redbreast whistles from a garden-croft,
And gathering swallows twitter in the skies.

1. Which genre of poetry is this poem?

   a. ballad
   b. elegy
   c. sonnet
   d. ode

93

2. Line 1 contains an example of

   a. assonance.
   b. hyperbole.
   c. alliteration.
   d. simile.

3. Lines 2–5 contain an example of

   a. personification.
   b. simile.
   c. metaphor.
   d. alliteration.

4. To which time of year is Keats referring in the first stanza?

   a. the end of autumn
   b. the beginning of winter
   c. the end of summer
   d. the beginning of autumn

5. In line 15, Keats's uses the word, "hair," to most likely represent

   a. wind.
   b. grain.
   c. flowers.
   d. grass.

6. Lines 19–20 contain an example of

   a. simile.
   b. metaphor.
   c. alliteration.
   d. consonance.

7. In line 25, the word, "stubble-plains," most likely refers to

   a. an unshaven face.
   b. harvested fields.
   c. storm clouds.
   d. groups of gnats.

8. Why does Keats ask, "Where are the songs of Spring?"

   a. He wishes spring would get here soon.
   b. He wonders how spring went so fast.
   c. He wants to emphasize autumn's songs.
   d. He likes spring's songs best of all.

9. Line 30 contains an example of

   a. assonance.
   b. consonance.
   c. hyperbole.
   d. onomatopoeia.

10. What is going to happen to the gnats mentioned in stanza 3?

   a. They are going to fly south.
   b. They are going to reproduce.
   c. They are going to die soon.
   d. They are going to hibernate.

11. To whom is Keats speaking in this poem?

   a. the readers
   b. autumn
   c. spring
   d. a woman

12. What overall mood is created from Keats's diction and figurative language in the first stanza? Use specific evidence from the text to support your answer.

   One possible answer:

   The reader feels a sense of contentment and fulfillment from the first stanza; Keats' uses diction to create this effect on the readers. Words such as "fruitfulness," "maturing," "load," "fill," "ripeness," "swell," "plump," "budding," and "o'er-brimmed" all create a sense of fullness and plenty. In addition, the apple trees are described as bending because of the weight of all the apples. Keats also uses personification and imagery to create satisfaction in the readers. The sun and autumn are described as "bosom buddies" who are conspiring to "load and bless." Also, Keats describes an illusion of warm days that will never cease and plentiful honey that can barely be confined in the bees' cells. Harmony, plenty, and warmth all lead the reader to feel a sense of contentment.

13. How does Keats create a change of tone in the second stanza? Use specific evidence from the text to support your answer.

One possible answer:

Keats uses diction, personification, alliteration, and assonance to create a slower, more lethargic tone in the second stanza. Words such as "careless," "half-reaped," "drowsed," "patient," "oozing," and "hours by hours" create the slower, lazy pace. The author is no longer focused on the ripeness of autumn but rather on the sluggishness of it. Autumn is described as sitting on the granary floor; the grain particles blown by the wind are described as wisps of hair gently being lifted as autumn languidly hangs around the granary. The softness of the wind, emphasized through the soft "w" sound in "winnowing wind" creates a carefree gentleness found throughout the second stanza. Lastly the long "o" sound repeated at the end of the stanza creates a slow, tired tone. Autumn is described as spending hours watching the last oozings of cider. Similar to the slowing flow of the cider, the season of autumn is also experiencing its final, slower moments.

14. What is the theme of this poem? Use specific evidence from the text to support your answer.

The theme of this poem is that autumn has its own beauty and value that may often be overlooked. As mentioned above, this is first developed as Keats paints a picture of autumn as a plentiful time of year through diction; autumn has its "later flowers" as well as "sweet kernels" and "warm days." Keats carefully takes those aspects that people especially admire in seasons such as summer and spring and associates them with the fall season as well.

The second stanza offers a different face of autumn. Again using diction and figurative language, he presents autumn as a restful time, perhaps after all of the fruits of the first stanza have been harvested. Keats describes autumn as sleeping to the pleasant fumes of poppies; later autumn is compared to the steadiness of a gleaner, one who slowly and carefully picks up grain after the reaper, in order to emphasize autumn's patience in everything from the brooks to the cider press. Keats fondly describes autumn's relaxed and peaceful demeanor, accentuating the positive aspects of the season.

The third stanza more aggressively develops autumn's worth. Keats' rhetorical questions ("Where are the songs of Spring? Ay where are they?") and following comments ("Think not of them; thou hast thy music too") at the beginning of the stanza illustrate his opinion that autumn has its own beauty and musicality. In an effort to demonstrate his point, he lists the sounds: the wailful choir of gnats, the bleating lamb, the singing crickets, and whistling redbreast.

Some students may also comment that Keats is talking about more than the season; many believe that Keats may have also been referring to the autumn of one's life, explaining that beauty and wonder can be found in more than just the springtime of youth.

15. Evaluate Keats's craft in this poem. How has he effectively or ineffectively put the components of a poem together to achieve an effect? Use specific evidence from the text to support your point.

Students may comment on the way Keats effectively structures his poem. He focuses on the beginning of autumn in the first stanza, continues after harvest in the second stanza, and then proceeds to the last moments before winter in the last stanza (as evident with the mourning gnats and full-grown lambs). This helps to emphasize that not just a section of autumn is praiseworthy, but rather all of the season. Students may also note the effective way autumn becomes a person in this poem. First of all, Keats chooses to speak directly to autumn as opposed to speaking to the reader about autumn. He asks the personified autumn questions and gives human features, such as hair, to autumn. Developing autumn as a living, breathing being with emotions adds to the theme by creating empathy for autumn within the reader. As Keats reflects on autumn's beauty and worth, the reader finds himself doing the same. Some students may also note that this quality supports the idea that Keats is talking about more than just the season. In either case, Keats's structure helps to achieve the overall effect.

97

FROM ACT I, SCENE IV OF *ROMEO AND JULIET*

by *William Shakespeare*

Romeo.
What, shall this speech be spoke for our
    excuse?
Or shall we on without apology?

Benvolio.
The date is out of such prolixity.
We'll have no Cupid hoodwink'd with a scarf,
Bearing a Tartar's painted bow of lath,
Scaring the ladies like a crowkeeper;
Nor no without-book prologue, faintly spoke
After the prompter, for our entrance;
But, let them measure us by what they will,
We'll measure them a measure, and be gone.

Romeo
Give me a torch. I am not for this ambling.
Being but heavy, I will bear the light.

Mercutio.
Nay, gentle Romeo, we must have you dance.

Romeo.
Not I, believe me. You have dancing shoes
With nimble soles; I have a soul of lead
So stakes me to the ground I cannot move.

Mercutio.
You are a lover. Borrow Cupid's wings
And soar with them above a common bound.

Romeo.
I am too sore enpierced with his shaft
To soar with his light feathers; and so bound
I cannot bound a pitch above dull woe.
Under love's heavy burthen do I sink.

Mercutio.
And, to sink in it, should you burthen love—
Too great oppression for a tender thing.

Romeo.
Is love a tender thing? It is too rough,
Too rude, too boist'rous, and it pricks like
    thorn.

Mercutio.
If love be rough with you, be rough with love.
Prick love for pricking, and you beat love
    down.
Give me a case to put my visage in.

A visor for a visor! What care I
What curious eye doth quote deformities?
Here are the beetle brows shall blush for me.

Benvolio.
Come, knock and enter; and no sooner in
But every man betake him to his legs.

Romeo.
A torch for me! Let wantons light of heart
Tickle the senseless rushes with their heels;
For I am proverb'd with a grandsire phrase,
I'll be a candle-holder and look on;
The game was ne'er so fair, and I am done.

Mercutio.
Tut! dun's the mouse, the constable's own
    word!
If thou art Dun, we'll draw thee from the mire
Of this sir-reverence love, wherein thou stick'st
Up to the ears. Come, we burn daylight, ho!

Romeo.
Nay, that's not so.

Mercutio.
I mean, sir, in delay
We waste our lights in vain, like lamps by day.
Take our good meaning, for our judgment sits
Five times in that ere once in our five wits.

Romeo.
And we mean well, in going to this masque;
But 'tis no wit to go.

Mercutio.
Why, may one ask?

Romeo.
I dreamt a dream to-night.

Mercutio.
And so did I.

Romeo.
Well, what was yours?

Mercutio.
That dreamers often lie.

Romeo.
In bed asleep, while they do dream things
    true.

99

1. What genre of fiction is this passage?

   a. novel
   b. novella
   c. short story
   d. drama

2. What time of day is it in the passage?

   a. early morning
   b. afternoon
   c. sunset
   d. night

3. How long does Benvolio plan to spend at the party?

   a. He wants to stay until the party ends.
   b. He wants to stay for one dance or so.
   c. He wants to stay until he falls in love.
   d. He doesn't plan on going to the party.

4. What is wrong with Romeo?

   a. He doesn't know how to dance very well.
   b. He doesn't have the right dancing shoes.
   c. He is suffering from a broken heart.
   d. He doesn't want Mercutio to come with him.

5. When Mercutio says, "Here are the beetle brows shall blush for me," he is using

   a. alliteration.
   b. assonance.
   c. onomatopoeia.
   d. consonance.

6. Why doesn't Romeo think they should go to this party?

   a. They were not invited to the party.
   b. He had a bad dream about it.
   c. He is not feeling very well.
   d. He is too tired to go to the party.

7. Mercutio complains that

   a. they are wasting too much time.
   b. it is getting too dark outside.
   c. he has been having bad dreams.
   d. the party is not going to be fun.

> A **PUN** is a play on word meaning. For example, Benjamin Franklin once said, "We must all hang together, or assuredly we shall all hang separately." In this quote, "hang" is first used in the sense of standing united or sticking together. However, the second "hang" could either be interpreted as being alone or literally hanging, as in being executed by being suspended by the neck.

8. Find two examples of puns in *Romeo and Juliet*. Explain their effect on the passage.

Students should be able to find multiple examples such as Romeo's second line: "Being but heavy, I will bear the light." "Heavy" could either be referring to the weight of the torch or to the weight of Romeo's soul. "Light" takes on two meanings as well: the literal torch that he wants to carry or those things that do not require exertion since Romeo is heartbroken. The pun begins to develop Romeo's mood in this scene; he is too upset about lost love to enjoy himself at the party. His soul's heaviness, first introduced in this pun, continues to be developed throughout the passage in other puns.

Another example of a pun comes at the end of the passage when Mercutio states, "That dreamers often lie." Mercutio accuses Romeo of trying to get out of going to the party without offending Romeo. "Lie" could be referring to the dreamers actually lying down as they dream or it could be referring to Romeo, a dreamer, as a liar. Mercutio may also be making the comment that dreams often do not portray the truth. The ambiguity of the statement allows Mercutio to get away with his comment.

9. Cupid is the Roman god of love and the son of Venus. He is a small, blindfolded, winged boy, carrying bow and arrows. The arrows, once they strike someone's heart, make the victim fall in love. How does this allusion to Roman mythology help to develop the passage?

The allusion develops Romeo's heartbroken nature. Benvolio first mentions Cupid when he demands that they will not ruin their charm by creating excuses or guises when going to the party; he insinuates that they are the Cupids entering the party. Romeo's comparison to the god of love comes again when Mercutio calls Romeo a lover and advises that he borrow Cupid's wings to soar above his worries. However, Romeo cleverly uses another aspect of Cupid's appearance to more accurately explain the way he feels; he cannot use the wings because he is too weighed down by the burden of Cupid's arrow. In other words, he is too in love with another.

10. Compare and contrast Romeo and Mercutio's views of love. Use specific evidence from the text to support your answer.

While both men understand the power of love, Romeo feels it is a tormenting and unbeatable thing whereas Mercutio sees it as vulnerable. Mercutio admits love's strength when he comments, "If love be rough with you, be rough with love." Understanding that love can be a powerful force, Mercutio also recognizes that man has the power to fight back. He even goes so far as to say it is quite a frail emotion, calling it a "tender thing" that is burdened by the weight of Romeo's obsession. Romeo, on the other hand, finds love to be unconquerable and supreme. He mentions that he is the one weighed down by love's burden. He uses the simile, "pricks like thorns," to describe love's effect, calling love rude and boisterous. Whereas Mercutio believes man can control love, Romeo suggests that this great power is beyond human domination.

"I Heard a Fly Buzz When I Died"

by Emily Dickinson

I heard a fly buzz when I died;   1
    The stillness round my form
Was like the stillness in the air
    Between the heaves of storm.

The eyes beside had wrung them dry,   5
    And breaths were gathering sure
For that last onset, when the king
    Be witnessed in his power.

I willed my keepsakes, signed away
    What portion of me I   10
Could make assignable,—and then
    There interposed a fly,

With blue, uncertain, stumbling buzz,
    Between the light and me;
And then the windows failed, and then   15
    I could not see to see.

1. Line 1 contains an example of

    a. rhyme.
    b. personification.
    c. hyperbole.
    d. onomatopoeia.

2. The eyes mentioned in line 5 most likely refer to

    a. the fly's eyes.
    b. the family's eyes.
    c. the king's eyes.
    d. the narrator's eyes.

3. In Line 15, the word, "windows," most likely refers to

    a. lights in the room.
    b. bedroom windows.
    c. the narrator's eyes.
    d. the fly's reflection.

4. Line 7 contains an example of

   a. oxymoron.
   b. personification.
   c. alliteration.
   d. hyperbole.

5. The poem is an example of

   a. a sonnet.
   b. a ballad.
   c. a lyric poem.
   d. an ode.

6. The narrator is speaking in the poem

   a. while she is dying.
   b. before she begins to die.
   c. after she has died.
   d. right before she sees the fly.

7. What effect does the dash in line 11 have on the poem?

   a. It speeds up the pace of the poem.
   b. It emphasizes the interruption of the fly.
   c. It imitates the buzzing sound of the fly.
   d. It causes the reader to stop and think.

8. From the first two stanzas, what prediction or expectation is presented? How does this prediction hold up in the final two stanzas? Be sure to use specific evidence from the text to support your answer.

   One possible answer:

   The first two stanzas offer the family's prediction or expectation for the dying narrator. Anticipation builds as Dickinson emphasizes the stillness not only around the narrator but also in the room. Words such as "king," "witness," and "power" all lead to the conclusion that the people around the narrator predict that God will soon come to take her away to heaven. However, some disappointment ensues in the final two stanzas as the reader realizes that the poem has ended without any presence of this higher being; in fact, the only thing to break the stillness is the buzzing of the fly.

9. What is the main theme of this poem? Be sure to use specific evidence from the text to support your answer.

One possible answer:

The theme of Dickinson's poem is the disappointment of death's final moments.   Everyone around her "gathering sure / for that last onset" creates anticipation; the word, "sure," indicates a faith in the momentous grandeur soon to take place. Even the narrator mentions that she "signed away / what portion of me I / could make assignable," indicating her belief that unlike her material possessions, her soul is handled by another. However, while the "king" should have broken the stillness of the room, instead it is the fly. The fly is often associated with those things dying or rotting. In addition, "Beelzebub," another name for the devil, translates into "the lord of the flies." The fly's interruption or replacement for the higher power is developed in the poem's final stanza: "With blue uncertain buzz, / between the light and me." While this line could either be seen as some darker power getting in the way of her awaited life after death or just the anticlimactic nature of her final moments, the expectations of the narrator are dashed. The poem ends with the narrator in a state of bewilderment instead of elation: "I could not see to see."

Question 1	Analyzing Sound Devices
Question 2	Drawing Conclusions
Question 3	Drawing Conclusions
Question 4	Analyzing Oxymoron
Question 5	Distinguishing Genres of Poetry
Question 6	Analyzing Point of View
Question 7	Evaluating Author's Craft
Question 8	Analyzing Predictions
Question 9	Interpreting Theme and Main Idea

THE LOTTERY TICKET

by Anton Chekov

Ivan Dmitritch, a middle-class man who lived with his family on an income of twelve hundred a year and was very well satisfied with his lot, sat down on the sofa after supper and began reading the newspaper.

"I forgot to look at the newspaper today," his wife said to him as she cleared the table.

"Look and see whether the list of drawings is there."

"Yes, it is," said Ivan Dmitritch; "but hasn't your ticket lapsed?"

"No; I took the interest on Tuesday."

"What is the number?"

"Series 9,499, number 26."

"All right . . . we will look . . . 9,499 and 26."

Ivan Dmitritch had no faith in lottery luck, and would not, as a rule, have consented to look at the lists of winning numbers, but now, as he had nothing else to do and as the newspaper was before his eyes, he passed his finger downwards along the column of numbers. And immediately, as though in mockery of his skepticism, no further than the second line from the top, his eye was caught by the figure 9,499! Unable to believe his eyes, he hurriedly dropped the paper on his knees without looking to see the number of the ticket, and, just as though someone had given him a douche of cold water, he felt an agreeable chill in the pit of the stomach; tingling and terrible and sweet!

"Masha, 9,499 is there!" he said in a hollow voice.

His wife looked at his astonished and panic-stricken face, and realized that he was not joking.

"9,499?" she asked, turning pale and dropping the folded tablecloth on the table.

"Yes, yes . . . it really is there!"

"And the number of the ticket?"

"Oh yes! There's the number of the ticket too. But stay . . . wait! No, I say! Anyway, the number of our series is there! Anyway, you understand. . . ."

Looking at his wife, Ivan Dmitritch gave a broad, senseless smile, like a baby when a bright object is shown it. His wife smiled too; it was as pleasant to her as to him that he only mentioned the series, and did not try to find out the number of the winning ticket. To torment and tantalize oneself with hopes of possible fortune is so sweet, so thrilling!

"It is our series," said Ivan Dmitritch, after a long silence. "So there is a probability that we have won. It's only a probability, but there it is!"

"Well, now look!"

"Wait a little. We have plenty of time to be disappointed. It's on the second line from the top, so the prize is seventy-five thousand. That's not money, but power, capital! And in a minute I shall look at the list, and there—26! Eh? I say, what if we really have won?"

The husband and wife began laughing and staring at one another in silence. The possibility of winning bewildered them; they could not have said, could not have dreamed, what they both needed that seventy-five thousand for, what they would buy, where they would go. They thought only of the figures 9,499 and 75,000 and pictured them in their imagination, while somehow they could not think of the happiness itself which was so possible.

Ivan Dmitritch, holding the paper in his hand, walked several times from corner to corner, and only when he had recovered from the first impression began dreaming a little.

"And if we have won," he said—"why, it will be a new life, it will be a transformation! The ticket is yours, but if it were mine I should, first of all, of course, spend twenty-five thousand on real property in the shape of an estate; ten thousand on immediate expenses, new furnishing . . . traveling . . . paying debts, and so on. . . . The other forty thousand I would put in the bank and get interest on it."

"Yes, an estate, that would be nice," said his wife, sitting down and dropping her hands in her lap.

"Somewhere in the Tula or Oryol provinces. . . . In the first place we shouldn't need a summer villa, and besides, it would always bring in an income."

And pictures came crowding on his imagination, each more gracious and poetical than the last. And in all these pictures he saw himself well fed, serene, healthy, felt warm, even hot! Here, after eating a summer soup, cold as ice, he lay on his back on the burning sand close to a stream or in the garden under a lime-tree. . . . It is hot. . . . His little boy and girl are crawling about near him, digging in the sand or catching ladybirds in the grass. He dozes sweetly, thinking of nothing, and feeling all over that he need not go to the office today, tomorrow, or the day after. Or, tired of lying still, he goes to the hayfield, or to the forest for mushrooms, or watches the peasants catching fish with a net. When the sun sets he takes a towel and soap and saunters to the bathing shed, where he undresses at his leisure, slowly rubs his bare chest with his hands, and goes into the water. And in the water, near the opaque soapy circles, little fish flit to and fro and green water-weeds nod their heads. After bathing there is tea with

cream and milk rolls. . . . In the evening a walk or vint with the neighbors.

"Yes, it would be nice to buy an estate," said his wife, also dreaming, and from her face it was evident that she was enchanted by her thoughts.

Ivan Dmitritch pictured to himself autumn with its rains, its cold evenings, and its St. Martin's summer. At that season he would have to take longer walks about the garden and beside the river, so as to get thoroughly chilled, and then drink a big glass of vodka and eat a salted mushroom or a soused cucumber, and then—drink another. . . . The children would come running from the kitchen-garden, bringing a carrot and a radish smelling of fresh earth. . . . And then, he would lie stretched full length on the sofa, and in leisurely fashion turn over the pages of some illustrated magazine, or, covering his face with it and unbuttoning his waistcoat, give himself up to slumber.

The St. Martin's summer is followed by cloudy, gloomy weather. It rains day and night, the bare trees weep, the wind is damp and cold. The dogs, the horses, the fowls—all are wet, depressed, downcast. There is nowhere to walk; one can't go out for days together; one has to pace up and down the room, looking despondently at the gray window. It is dreary!

Ivan Dmitritch stopped and looked at his wife.

"I should go abroad, you know, Masha," he said.

And he began thinking how nice it would be in late autumn to go abroad somewhere to the South of France . . . to Italy . . . to India!

"I should certainly go abroad too," his wife said. "But look at the number of the ticket!"

108

"Wait, wait! . . ."

He walked about the room and went on thinking. It occurred to him: what if his wife really did go abroad? It is pleasant to travel alone, or in the society of light, careless women who live in the present, and not such as think and talk all the journey about nothing but their children, sigh, and tremble with dismay over every farthing. Ivan Dmitritch imagined his wife in the train with a multitude of parcels, baskets, and bags; she would be sighing over something, complaining that the train made her head ache, that she had spent so much money. . . . At the stations he would continually be having to run for boiling water, bread and butter. . . . She wouldn't have dinner because of its being too dear. . . .

"She would begrudge me every farthing," he thought, with a glance at his wife. "The lottery ticket is hers, not mine! Besides, what is the use of her going abroad? What does she want there? She would shut herself up in the hotel, and not let me out of her sight. . . . I know!"

And for the first time in his life his mind dwelt on the fact that his wife had grown elderly and plain, and that she was saturated through and through with the smell of cooking, while he was still young, fresh, and healthy, and might well have got married again.

"Of course, all that is silly nonsense," he thought; "but . . . why should she go abroad? What would she make of it? And yet she would go, of course. . . . I can fancy. . . . In reality it is all one to her, whether it is Naples or Klin. She would only be in my way. I should be dependent upon her. I can fancy how, like a regular woman, she will lock the money up as soon as she gets it. . . . She will look after her relations and grudge me every farthing."

Ivan Dmitritch thought of her relations. All those wretched brothers and sisters and aunts and uncles would come crawling about as soon as they heard of the winning ticket, would begin whining like beggars, and fawning upon them with oily, hypocritical smiles. Wretched, detestable people! If they were given anything, they would ask for more; while if they were refused, they would swear at them, slander them, and wish them every kind of misfortune.

Ivan Dmitritch remembered his own relations, and their faces, at which he had looked impartially in the past, struck him now as repulsive and hateful.

"They are such reptiles!" he thought.

And his wife's face, too, struck him as repulsive and hateful. Anger surged up in his heart against her, and he thought malignantly:

"She knows nothing about money, and so she is stingy. If she won it she would give me a hundred roubles, and put the rest away under lock and key."

And he looked at his wife, not with a smile now, but with hatred. She glanced at him too, and also with hatred and anger. She had her own daydreams, her own plans, her own reflections; she understood perfectly well what her husband's dreams were. She knew who would be the first to try to grab her winnings.

"It's very nice making daydreams at other people's expense!" is what her eyes expressed. "No, don't you dare!"

Her husband understood her look; hatred began stirring again in his breast, and in order to annoy his wife he glanced quickly, to spite her at the fourth page on the newspaper and read out triumphantly:

"Series 9,499, number 46! Not 26!"

Hatred and hope both disappeared at once, and it began immediately to seem to Ivan Dmitritch and his wife that their rooms were dark and small and low-pitched, that the supper they had been eating was not doing them good, but lying heavy on their stomachs, that the evenings were long and wearisome. . . .

"What the devil's the meaning of it?" said Ivan Dmitritch, beginning to be ill-humored. "Wherever one steps there are bits of paper under one's feet, crumbs, husks. The rooms are never swept! One is simply forced to go out. Damnation take my soul entirely! I shall go and hang myself on the first aspen-tree!"

1. This short story is written in

   a. first person.
   b. third person limited.
   c. *third person omniscient.*
   d. objective.

2. The climax of the story is when

   a. Ivan finds out that 9,499 is the series number.
   b. Ivan dreams about living in his estate.
   c. *Ivan first sees his wife as inadequate.*
   d. Ivan shouts out the final number.

3. Ivan Dmitritch can be described as a

   a. flat, static character.
   b. flat, dynamic character.
   c. round, static character.
   d. *round, dynamic character.*

4. The author's main purpose of this story is to

   a. persuade people to play the lottery.
   b. *give an opinion about the effect of greed.*
   c. inform people on the lottery process.
   d. give an opinion about lottery tickets.

5. The narrator notes that Ivan "gave a broad, senseless smile, like a baby when a bright object is shown it" upon first discovering the number 9,499 in the newspaper. What effect does this simile create?

   a. It emphasizes how immature Ivan is.
   b. *It emphasizes Ivan's pure excitement.*
   c. It emphasizes the lottery's worth.
   d. It emphasizes Ivan's youthful face.

6. Why does the narrator feel the couple does not look right away to see if they have won?

   a. They love to torment themselves with hope of fortune.
   b. They are too excited to look in the newspaper.
   c. They already know that they have lost the lottery.
   d. They know they will be disappointed with the amount.

7. Why does Ivan reveal the last number triumphantly?

   a. They have won some money for being close.
   b. He's glad his wife didn't win the money.
   c. He's glad he finally gets to go on a walk.
   d. He's glad his wife can get back to cleaning.

8. From the last paragraph the audience can infer that Ivan

   a. wishes he had purchased the ticket.
   b. doesn't like to be around a messy house.
   c. no longer feels content with his life.
   d. is mad they made a big deal of the ticket.

9. When Ivan first discovers that he may have won the lottery the narrator says, "he felt an agreeable chill in the pit of the stomach; tingling and terrible and sweet." Explain the meaning of this paradox and how it helps to develop the short story.

One possible answer:

The paradox helps to capture both the ultimate joy and the ultimate pain of hope. In the hopes of winning the money, Ivan can't help but be elated by all of the opportunities that could lie ahead. However, with the promise of hope also comes the possibility that he has not won. In addition, the elation of possibly winning only makes losing even more painful. This idea of sweet torture comes again when the narrator notes, "To torment and tantalize oneself with hopes of possible fortune is so sweet, so thrilling!" This development prepares the reader for the ending when the couple's hope is gone, and they are left with the painful inadequacies they both feel towards their lives.

10. When Ivan first mentions that he would buy an estate, Chekov writes, "'Yes, an estate, that would be nice,' said his wife, sitting down and dropping her hands in her lap." What do you think is the reason for her response? Use specific evidence from the text to support your answer.

One possible answer:

The wife recognizes the reality of their relationship in the presence of a hopeful fortune: they do not have a partnership. This is first made clear when Ivan comments, "The ticket is yours, but if it were mine . . . " Immediately he begins to think of his life with the lottery winnings, a daydream that the reader notes doesn't include his wife. In addition he later comments he "might well have got married again." Sitting down and dropping hands is not the body language of an ecstatic person; the wife feels slighted by his initial reaction. Later in the story, the narrator even notes that her eyes seem to be saying, "It's very nice making daydreams at other people's expense!" "No, don't you dare!" The wife's reaction comes as she slowly realizes that she is not part of Ivan's lottery-winning fantasy.

11. How would you describe Ivan's life on the imaginative estate? Consider the connotation of words used in the description to make your point. How does it compare to his current lifestyle?

Ivan's life would be one of relaxation and laziness. The narrator begins by saying that he would "lay on his back" and doze sweetly. He continues to use words and phrases such as "saunters," "undresses at his leisure," and "slowly rubs his bare chest" to describe Ivan's wishes. Ivan imagines his estate in the autumn with the narrator noting, "he would lie stretched full length on the sofa, and in leisurely fashion turn over the pages of some illustrated magazine, or, covering his face with it and unbuttoning his waistcoat, give himself up to slumber." The repetition of "leisure," along with words connoting slowness such as "saunters" and "slowly," help to create this effect. While the reader only gets a small glimpse of Ivan's daily life, it also appears ironically to be fairly relaxing. The narrator notes, "Ivan Dmitritch had no faith in lottery luck, and would not, as a rule, have consented to look at the lists of winning numbers, but now, as he had nothing else to do and as the newspaper was before his eyes, he passed his finger downwards along the column of numbers." The newspaper in front of him at the beginning of the story echoes Ivan's daydream of lying stretched on the sofa reading a magazine. The major difference seems to be the presence of his wife; as noted earlier, she doesn't appear in his daydreams until she specifically invites herself to go abroad with him.

12. What is the effect of the lottery on the couple? Use specific evidence from the text.

The hope of winning the lottery causes the couple to realize their unhappiness with each other and their surroundings. The beginning of the story opens with the important comment, "Ivan Dmitritch, a middle-class man who lived with his family on an income of twelve hundred a year and was very well satisfied with his lot. . . ."

In addition, the wife is first introduced to the reader as "clearing off the table," no doubt performing her household duties. When the couple first finds out about the possibility of winning the lottery, they are described as smiling and laughing with each other.

This satisfied beginning contrasts sharply to the way Ivan and his wife feel after the hopes of the lottery are dashed. The narrator notes, "And he looked at his wife, not with a smile now, but with hatred. She glanced at him too, and also with hatred and anger." The possibility of money changes their relationship from one of companionship to one of animosity. In addition, neither of them are happy with the current situation: ". . . and it began immediately to seem to Ivan Dmitritch and his wife that their rooms were dark and small and low-pitched, that the supper they had been eating was not doing them good." Ivan continues to show his newly-found disgust for his wife when he notes, "The rooms are never swept! One is simply forced to go out." While Ivan seemed perfectly content with his place and his wife in the beginning, by the end of the story neither seems good enough. The hope of winning the lottery has had only a negative impact on the couple's view of their lives.

13. What is the main theme of this short story? Use specific evidence from the text to support your answer.

One possible answer:

The story's main theme deals with the effect that greed can have on relationships. As noted above, Ivan is described by the narrator as "satisfied" at the beginning of the story. In addition, at first the couple seems to enjoy the hope of winning: ". . . it was as pleasant to her as to him that he only mentioned the series, and did not try to find out the number of the winning ticket." However, in less than two paragraphs Ivan already has developed fantasies of a life without his wife. In addition, he begins to loathe his wife's presence; "She would begrudge me every farthing." Not only is Ivan's relationship with his wife affected, but his relationship with his relatives is affected as well. He notes that his wife's family members are "wretched, detestable people" who if "given anything . . . would ask for more." He even begins to view his own family differently. " Ivan Dmitritch remembered his own relations, and their faces, at which he had looked impartially in the past, struck him now as repulsive and hateful." Anyone who might get in the way of him having all of the wealth has now become a "reptile" to him. While the wife's thoughts are not as well known, the narrator does note, ". . . she had her own daydreams, her own plans, her own reflections." She now looks at him with hate and anger. Greed for money had changed the relationships presented in the story.

14. What is your prediction for the couple after the short story ends? Use specific evidence from the text to support your prediction.

Most students will predict an unhappy future for the couple. Some students may feel that the couple will stay together since, when they didn't win the lottery, the "hatred and hope both disappeared at once." However, most students will agree that if the couple does stay together that they will continue to be miserable. Both of them note that "their rooms were dark and small and low-pitched, that the supper they had been eating was not doing them good, but lying heavy on their stomachs, that the evenings were long and wearisome." They are no longer content with their lives; in addition, the husband seems particularly miserable, screaming at his wife about the unkempt nature of the house.

Some students may believe that the two will no longer be together. Ivan's disturbing last lines, "Damnation take my soul entirely! I shall go and hang myself on the first aspen-tree!" may cause some students to assume that he had become so desperate for his imagined new life that he might end his miserable one. Other students will take this less literally, saying that the actual damnation is that he will have to continue to live his unhappy life with his wife and house even though he has caught a glimpse of a different life. Students may predict that even though Ivan may decide to live out his unhappy existence doesn't mean that his wife will necessarily stay with him. Recognizing her husband's greed ("She knew who would be the first to try to grab her winnings"), wanting to realize her own dreams, and refusing to live with her husband's scrutiny, she may decide to leave the marriage.

Question 1	Analyzing Point of View
Question 2	Analyzing Conflict, Plot, and Setting
Question 3	Analyzing Character
Question 4	Analyzing Author's Purpose
Question 5	Analyzing Figurative Language
Question 6	Recognizing Author's Beliefs/Bias
Question 7	Drawing Conclusions
Question 8	Making Inferences
Question 9	Analyzing Paradox
Question 10	Analyzing Character/Making Inferences
Question 11	Analyzing Diction/Compare and Contrast
Question 12	Analyzing Cause and Effect
Question 13	Interpreting Theme/Main Idea
Question 14	Making Predictions

115

FROM ACT III, SCENE III OF *HAMLET*

by William Shakespeare

[Enter Polonius.]

Polonius.
My lord, he's going to his mother's closet:
Behind the arras I'll convey myself
To hear the process; I'll warrant she'll tax him
    home:
And, as you said, and wisely was it said,
'Tis meet that some more audience than a
    mother,
Since nature makes them partial, should
    o'erhear
The speech, of vantage. Fare you well, my liege:
I'll call upon you ere you go to bed,
And tell you what I know.

King.
Thanks, dear my lord.
[Exit Polonius.]
O, my offence is rank, it smells to heaven;
It hath the primal eldest curse upon't,—
A brother's murder!—Pray can I not,
Though inclination be as sharp as will:
My stronger guilt defeats my strong intent;
And, like a man to double business bound,
I stand in pause where I shall first begin,
And both neglect. What if this cursed hand
Were thicker than itself with brother's blood,—
Is there not rain enough in the sweet heavens
To wash it white as snow? Whereto serves
    mercy
But to confront the visage of offence?
And what's in prayer but this twofold force,—
To be forestalled ere we come to fall,
Or pardon'd being down? Then I'll look up;
My fault is past. But, O, what form of prayer
Can serve my turn? Forgive me my foul
    murder!—
That cannot be; since I am still possess'd
Of those effects for which I did the murder,—
My crown, mine own ambition, and my queen.
May one be pardon'd and retain the offence?
In the corrupted currents of this world
Offence's gilded hand may shove by justice;
And oft 'tis seen the wicked prize itself
Buys out the law; but 'tis not so above;
There is no shuffling;—there the action lies

In his true nature; and we ourselves compell'd,
Even to the teeth and forehead of our faults,
To give in evidence. What then? what rests?
Try what repentance can: what can it not?
Yet what can it when one cannot repent?
O wretched state! O bosom black as death!
O limed soul, that, struggling to be free,
Art more engag'd! Help, angels! Make assay:
Bow, stubborn knees; and, heart, with strings of
    steel,
Be soft as sinews of the new-born babe!
All may be well.

[Retires and kneels.]

[Enter Hamlet.]

Hamlet.
Now might I do it pat, now he is praying;
And now I'll do't;—and so he goes to heaven;
And so am I reveng'd.—that would be scann'd:
A villain kills my father; and for that,
I, his sole son, do this same villain send
To heaven.
O, this is hire and salary, not revenge.
He took my father grossly, full of bread;
With all his crimes broad blown, as flush as
    May;
And how his audit stands, who knows save
    heaven?
But in our circumstance and course of thought,
'Tis heavy with him: and am I, then, reveng'd,
To take him in the purging of his soul,
When he is fit and season'd for his passage?
No.
Up, sword, and know thou a more horrid hent:
When he is drunk asleep; or in his rage;
Or in the incestuous pleasure of his bed;
At gaming, swearing; or about some act
That has no relish of salvation in't;—
Then trip him, that his heels may kick at
    heaven;
And that his soul may be as damn'd and black
As hell, whereto it goes. My mother stays:
This physic but prolongs thy sickly days.

[Exit.]

[The King rises and advances.]

King.
My words fly up, my thoughts remain below:
Words without thoughts never to heaven go.

[Exit.]

1. What genre of fiction is this?

    a. novel
    b. novella
    c. short story
    d. drama

2. In this case, the word, "rank," carries the connotation of

    a. organized.
    b. growing.
    c. odorous.
    d. completed.

3. What has the king done?

    a. insulted his own family members
    b. thought about killing his brother
    c. spied on Hamlet's mother
    d. murdered his own brother

4. Why is the king kneeling down?

    a. to pray
    b. to rest
    c. to pick up something
    d. to sleep

5. "Bow, stubborn knees" contains an example of

    a. onomatopoeia.
    b. personification.
    c. consonance.
    d. alliteration.

6. Which is **not** an effect of the king's crime?

    a. He became king.
    b. He married the queen.
    c. He upset Hamlet.
    d. He lost his crown.

7. Why doesn't Hamlet want to kill the king at this moment?

    a. He is worried about his mother.
    b. The king has just confessed his sins.
    c. He feels too tired at the moment.
    d. He wants to wait until the king is alone.

8. "What if this cursed hand/ Were thicker than itself with brother's blood,—/ Is there not rain enough in the sweet heavens/To wash it white as snow?" What type of figurative language is in this excerpt? Explain the effect of the excerpt on the entire passage.

Shakespeare uses a simile and symbolism to emphasize the king's inability to be forgiven for his sin. The king describes his hand as "cursed" when asking himself if he could ever wash his brother's blood from his hands. He questions whether or not even all the rain in heaven could wash them clean. The blood is symbolic of the sin or guilt the king has for killing his brother; the fact that he wonders if even all the rain in the sweet heavens could wash him clean indicates his own doubt about whether or not his sin can ever be forgiven. White in this instance is symbolic of purity. Using a simile that compares his desired whiteness to snow, Shakespeare emphasizes the king's desire to return to a cleaner, more innocent time. This figurative language sets the stage for the rest of the king's soliloquy in which he wanders how he can be forgiven when he is "still possess'd/ Of those effects for which I did the murder" and attempts to pray for forgiveness, ultimately realizing that he cannot receive it.

9. What is the king's problem? Is his solution to his problem effective or ineffective? Why? Use specific evidence from the text to support your answer.

One possible answer:
The king's problem is that he wants to be forgiven for his sins; however, he still wants to keep the benefits of his sin: the crown, the queen, and ambition. The king realizes that getting out of trouble on earth is different from doing this in heaven: "In the corrupted currents of this world/ Offence's gilded hand may shove by justice;/ And oft 'tis seen the wicked prize itself/ Buys out the law; but 'tis not so above." While he may be able to pay off people on earth, the king cannot buy his way into heaven. His solution is to pray for forgiveness. However, this solution is ineffective. The last couplet of the scene, "My words fly up, my thoughts remain below:/ Words without thoughts never to heaven go," indicates that the solution has failed because he doesn't really feel sorry for what he has done. This is further indicated when he addresses his own body (stubborn knees, heart's strings of steel) to cooperate in asking for forgiveness. The king forces himself to pray, hoping that the illusion of prayer will be good enough so he will be forgiven; however, it is not.

10. What type of irony is presented in this passage? Explain the effect of the irony on the entire passage.

Shakespeare uses dramatic irony in this passage: Hamlet stalls in killing the king because he does not want to kill him when all of the king's sins have been forgiven (therefore sending him to heaven). However, the audience finds out that the king has not been forgiven of his sins because he was not sincerely praying. The irony helps to develop the delay Hamlet has in avenging his father. Hamlet notes that his own father was taken before he had a chance to ask forgiveness for his sins, so that killing the king now and sending him to heaven would not be true revenge. However, Hamlet spends so much time thinking about how to properly avenge his father than he passes up an easy opportunity to do so. Because the audience knows that he passed up a perfect moment for revenge (since the king hadn't been forgiven), the irony emphasizes Hamlet's tendency to put off the revenge.

Passage I: "London 1802"

by William Wordsworth

Milton! thou shouldst be living at this hour;   1
England hath need of thee: she is a fen
Of stagnant waters: altar, sword, and pen,
Fireside, the heroic wealth of hall and bower,
Have forfeited their ancient English dower   5
Of inward happiness. We are selfish men;
Oh! raise us up, return to us again;
And give us manners, virtue, freedom, power.
Thy soul was like a Star, and dwelt apart;
Thou hadst a voice whose sound was like the sea: 10
Pure as the naked heavens, majestic, free,
So didst thou travel on life's common way,
In cheerful godliness; and yet thy heart
The lowliest duties on herself did lay.

Passage II: "England 1819"

by Percy Shelley

An old, mad, blind, despised, and dying king,—   1
Princes, the dregs of their dull race, who flow
Through public scorn,—mud from a muddy spring,—
Rulers who neither see, nor feel, nor know,
But leech-like to their fainting country cling,   5
Till they drop, blind in blood, without a blow,—
A people starved and stabbed in the untilled field,—
An army, which liberticide and prey
Makes as a two-edged sword to all who wield,—
Golden and sanguine laws which tempt and slay;   10
Religion Christless, Godless—a book sealed;
A Senate, Time's worst statute unrepealed,—
Are graves, from which a glorious Phantom may
Burst, to illumine our tempestuous day.

120

Passage I

1. The word, "fen," in this passage connotes

    a. clarity.
    b. stillness.
    c. quickness.
    d. turmoil.

2. What does Wordsworth mean when he says, "altar, sword, and pen"?

    a. He is referring to the country's need for more of these types of items.
    b. He is referring to the country's need to share these items with others.
    c. He is referring to the fact that the country no longer needs these items.
    d. He is referring to the church, the army, and the state, and not to the items themselves.

3. What kind of tone is created in the poem by words like "thy" and "thou"?

    a. whimsical
    b. forlorn
    c. formal
    d. bitter

4. In the last three lines of the poem which of Milton's qualities does Wordsworth admire?

    a. his desire to travel
    b. his good manners
    c. his strong singing voice
    d. his persevering nature

Passage II

5. What does Shelley mean when he says, "mud from a muddy spring"?

    a. He means that the princes are similar to the corrupted kings.
    b. He means England's landscape is dirty from the rain.
    c. He means the public is mean and nasty to the princes.
    d. He means things are unclear for the country right now.

6. Line 1 contains an example of

    a. personification.
    b. consonance.
    c. onomatopoeia.
    d. simile.

7. "But leech-like to their fainting country cling,/Till they drop, blind in blood, without a blow." This simile emphasizes the

    a. poor state of the country.
    b. greed of the ruling class.
    c. number of dying royalty.
    d. bloodiness of the time.

8. Line 6 contains an example of

    a. onomatopoeia.
    b. personification.
    c. alliteration.
    d. simile.

9. How does Shelley feel about the Senate?

    a. They are not overturning bad laws.
    b. They are too old to make decisions.
    c. They will get the job done in time.
    d. They are working to make things better.

Passages I and II

10. Analyze how Wordsworth uses figurative language in "London 1802" in order to create a specific effect. Use examples from the text to support your answer.

One possible answer:

Wordsworth's figurative language helps to show the contrast between London and Milton. He begins with the metaphor, "she is a fen of stagnant waters." This metaphor paints London as a swampland where things are not moving and progress is not being made. This contrasts sharply to Wordsworth's simile describing Milton: "Thou hadst a voice whose sound was like the sea." While London is compared to a bog, Milton represents a rolling, moving sea. While London seems to be stuck in its current mess, Milton's voice is presented as free and as changing as the ocean. Milton continues to be described through similes: "thy soul was like a star, and dwelt apart" and "Pure as the naked heavens, majestic, free." Both of these represent qualities far different from those of a swampland; instead of being stuck in a sticky, filthy marsh, Milton represents a purity and freedom from a corruption that weighs a person down. This contrast between Milton and London is important to Wordsworth's point: Wordsworth calls for Milton's type of spirit to help the ailing London.

11. Why does Wordsworth address John Milton, a famous poet from the 1600s, in his poem? What effect does this have on the poem?

Wordsworth addresses Milton because he represents the type of thinking and spirit that Wordsworth believes England needs. He calls the men around him selfish, saying that they have given up their natural gift to be happy, opting to leave things unchanged ("stagnant waters") rather than to make necessary modifications. Milton was a strong voice in his own time, advocating for religious and social change. Even though Milton had his own problems to deal with (being thrown in jail and going blind), he still managed to travel through life in "cheerful godliness" with a voice "like the sea." He was not willing to give up his natural right to be happy. In this poem Wordsworth calls on Milton's perseverance to inspire both him and the people of his time. In this way the poet gives the people of his time an example to model without directly instructing them to behave a certain way.

12. Shelley's "England 1819" was written shortly after the Peterloo Massacre of August 16, 1819, when troops charged into a crowd at a public meeting in England. What connections can you make between the poem and the massacre, hinting that Shelley may have been specifically addressing this incident?

Students should make a number of connections between the poem and the massacre. First of all, Shelley uses words with the connotation of an attack: "blow," "stabbed," "sword," and "slay." In addition he directly refers to those people "starved and stabbed in an untilled field." Shelley also mentions the army that has become a double-edged sword. While normally an army would protect the people, this army has become an element of liberticide, or the destruction of civil liberty, such as on the day of the massacre when the troops ended up killing innocent people who were there to discuss their rights. Lastly the poem directly refers to laws that "tempt and slay" as well as "Time's worst statute" that remains "unrepealed." This may very well be referring to laws such as the "corn laws" that many had wanted to discuss at the public meeting.

13. Compare and contrast the two sonnets. What similarities and differences do you notice in the structure and organization of the sonnet? Use specific evidence from the two texts to support your answer.

While students may not know the difference between a Shakespearean sonnet and a Petrarchan sonnet by name, they should be able to distinguish how the two different sonnets are organized. First of all, the poems are similar in that they are both 14 lines and follow a problem-solution-type format. However, students should note that the two poems have quite different rhyme schemes. Wordsworth's poem has the rhyme scheme of abba abba cdd ece. This is a typical rhyme scheme of a Petrarchan, or Italian, sonnet with just a slight variation in the last four lines (normally ecde, ccdc, or edce). Shelley's poem, however, follows more the rhyme scheme of the Shakespearean sonnet, although with noticeable variations: ababab cdcd ee gg. (The normal Shakespearean sonnet follows the abab cdcd efef gg rhyme scheme.) Most importantly, however, is the difference in how the problem-solution format is set up. In Wordsworth's Petrarchan-like format, the problem is presented in the first eight lines and resolved in the last six. For example, Wordsworth spends the first eight lines describing the problem with London and the last six lines focusing on those qualities of Milton that would benefit London if the people would adopt them. Shelley's poem, however, takes the form of a Shakespearean sonnet by presenting the problem for the first twelve lines of the poem, only revealing the solution in the last two lines: "Are graves, from which a glorious Phantom may / Burst, to illumine our tempestuous day." Shelley says that all of these terrible things will only inspire some rebirth that will bring the community to a better place. While both poems may be in the form of sonnets, they have quite different organizational patterns.

14. Both of these poems were written during the English Romantic time period. Using the two poems above, what generalizations can you make about the time period and those that lived in it? Use specific evidence from the two texts to support your answer.

Students will most likely note the time period as a call for change. In both poems the narrators call for some kind of reform. Wordsworth addresses Milton and his qualities as the way to change while Shelley refers to the "glorious phantom" that will help to fix the problem. More specifically, each author expresses discontent with the ruling bodies of the time. Wordsworth says that the "pen" and "heroic wealth of hall" have forfeited their natural happiness and have become selfish. The pen and heroic wealth may very well be referring to the lawmakers and other ruling class members who have become a "fen." Shelley picks up on this point in a stronger way by saying that the rulers are like leeches that suck the people dry of all their resources and then fall off without much concern. Shelley also addresses lawmakers specifically by saying that "Time's worst statute" remains "unrepealed." The discontent of the people with the selfish ruling class is just one generalization of the time period.

In addition to government, both poems address religion at that time: again, both poems suggest that changes need to be made in the way religion is practiced. Wordsworth's poem refers to the "altar" being stagnant or, in other words, the church. Similarly, Shelley addresses the church institution when he says, " Religion Christless, Godless—a book sealed" suggesting that the way religion is currently being practiced does not follow the Bible. Both authors address religious concerns in the time period.

Lastly, both poems express problems with the armies of the time. Wordsworth recognizes a need for change in the sword, or the army, while Shelley offers a much more poignant description of the force saying, "An army, which liberticide and prey / Makes as a two-edged sword to all who wield," and referring to people being stabbed in fields. Both authors paint a picture of the time period by focusing on people's discontent with major institutions such as the legal system, armed forces, and religion. They both show a lack of progress or even a death in the improvement of society for the people during this time by using images such as "fen of stagnant waters" and "grave."

15. Which poem do you think is better crafted? Use specific evidence from the text to support your point.

Students' answers will vary. Some may feel that Wordsworth's poem flows more smoothly from beginning to end with the use of the metaphor in lines 2-6 and the focus on Milton for much of the rest of the poem; in contrast, Shelley's poem is more a succession of images put in front of the reader. Some may also feel the last two lines of Shelley's poem seem dwarfed by the heavy images present in the other twelve lines. Others, however, will appreciate Shelley's much more specific description of the problems, recognizing that those who read about the horrible deeds in the poem may be inspired to become part of the phantom rising from the grave with new energy and ideas, as distinct from Wordsworth's poem where more attention has been placed on Milton.

Question 1	Analyzing Diction
Question 2	Making Inferences
Question 3	Analyzing Development of Tone/Mood
Question 4	Summarizing and Paraphrasing
Question 5	Drawing Conclusions
Question 6	Analyzing Figurative Language
Question 7	Analyzing Figurative Language
Question 8	Analyzing Sound Devices and Rhythm
Question 9	Recognizing Author's Beliefs/Bias
Question 10	Analyzing Figurative Language
Question 11	Interpreting References from Culture/Past
Question 12	Examining Cultures/Historical Periods
Question 13	Comparing and Contrasting/Text Structure
Question 14	Making Generalizations/Examining Cultures and Historical Periods
Question 15	Evaluating Author's Craft

FROM BOOK IX OF HOMER'S *THE ODYSSEY*

'Now when early Dawn shone forth, the rosy-fingered, again he kindled the fire and milked his goodly flocks all orderly, and beneath each ewe set her lamb. Anon when he had done all his work busily, again he seized yet other two men and made ready his mid-day meal. And after the meal, lightly he moved away the great door-stone, and drave his fat flocks forth from the cave, and afterwards he set it in his place again, as one might set the lid on a quiver. Then with a loud whoop, the Cyclops turned his fat flocks towards the hills; but I was left devising evil in the deep of my heart, if in any wise I might avenge me, and Athene grant me renown.

'And this was the counsel that showed best in my sight. There lay by a sheep-fold a great club of the Cyclops, a club of olive wood, yet green, which he had cut to carry with him when it should be seasoned. Now when we saw it we likened it in size to the mast of a black ship of twenty oars, a wide merchant vessel that traverses the great sea gulf, so huge it was to view in bulk and length. I stood thereby and cut off from it a portion as it were a fathom's length, and set it by my fellows, and bade them fine it down, and they made it even, while I stood by and sharpened it to a point, and straightway I took it and hardened it in the bright fire. Then I laid it well away, and hid it beneath the dung, which was scattered in great heaps in the depths of the cave. And I bade my company cast lots among them, which of them should risk the adventure with me, and lift the bar and turn it about in his eye, when sweet sleep came upon him. And the lot fell upon those four whom I myself would have been fain to choose, and I appointed myself to be the fifth among them. In the evening he came shepherding his flocks of goodly fleece, and presently he drave his fat flocks into the cave each and all, nor left he any without in the deep court-yard, whether through some foreboding, or perchance that the god so bade him do. Thereafter he lifted the huge door-stone and set it in the mouth of the cave, and sitting down he milked the ewes and bleating goats, all orderly, and beneath each ewe he placed her young. Now when he had done all his work busily, again he seized yet other two and made ready his supper. Then I stood by the Cyclops and spake to him, holding in my hands an ivy bowl of the dark wine:

' "Cyclops, take and drink wine after thy feast of man's meat, that thou mayest know what manner of drink this was that our ship held. And lo, I was bringing it thee as a drink offering, if haply thou mayest take pity and send me on my way home, but thy mad rage is past all sufferance. O hard of heart, how may another of the many men there be come ever to thee again, seeing that thy deeds have been lawless?"

'So I spake, and he took the cup and drank it off, and found great delight in drinking the sweet draught, and asked me for it yet a second time:

' "Give it me again of thy grace, and tell me thy name straightway, that I may give thee a stranger's gift, wherein thou mayest be glad. Yea for the earth, the grain-giver, bears for the Cyclopes the mighty clusters of the juice of the grape, and the rain of Zeus gives them increase, but this is a rill of very nectar and ambrosia."

'So he spake, and again I handed him the dark wine. Thrice I bare and gave it him, and thrice in his folly he drank it to the lees. Now when the wine had got about the wits of the Cyclops, then did I speak to him with soft words:

' "Cyclops, thou askest me my renowned name, and I will declare it unto thee, and do thou grant me a stranger's gift, as thou didst promise. Noman is my name, and Noman they call me, my father and my mother and all my fellows."

'So I spake, and straightway he answered me out of his pitiless heart:

' "Noman will I eat last in the number of his fellows, and the others before him: that shall be thy gift."

'Therewith he sank backwards and fell with face upturned, and there he lay with his great neck bent round, and sleep, that conquers all men, overcame him. And the wine and the fragments of men's flesh issued forth from his mouth, and he vomited, being heavy with wine. Then I thrust in that stake under the deep ashes, until it should grow hot, and I spake to my companions comfortable words, lest any should hang back from me in fear. But when that bar of olive wood was just about to catch fire in the flame, green though it was, and began to glow terribly, even then I came nigh, and drew it from the coals, and my fellows gathered about me,

128

and some god breathed great courage into us. For their part they seized the bar of olive wood, that was sharpened at the point, and thrust it into his eye, while I from my place aloft turned it about, as when a man bores a ship's beam with a drill while his fellows below spin it with a strap, which they hold at either end, and the auger runs round continually. Even so did we seize the fiery-pointed brand and whirled it round in his eye, and the blood flowed about the heated bar. And the breath of the flame singed his eyelids and brows all about, as the ball of the eye burnt away, and the roots thereof crackled in the flame. And as when a smith dips an axe or adze in chill water with a great hissing, when he would temper it—for hereby anon comes the strength of iron—even so did his eye hiss round the stake of olive. And he raised a great and terrible cry, that the rock rang around, and we fled away in fear, while he plucked forth from his eye the brand bedabbled in much blood. Then maddened with pain he cast it from him with his hands, and called with a loud voice on the Cyclopes, who dwelt about him in the caves along the windy heights. And they heard the cry and flocked together from every side, and gathering round the cave asked him what ailed him:

' "What hath so distressed thee, Polyphemus, that thou criest thus aloud through the immortal night, and makest us sleepless? Surely no mortal driveth off thy flocks against thy will: surely none slayeth thyself by force or craft?"

'And the strong Polyphemus spake to them again from out the cave: "My friends, Noman is slaying me by guile, nor at all by force."

'And they answered and spake winged words: "If then no man is violently handling thee in thy solitude, it can in no wise be that thou shouldest escape the sickness sent by mighty Zeus. Nay, pray thou to thy father, the lord Poseidon."

'On this wise they spake and departed; and my heart within me laughed to see how my name and cunning counsel had beguiled them. But the Cyclops, groaning and travailing in pain, groped with his hands, and lifted away the stone from the door of the cave, and himself sat in the entry, with arms outstretched to catch, if he might, any one that was going forth with his sheep, so witless, methinks, did he hope to find me. But I advised me how all might be for the very best, if perchance I might find a way of escape from

129

death for my companions and myself, and I wove all manner of craft and counsel, as a man will for his life, seeing that great mischief was nigh. And this was the counsel that showed best in my sight. The rams of the flock were well nurtured and thick of fleece, great and goodly, with wool dark as the violet. Quietly I lashed them together with twisted withies, whereon the Cyclops slept, that lawless monster. Three together I took: now the middle one of the three would bear each a man, but the other twain went on either side, saving my fellows. Thus every three sheep bare their man. But as for me I laid hold of the back of a young ram who was far the best and the goodliest of all the flock, and curled beneath his shaggy belly there I lay, and so clung face upward, grasping the wondrous fleece with a steadfast heart. So for that time making moan we awaited the bright Dawn.

'So soon as early Dawn shone forth, the rosy-fingered, then did the rams of the flock hasten forth to pasture, but the ewes bleated unmilked about the pens, for their udders were swollen to bursting. Then their lord, sore stricken with pain, felt along the backs of all the sheep as they stood up before him, and guessed not in his folly how that my men were bound beneath the breasts of his thick-fleeced flocks. Last of all the sheep came forth the ram, cumbered with his wool, and the weight of me and my cunning. And the strong Polyphemus laid his hands on him and spake to him saying:

' "Dear ram, wherefore, I pray thee, art thou the last of all the flocks to go forth from the cave, who of old wast not wont to lag behind the sheep, but wert ever the foremost to pluck the tender blossom of the pasture, faring with long strides, and wert still the first to come to the streams of the rivers, and first did long to return to the homestead in the evening? But now art thou the very last. Surely thou art sorrowing for the eye of thy lord, which an evil man blinded, with his accursed fellows, when he had subdued my wits with wine, even Noman, whom I say hath not yet escaped destruction. Ah, if thou couldst feel as I, and be endued with speech, to tell me where he shifts about to shun my wrath; then should he be smitten, and his brains be dashed against the floor here and there about the cave, and my heart be lightened of the sorrows which Noman, nothing worth, hath brought me!"

'Therewith he sent the ram forth from him, and when we had gone but a little way from the cave and from the yard,

first I loosed myself from under the ram and then I set my
fellows free. And swiftly we drave on those stiff-shanked
sheep, so rich in fat, and often turned to look about, till
we came to the ship. And a glad sight to our fellows were
we that had fled from death, but the others they would have
bemoaned with tears; howbeit I suffered it not, but with
frowning brows forbade each man to weep. Rather I bade them
to cast on board the many sheep with goodly fleece, and to
sail over the salt seawater. So they embarked forthwith,
and sate upon the benches, and sitting orderly smote the
gray seawater with their oars. But when I had not gone so
far, but that a man's shout might be heard, then I spoke
unto the Cyclops taunting him:

' "Cyclops, so thou wert not to eat the company of a
weakling by main might in thy hollow cave! Thine evil deeds
were very sure to find thee out, thou cruel man, who hadst
no shame to eat thy guests within thy gates, wherefore Zeus
hath requited thee, and the other gods."

'So I spake, and he was mightily angered at heart, and he
brake off the peak of a great hill and threw it at us, and
it fell in front of the dark-prowed ship. And the sea
heaved beneath the fall of the rock, and the backward flow
of the wave bare the ship quickly to the dry land, with the
wash from the deep sea, and drave it to the shore.

1. "Now when we saw it we/ likened it in size to the mast of a black ship of twenty/oars,
   a wide merchant vessel that traverses the great sea/gulf, so huge it was to view in
   bulk and length." These lines contain an example of

   a. metaphor.
   b. simile.
   c. onomatopoeia.
   d. personification.

2. "Then/ with a loud whoop, the Cyclops turned his fat flocks/ towards the hills." These
   lines contain an example of

   a. metaphor.
   b. simile.
   c. onomatopoeia.
   d. personification.

131

3. Which is seemingly the biggest problem for Odysseus and his men in their escape?

   a. getting back to their ship once out of the cave
   b. getting the large rock in the cave's entrance moved
   c. getting the Cyclops to drink a lot so he gets drunk
   d. figuring out how to trick the clever Cyclops

4. Which is **not** an effect of Odysseus lying that his name is Noman?

   a. The Cyclops promises to eat Odysseus last.
   b. The Cyclops gives Odysseus a stranger's gift.
   c. The other Cyclopes misunderstand Polyphemus.
   d. The Cyclops asks many times for more wine.

5. The quote "bound beneath the breasts of his thick-fleeced flocks" contains an example of

   a. alliteration.
   b. consonance.
   c. personification.
   d. onomatopoeia.

6. Odysseus thinks that the Cyclops is

   a. clever.
   b. a baby.
   c. ruthless.
   d. fair.

7. "But as for me I laid hold of the back of a young/ ram who was far the best and the goodliest of all the/ flock, and curled beneath his shaggy belly there I lay." This quote illustrates that Odysseus

   a. puts his men's needs above his own.
   b. puts his own needs above those of his men.
   c. likes rams better than sheep.
   d. is cleverer than the other men.

8. Which of these is **not** part of the solution to Odysseus' problem?

   a. He stabs the Cyclops in the eye.
   b. He rides the ram out of the cave.
   c. He lures the other Cyclopes to the cave.
   d. He tells the Cyclops that his name is Noman.

9. The Cyclops finds the ram's behavior unusual because the ram

   a. is walking with long strides.
   b. feels sorry for the Cyclopes.
   c. is hungry and wants to eat.
   d. is the last out of the cave.

10. How does Odysseus feel about the Cyclops' sheep?

    a. ***They are very valuable to him and his men.***
    b. They are smaller than the average-size sheep.
    c. They are only good to help the men escape.
    d. They are being held captive like him and his men.

11. Why does the Cyclops throw part of a hill at Odysseus and his men?

    a. He regains part of his eyesight, finally seeing the men.
    b. He does not want to be punished by the god Zeus.
    c. ***He is teased by Odysseus for allowing them to escape.***
    d. He wants to push Odysseus far out into the sea.

12. How does Homer bring to life the moment when Odysseus shoves the stake into the Cyclops' eye? Evaluate the effectiveness of the author's craft in this section. Use specific evidence from the text to support your answer.

One possible answer:

Homer is very effective in bringing the scene to life because he captures both the sights and sounds of the moment through figurative language and sound devices. He first uses similes to capture the sight of the men shoving the olive wood into the monster's eye; he compares the moment to "when a man bores a ship's / beam with a drill while his fellows below spin it with a / strap, which they hold at either end, and the auger runs / round continually." This simile allows the audience to envision the twisting motion with which the men pierce the Cyclops' eye. This vision is enhanced through the use of imagery. Homer describes the "blood flowing around the heated bar" and the eyeball being "burnt away." In addition, Homer uses a simile to capture the grotesque sound: "And as when a smith dips an axe or adze in chill water with / a great hissing, when he would temper it—for hereby anon / comes the strength of iron—even so did his eye hiss round / the stake of olive." Even though Homer's readers today may not be blacksmiths, most have heard the hissing of something scalding hot being cooled down with water. To capture the sound even more, he uses onomatopoeia, describing the roots of the eye as crackling. All of these literary devices enhance the scene, creating an unforgettable moment in the text.

133

13. How does the tone change during the Cyclops' speech to the ram? Use specific
    evidence from the text to support your answer.

The tone changes from affectionate to fierce during the Cyclops' speech to the ram. The affectionate tone is developed from the start as the Cyclops refers to the ram as "dear ram." This warmth continues as the monster seems concerned that something may be wrong with the ram: "but wert ever the / foremost to pluck the tender blossom of the pasture, faring / with long strides, and wert still the first to come to the / streams of the rivers, and first did long to return to the / homestead in the evening?" Words such as "tender," "blossom," and "homestead" all wrapped up in a question of concern create the tender tone. However, the tone of the speech quickly changes when the Cyclops thinks of Odysseus. Words in the last lines of the speech, such as "evil," "accursed," "destruction," "wrath," and "dashed" create a more violent tone. The reader notes that what had earlier been the "homestead" is now called the "cave," and the Cyclops has gone from asking tender questions to making violent exclamations.

14. Analyze the use of irony in this passage. Identify specific examples of irony, the type
    of irony, and the effect on the passage.

Homer effectively uses dramatic irony in the passage to emphasize Odysseus' cleverness. The first instance of dramatic irony happens when the Cyclops yells to his fellow monsters, "My friends, Noman is slaying me by guile, nor at all / by force." The other Cyclopes believe that he is saying that no man is causing him trouble, so they return to their caves; however, the audience understands what is really going on and now fully realizes the ingenuity of Odysseus' lie about his name earlier in the passage. A second instance of dramatic irony comes at the end of the passage when the Cyclops is talking to the ram. He comments, "Ah, if thou couldst feel as I, and / be endued with speech, to tell me where he shifts about to / shun my wrath". The audience knows that Odysseus is underneath the ram, making the Cyclops appear even more foolish and Odysseus appear even more cunning since Odysseus lies within the monster's grasp but will still escape.

134

15. How does Homer use indirect characterization to develop Odysseus' main traits? Use specific evidence from the text to support your answer.

One possible answer:

Homer uses indirect characterization to develop Odysseus as an ingenious but self-involved character. Odysseus' cleverness is mainly shown through his actions and what he says. Odysseus is the one that plans to get the Cyclops drunk in order to easily poke out his eye. His quick thinking also causes him to lie about his name to eliminate the threat of the other Cyclopes, and to tie the men underneath the sheep so that they can escape undetected. All of these examples allow the audience to understand his strengths.

Although Homer develops Odysseus' strengths, he also develops Odysseus' self-involved side. From the beginning of the passage Odysseus doesn't mention devising a plan to get his men to safety, but rather he says, " I was left devising evil in the deep / of my heart, if in any wise I might avenge me." Odysseus seems more concerned to pay back the Cyclops than to safely escape. In addition, he seems to enjoy the challenge commenting, "On this wise they spake and departed; and my heart within / me laughed to see how my name and cunning counsel had / beguiled them." Through what he says, the audience begins to understand Odysseus' selfish nature. This quality is emphasized through the character's actions at the end of the passage. Even though the men have all escaped, they are still within reach of the monster's harm. However, Odysseus cannot help but taunt the Cyclops saying, "Cyclops, so thou wert not to eat the company of a / weakling by main might in thy hollow cave!" If Odysseus were truly worried about his men's safety, he would not have attracted the Cyclops' attention. This action has a negative effect on the whole crew as they are pushed back to the Cyclops' island after the Cyclops throws a rock toward their boat in anger. The character's comments and actions both help to develop Odysseus' strengths and weaknesses in the passage.

"The Haunted Oak"

by Paul Laurence Dunbar

Pray why are you so bare, so bare,   1
    Oh, bough of the old oak-tree;
And why, when I go through the shade you throw,
    Runs a shudder over me?

My leaves were green as the best, I trow,   5
    And sap ran free in my veins,
But I saw in the moonlight dim and weird
    A guiltless victim's pains.

I bent me down to hear his sigh;
    I shook with his gurgling moan,   10
And I trembled sore when they rode away,
    And left him here alone.

They'd charged him with the old, old crime,
    And set him fast in jail:
Oh, why does the dog howl all night long,   15
    And why does the night wind wail?

He prayed his prayer and he swore his oath,
    And he raised his hand to the sky;
But the beat of hoofs smote on his ear,
    And the steady tread drew nigh.   20

Who is it rides by night, by night,
    Over the moonlit road?
And what is the spur that keeps the pace,
    What is the galling goad?

And now they beat at the prison door,   25
    "Ho, keeper, do not stay!
We are friends of him whom you hold within,
    And we fain would take him away

From those who ride fast on our heels
    With mind to do him wrong;
They have no care for his innocence,   30
    And the rope they bear is long."

They have fooled the jailer with lying words,
    They have fooled the man with lies;
The bolts unbar, the locks are drawn,   35
    And the great door open flies.

137

Now they have taken him from the jail,
    And hard and fast they ride,
And the leader laughs low down in his throat,
    As they halt my trunk beside.   40

Oh, the judge, he wore a mask of black,
    And the doctor one of white,
And the minister, with his oldest son,
    Was curiously bedight.

Oh, foolish man, why weep you now?   45
    'Tis but a little space,
And the time will come when these shall dread
    The mem'ry of your face.

I feel the rope against my bark,
    And the weight of him in my grain,   50
I feel in the throe of his final woe
    The touch of my own last pain.

And never more shall leaves come forth
    On a bough that bears the ban;
I am burned with dread, I am dried and dead,   55
    From the curse of a guiltless man.

And ever the judge rides by, rides by,
    And goes to hunt the deer,
And ever another rides his soul
    In the guise of a mortal fear.   60

And ever the man he rides me hard,
    And never a night stays he;
For I feel his curse as a haunted bough
    On the trunk of a haunted tree.

1. Which genre of poetry is this poem?

    a. sonnet
    b. ode
    c. ballad
    d. elegy

2. What prompts the opening question in stanza 1?

    a. The narrator is climbing the tree.
    b. The narrator is cutting down the tree.
    c. The tree gives the narrator chills.
    d. The tree speaks to the narrator.

3. Who is speaking in stanza 2?

    a. the haunted tree
    b. the stanza 1 narrator
    c. the guiltless man
    d. the townspeople

4. To which historical time period is this poem referring?

    a. the American Revolution
    b. settlers' colonization of America
    c. post–Civil War, late 1800s
    d. modern period, late 1900s

5. Which type of figurative language is used in this poem?

    a. simile
    b. metaphor
    c. hyperbole
    d. personification

6. The word, "wail," in line 16 carries the connotation of

    a. pain.
    b. happiness.
    c. hate.
    d. confusion.

7. How do the men acquire their victim?

    a. They sneak up on him in a field.
    b. They claim to be his friends.
    c. They pretend like they're the jailers.
    d. They tie him up with a long rope.

139

8. What happens to the victim?

    a. He is tied to the tree and left to die.
    b. He is hunted down like a deer.
    c. He is taken to the jail for execution.
    d. *He is hanged on a large oak tree.*

9. From stanza 11, a person can infer that

    a. *the town's leaders are a part of it.*
    b. the minister is trying to stop them.
    c. the court decided on this punishment.
    d. the victim is extremely injured.

10. What is the tone as the story is told?

    a. neutral
    b. *mournful*
    c. aggressive
    d. peaceful

11. How do the sound devices and rhythm of the poem add to the poem's effect? Use specific evidence from the text to support your answer.

One possible answer:

The sound devices help to create the sad tone of the poem. Dunbar uses a number of onomatopoeic words such as "gurgling," "sigh," "howl," and "wail" that connote sadness and suffering. In addition, he uses alliteration and consonance to create this effect. The narrator notes, " And the leader laughs low down in his throat". The alliterative "l" sound creates a sinister tone to the leader's laugh. Later the narrator notes, "On a bough that bears the ban / I am burned with dread, I am dried and dead"; the hard "b" and "d" sound created through alliteration and consonance emphasize the painful effects on the tree. Not only does the author use these sound devices, but he also uses the element of strongly-patterned rhyme and rhythm to create a similar effect. The rhyme and rhythm first emphasize the unstoppable nature of the men as they attack their victim: " And what is the spur that keeps the pace, / What is the galling goad." Later it becomes a reminder of the lingering effect of the victim's death. As the strong beat and rhyme continue on, so does the haunting effect of the crime: "For I feel his curse as a haunted bough / On the trunk of a haunted tree." Both the rhyme and rhythm show the continuous suffering.

12. Paraphrase lines 57–60. Why does the author include these lines?

One possible answer:

The author includes these lines in order to show the effect of the murder on humanity. The judge, presumably one of the leaders of the lynch mob, often rides by the tree on his way to hunt deer; however, the spirit of those whom he has murdered haunts him by making him deathly afraid. The author wants to emphasize that the crimes committed will continue to haunt humanity long after they were committed.

13. How would the poem be different if the author had not included the first stanza but instead started with the second stanza? Evaluate the author's craft in including this first stanza.

One possible answer:

Beginning with a question effectively grabs the reader's attention. It builds suspense by creating wonder in the reader. Why does the tree appear to be dying, or why does the passerby feel an eerie feeling as s / he passes by? The reader is filled with an ominous feeling only then to realize the horrifying truth. The tree had been used to lynch an innocent, presumably black, man. If the author had left out the first stanza, this suspense would have been lost. In addition, the first stanza is effective because it introduces the idea that all humankind will be affected by the crime, not just the tree. The innocent passerby shudders as s / he passes by the tree, haunted by the crimes that have occurred. If the first stanza had not been there, this idea would not have been introduced until stanza 12. Lastly, the fact that the tree is recounting the events it has witnessed to a person further emphasizes the connectedness of the natural world and the permanence of the tree's story in that world. Without the first stanza, all of these ideas would not have been developed nearly as well.

14. What is the theme of this poem? Use specific evidence from the text to support your answer.

One possible answer:

The main theme of this poem is that all humanity and all of the natural world will continue to be haunted by the committed hate crimes. This is made evident immediately from the first stanza when the passerby is described as shuddering as s/he passes the tree: although the observer may not yet know the details of the crime, s/he is still feels a lingering effect. This continues to be emphasized as the tree trembles, the dog howls, and the wind wails. All aspects of nature have been horrified and somehow changed.

Not only are the natural elements and the onlooker affected, but the men who committed the crime have also been changed. The tree speaks to the victim as he is about to be hanged: "Oh, foolish man, why weep you now? / 'Tis but a little space, / And the time will come when these shall dread / The mem'ry of your face." The tree seems to know before the man does that the crime committed against him will continue to disturb the perpetrators. This is exemplified as the judge rides to hunt deer while "ever another rides his soul / In the guise of a mortal fear." Even though the judge engages in sports and play, he is tormented by the memories of the time when he hunted his own man.

Finally, the tree's closing words connote the lasting impact of the misdeed.   The tree indicates its own pain as the man is murdered, as well as the suggestion that it has died from the crime committed: "I am burned with dread, I am dried and dead." In addition, the tree uses these words—"cursed" twice, "haunted" twice, and "ban" in the final stanzas— to indicate an eternal consequence. These words, combined with the strong presence of a continuous rhythm and rhyme, signify an unremitting guilt and sadness felt by all from the offenses against this man and against all the others who have suffered from other people's prejudices.

Cask of Amontillado

by Edgar Allen Poe

The thousand injuries of Fortunato I had borne as I best could; but when he ventured upon insult, I vowed revenge. You, who so well know the nature of my soul, will not suppose, however, that I gave utterance to a threat. At length I would be avenged; this was a point definitively settled—but the very definitiveness with which it was resolved, precluded the idea of risk. I must not only punish, but punish with impunity. A wrong is unredressed when retribution overtakes its redresser. It is equally unredressed when the avenger fails to make himself felt as such to him who has done the wrong.

It must be understood, that neither by word nor deed had I given Fortunato cause to doubt my good will. I continued, as was my wont, to smile in his face, and he did not perceive that my smile now was at the thought of his immolation.

He had a weak point—this Fortunato—although in other regards he was a man to be respected and even feared. He prided himself on his connoisseurship in wine. Few Italians have the true virtuoso spirit. For the most part their enthusiasm is adopted to suit the time and opportunity—to practice imposture upon the British and Austrian millionaires. In painting and gemmary, Fortunato, like his countrymen, was a quack—but in the matter of old wines he was sincere. In this respect I did not differ from him materially: I was skilful in the Italian vintages myself, and bought largely whenever I could.

It was about dusk, one evening during the supreme madness of the carnival season, that I encountered my friend. He accosted me with excessive warmth, for he had been drinking much. The man wore motley. He had on a tight-fitting parti-striped dress, and his head was surmounted by the conical cap and bells. I was so pleased to see him, that I thought I should never have done wringing his hand.

I said to him—"My dear Fortunato, you are luckily met. How remarkably well you are looking today! But I have received a pipe of what passes for Amontillado, and I have my doubts."

"How?" said he. "Amontillado? A pipe? Impossible! And in the middle of the carnival!"

"I have my doubts," I replied; "and I was silly enough to pay the full Amontillado price without consulting you in the matter. You were not to be found, and I was fearful of losing a bargain."

"Amontillado!"

"I have my doubts."

"Amontillado!"

"And I must satisfy them."

"Amontillado!"

"As you are engaged, I am on my way to Luchesi. If any one has a critical turn, it is he. He will tell me—"

"Luchesi cannot tell Amontillado from Sherry."

"And yet some fools will have it that his taste is a match for your own."

"Come, let us go."

"Whither?"

"To your vaults."

"My friend, no; I will not impose upon your good nature. I perceive you have an engagement. Luchesi—"

"I have no engagement; —come."

"My friend, no. It is not the engagement, but the severe cold with which I perceive you are afflicted. The vaults are insufferably damp. They are encrusted with nitre."

144

"Let us go, nevertheless. The cold is merely nothing. Amontillado! You have been imposed upon. And as for Luchesi, he cannot distinguish Sherry from Amontillado."

Thus speaking, Fortunato possessed himself of my arm. Putting on a mask of black silk, and drawing a roquelaire closely about my person, I suffered him to hurry me to my palazzo.

There were no attendants at home; they had absconded to make merry in honor of the time. I had told them that I should not return until the morning, and had given them explicit orders not to stir from the house. These orders were sufficient, I well knew, to insure their immediate disappearance, one and all, as soon as my back was turned.

I took from their sconces two flambeaux, and giving one to Fortunato, bowed him through several suites of rooms to the archway that led into the vaults. I passed down a long and winding staircase, requesting him to be cautious as he followed. We came at length to the foot of the descent, and stood together on the damp ground of the catacombs of the Montresors.

The gait of my friend was unsteady, and the bells upon his cap jingled as he strode.

"The pipe," said he.

"It is farther on," said I; "but observe the white web-work which gleams from these cavern walls."

He turned towards me, and looked into my eyes with two filmy orbs that distilled the rheum of intoxication.

"Nitre?" he asked, at length.

"Nitre," I replied. "How long have you had that cough?"

"Ugh! ugh! ugh!—ugh! ugh! ugh!—ugh! ugh! ugh!—ugh! ugh! ugh!—ugh! ugh! ugh!"

My poor friend found it impossible to reply for many minutes.

"It is nothing," he said, at last.

"Come," I said, with decision, "we will go back ; your health is precious. You are rich, respected, admired, beloved; you are happy, as once I was. You are a man to be missed. For me it is no matter. We will go back; you will be ill, and I cannot be responsible. Besides, there is Luchesi—"

"Enough," he said; "the cough is a mere nothing; it will not kill me. I shall not die of a cough."

"True—true," I replied; "and, indeed, I had no intention of alarming you unnecessarily—but you should use all proper caution. A draught of this Medoc will defend us from the damps."

Here I knocked off the neck of a bottle which I drew from a long row of its fellows that lay upon the mould.

"Drink," I said, presenting him the wine.

He raised it to his lips with a leer. He paused and nodded to me familiarly, while his bells jingled.

"I drink," he said, "to the buried that repose around us."

"And I to your long life."

He again took my arm, and we proceeded.

"These vaults," he said, "are extensive."

"The Montresors," I replied, "were a great and numerous family."

"I forget your arms."

"A huge human foot d'or, in a field azure; the foot crushes a serpent rampant whose fangs are imbedded in the heel."

"And the motto?"

"*Nemo me impune lacessit.*"

145

"Good!" he said.

The wine sparkled in his eyes and the bells jingled. My own fancy grew warm with the Medoc. We had passed through walls of piled bones, with casks and puncheons intermingling, into the inmost recesses of the catacombs. I paused again, and this time I made bold to seize Fortunato by an arm above the elbow.

"The nitre!" I said: "see, it increases. It hangs like moss upon the vaults. We are below the river's bed. The drops of moisture trickle among the bones. Come, we will go back ere it is too late. Your cough—"

"But first, another draught of the Medoc."

I broke and reached him a flagon of De Grâve. He emptied it at a breath. His eyes flashed with a fierce light. He laughed and threw the bottle upwards with a gesticulation I did not understand.

I looked at him in surprise. He repeated the movement – a grotesque one.

"You do not comprehend?" he said.

"Not I," I replied.

"Then you are not of the brotherhood."

"How?"

"You are not of the masons."

"Yes, yes," I said, "yes, yes."

"You? Impossible! A mason?"

"A mason," I replied.

"A sign," he said.

"It is this," I answered, producing a trowel from beneath the folds of my roquelaire.

"You jest," he exclaimed, recoiling a few paces. "But let us proceed to the Amontillado."

"Be it so," I said, replacing the tool beneath the cloak, and again offering him my arm. He leaned upon it heavily. We continued our route in search of the Amontillado. We passed through a range of low arches, descended, passed on, and descending again, arrived at a deep crypt, in which the foulness of the air caused our flambeaux rather to glow than flame.

At the most remote end of the crypt there appeared another less spacious. Its walls had been lined with human remains, piled to the vault overhead, in the fashion of the great catacombs of Paris. Three sides of this interior crypt were still ornamented in this manner. From the fourth the bones had been thrown down, and lay promiscuously upon the earth, forming at one point a mound of some size. Within the wall thus exposed by the displacing of the bones, we perceived a still interior recess, in depth about four feet, in width three, in height six or seven. It seemed to have been constructed for no especial use in itself, but formed merely the interval between two of the colossal supports of the roof of the catacombs, and was backed by one of their circumscribing walls of solid granite.

It was in vain that Fortunato, uplifting his dull torch, endeavored to pry into the depths of the recess. Its termination of the feeble light did not enable us to see.

"Proceed," I said; "herein is the Amontillado. As for Luchesi—"

"He is an ignoramus," interrupted my friend, as he stepped unsteadily forward, while I followed immediately at his heels. In an instant he had reached the extremity of the niche, and finding his progress arrested by the rock, stood stupidly bewildered. A moment more and I had fettered him to the granite. In its surface were two iron staples, distant from each other about two feet, horizontally. From one of these depended a short chain, from the other a padlock. Throwing the links about his waist, it was but the work of a few

146

seconds to secure it. He was too much astounded to resist. Withdrawing the key I stepped back from the recess.

"Pass your hand," I said, "over the wall; you cannot help feeling the nitre. Indeed it is very damp. Once more let me implore you to return. No? Then I must positively leave you. But I must first render you all the little attentions in my power."

"The Amontillado!" ejaculated my friend, not yet recovered from his astonishment.

"True," I replied; "the Amontillado."

As I said these words I busied myself among the pile of bones of which I have before spoken. Throwing them aside, I soon uncovered a quantity of building stone and mortar. With these materials and with the aid of my trowel, I began vigorously to wall up the entrance of the niche.

I had scarcely laid the first tier of my masonry when I discovered that the intoxication of Fortunato had in a great measure worn off. The earliest indication I had of this was a low moaning cry from the depth of the recess. It was not the cry of a drunken man. There was then a long and obstinate silence. I laid the second tier, and the third, and the fourth; and then I heard the furious vibrations of the chain. The noise lasted for several minutes, during which, that I might hearken to it with the more satisfaction, I ceased my labors and sat down upon the bones. When at last the clanking subsided, I resumed the trowel, and finished without interruption the fifth, the sixth, and the seventh tier. The wall was now nearly upon a level with my breast. I again paused, and holding the flambeaux over the mason-work, threw a few feeble rays upon the figure within.

A succession of loud and shrill screams, bursting suddenly from the throat of the chained form, seemed to thrust me violently back. For a brief moment I hesitated—I

trembled. Unsheathing my rapier, I began to grope with it about the recess: but the thought of an instant reassured me. I placed my hand upon the solid fabric of the catacombs, and felt satisfied. I reapproached the wall. I replied to the yells of him who clamored. I re-echoed—I aided —I surpassed them in volume and in strength. I did this, and the clamorer grew still.

It was now midnight, and my task was drawing to a close. I had completed the eighth, the ninth, and the tenth tier. I had finished a portion of the last and the eleventh; there remained but a single stone to be fitted and plastered in. I struggled with its weight; I placed it partially in its destined position. But now there came from out the niche a low laugh that erected the hairs upon my head. It was succeeded by a sad voice, which I had difficulty in recognizing as that of the noble Fortunato. The voice said—

"Ha! ha! ha!—he! he!—a very good joke indeed—an excellent jest. We will have many a rich laugh about it at the palazzo— he! he! he!—over our wine—he! he! he!"

"The Amontillado!" I said.

"He! he! he!—he! he! he!—yes, the Amontillado. But is it not getting late? Will not they be awaiting us at the palazzo, the Lady Fortunato and the rest? Let us be gone."

"Yes," I said, "let us be gone."

"For the love of God, Montresor!"

"Yes," I said, "for the love of God!"

But to these words I hearkened in vain for a reply. I grew impatient. I called aloud—

"Fortunato!"

No answer. I called again—

"Fortunato!"

No answer still. I thrust a torch through the remaining aperture and let it fall within. There came forth in return only a jingling of the bells. My heart grew sick— on account of the dampness of the catacombs. I hastened to make an end of my labor. I forced the last stone into its position; I plastered it up. Against the new masonry I re-erected the old rampart of bones. For the half of a century no mortal has disturbed them. *In pace requiescat!*

1. Which genre of fiction is this?

   a. novel
   b. novella
   c. drama
   d. short story

2. In which point of view is the passage written?

   a. first person
   b. third person omniscient
   c. third person limited
   d. objective

3. What is Amontillado?

   a. a cigar
   b. a wine
   c. a cheese
   d. a jewel

4. Why does the narrator mention Luchesi?

   a. He wants Luchesi's opinion about his purchase.
   b. He wants Luchesi to help Fortunato's cold.
   c. He wants to make Fortunato jealous.
   d. He wants to find Luchesi at the party.

5. How does Montresor feel about revenge?

   a. He feels it is a bad idea to ever get revenge on someone.
   b. He feels it is only good if the avenger is not punished.
   c. He feels it is only good if the avenger gets an apology.
   d. He feels it is only good in the most severe cases of insult.

6. How is Fortunato characterized in this passage?

   a. a very smart man
   b. a very concerned man
   c. a very foolish man
   d. a very witty man

7. Montresor notes, "I had told them that I should not return until the morning, and had given them explicit orders not to stir from the house. These orders were sufficient, I well knew, to insure their immediate disappearance, one and all, as soon as my back was turned." What does this quote illustrate about Montresor's opinion of human nature?

   a. People don't listen very well when others speak.
   b. People do not like sitting still for very long.
   c. People do not like their bosses very much.
   d. People often do things they are told not to do.

8. At one point Montresor reveals a trowel to Fortunato. This moment in the text

   a. creates suspense.
   b. resolves the conflict.
   c. identifies the conflict.
   d. develops the setting.

9. Which moment in the text **best** represents the climax?

   a. Montresor convinces Fortunato to enter the catacombs.
   b. Fortunato asks Montresor about his family crest.
   c. Fortunato realizes the whole thing is not a joke.
   d. Montresor chains Fortunato to the catacombs' walls.

10. "A succession of loud and shrill screams, bursting suddenly from the throat of the chained form, seemed to thrust me violently back. For a brief moment I hesitated—I trembled. Unsheathing my rapier, I began to grope with it about the recess: but the thought of an instant reassured me. I placed my hand upon the solid fabric of the catacombs, and felt satisfied." The narrator feels reassured because

   a. he has the means to kill Fortunato if he needs to do it.
   b. the catacomb walls are thick, so no one will hear the screams.
   c. the catacombs make him feel at home and safe from danger.
   d. he realizes that no one but these two are down in the catacombs.

149

does the setting add to the overall story? Use specific details from the text to ~~support~~ ort your answer.

The story takes place during carnival season in some Italian city; most of the story occurs in the catacombs beneath Montresor's place. The time of the story is important because it allows Montresor to get away with his crime; since everyone is partying, no one pays attention as he lures Fortunato down into the catacombs. Likewise, Montresor's place is absent of any attendants because they have all left to enjoy the festivities. Therefore, Montresor carries out the crime without any witnesses. The catacombs are an appropriate place for most of the story because they help to create the frightening mood. The catacombs themselves are dangerously dark and covered with nitre, capturing the evil and danger that surrounds Fortunato as he proceeds into the catacombs. The reader notes that as the nitre on the walls increases, the danger for Fortunato also increases. The narrator comments as they reach the crypt, "the foulness of the air caused our flambeaux rather to glow than flame," further foreshadowing the frightening, dark crime that is soon to take place. In addition, death is indicated in the bones that line the walls in the catacombs' inner recesses.

12. How does the connotation of Montresor's diction when he is speaking to Fortunato help mask his true intent?

Montresor only uses words with a positive, friendly connotation when talking with Fortunato. He first addresses Fortunato as "my dear Fortunato." Later he refers to Fortunato as his friend in multiple instances. Oddly, not only does he refer to his friend in his dialogue with his enemy, but also in his comments to the audience as in "The gait of my friend was unsteady", seemingly trying to disguise his intentions even to his own audience. In addition, Montresor continuously praises Fortunato while making himself appear more foolish. He comments, "and I was silly enough to pay the full Amontillado price without consulting you in the matter" and "And yet some fools will have it that his taste is a match for your own," exalting Fortunato's abilities above Luchesi's and his own talent for wine tasting. Later he dotes, "You are rich, respected, admired, beloved." Using only words with a positive connotation in speaking about Fortunato, Montresor successfully fools his enemy.

150

13. How is irony used in this passage to create an effect? Use specific evidence from the text to support your answer.

Situational, verbal, and dramatic ironies are all used to build suspense in the text as Fortunato is led to his death. First of all, Fortunato's name, quite similar to the word, "fortunate," creates situational irony. The audience would expect the author to give such a name to a lucky character in the text; however, the opposite is true. Suspense begins to build as the audience realizes that this "fortunate" man is about ready to meet an unfortunate end. Verbal irony builds this point as well when Montresor comments upon meeting Fortunato, "My dear Fortunato, you are luckily met. How remarkably well you are looking today." The reader quickly realizes that Fortunato is not lucky to have run into Montresor, nor is he looking well, considering that he is sick with a severe cold. Dramatic irony later plays a role in the suspense as Fortunato announces, "I shall not die of a cough." As Montresor responds, " 'Tis true," the audience knows that while Fortunato thinks that Montresor is merely agreeing that the cough is not serious, the truth is that he intends to kill Fortunato. Dramatic irony also builds the suspense of Fortunato's death when Montresor drinks to Fortunato's "long life." The audience knows that Fortunato's life will not be long, creating tension in the text.

14. How reliable is the narrator? Provide evidence from the text to support your answer.

Students answers may vary, but most will say that the narrator is unreliable. Montresor leaves out important details of the story which would have supported his actions, such as the specific injury that Fortunato had inflicted upon him. In addition, the narrator shows signs of madness: he smiles at the thought of destroying Fortunato; he pauses in building the wall to enjoy Fortunato's panic as he tries to get out of the chains; and he taunts Fortunato by screaming back at him when Fortunato starts to yell.

15. Poe uses two lines of Latin during the passage: *Nemo me impune lacessit* meaning "No one provokes me with impunity"; and *In pace requiescat* meaning "May he or she rest in peace." How do the Latin quotes and the rest of the passage develop the overall theme of the text? Use specific evidence from the text to support your answer.

One possible answer:

The main theme of the story is that revenge doesn't hurt just the person receiving the revenge but also the avenger. This is first introduced when the narrator comments that revenge is only successful when the avenger is not punished or harmed in any way. However, even though Montresor seems to know this and get away with his crimes, small clues reveal that even his "perfect crime" has not been without harm to himself. First of all, the narrator tells this story fifty years after the crime had been committed. Telling the story years after the event suggests that the narrator has not been able to forget his crime and to move on with his life.

In addition, while Montresor seems to commit most of the crime with ease, right as he is about to put in the last brick he notes, "My heart grew sick—on account of the dampness of the catacombs." While the narrator attributes his feeling to the physical dampness of his surroundings, the audience realizes that the words along with the pause (indicated by the dash) are more logically attributed to the completion of this revenge.

Lastly, the Latin sayings help to illustrate the theme. While Montresor's family crest suggests that punishment is the only way to deal with any kind of offense, Montresor's final line indicates that revenge may actually be more hurtful than helpful. While the reader may first assume that the narrator means that Fortunato should rest in peace, another interpretation is the narrator's own hope that he himself may rest in peace after committing his crime, perhaps receiving relief when he finally tells his story fifty years after it took place. Others may comment that his madness throughout the text also shows the effect that stewing over revenge for so long has had on him.

FROM *DAVID CROCKETT: HIS LIFE AND ADVENTURES*

by John S.C. Abbott

A little more than a hundred years ago, a poor man, by the name of Crockett, embarked on board an emigrant-ship, in Ireland, for the New World. He was in the humblest station in life. But very little is known respecting his uneventful career excepting its tragical close. His family consisted of a wife and three or four children. Just before he sailed, or on the Atlantic passage, a son was born, to whom he gave the name of John. The family probably landed in Philadelphia, and dwelt somewhere in Pennsylvania, for a year or two, in one of those slab shanties, with which all are familiar as the abodes of the poorest class of Irish emigrants.

After a year or two, Crockett, with his little family, crossed the almost pathless Alleghanies. Father, mother, and children trudged along through the rugged defiles and over the rocky cliffs, on foot. Probably a single pack-horse conveyed their few household goods. The hatchet and the rifle were the only means of obtaining food, shelter, and even clothing. With the hatchet, in an hour or two, a comfortable camp could be constructed, which would protect them from wind and rain. The campfire, cheering the darkness of the night, drying their often wet garments, and warming their chilled limbs with its genial glow, enabled them to enjoy that almost greatest of earthly luxuries, peaceful sleep.

The rifle supplied them with food. The fattest of turkeys and the most tender steaks of venison, roasted upon forked sticks, which they held in their hands over the coals, feasted their voracious appetites. This, to them, was almost sumptuous food. The skin of the deer, by a rapid and simple process of tanning, supplied them with moccasins, and afforded material for the repair of their tattered garments.

We can scarcely comprehend the motive which led this solitary family to push on, league after league, farther and farther from civilization, through the trackless forests. At length they reached the Holston River. This stream takes its rise among the western ravines of the Alleghanies, in Southwestern Virginia. Flowing hundreds of miles through one of the most solitary and romantic regions upon the globe, it finally unites with the Clinch River, thus forming the majestic Tennessee.

One hundred years ago, this whole region, west of the Alleghanies, was an unexplored and an unknown wilderness. Its silent rivers, its forests, and its prairies were crowded with game. Countless Indian tribes, whose names even had never been heard east of the Alleghanies, ranged this vast expanse, pursuing, in the chase, wild beasts scarcely more savage than themselves.

The origin of these Indian tribes and their past history are lost in oblivion. Centuries have come and gone, during which joys and griefs, of which we now can know nothing, visited their humble lodges. Providence seems to have raised up a peculiar class of men, among the descendants of the emigrants from the Old World, who, weary of the restraints of civilization, were ever ready to plunge into the wildest depths of the wilderness, and to rear their lonely huts in the midst of all its perils, privations, and hardships.

This solitary family of the Crocketts followed down the northwestern banks of the Hawkins River for many a weary mile, until they came to a spot which struck their fancy as a suitable place to build their Cabin. In subsequent years a small village called Rogersville was gradually reared upon this spot, and the territory immediately around was organized into what is now known as Hawkins County. But then, for leagues in every direction, the solemn forest stood in all its grandeur. Here Mr. Crockett, alone and unaided save by his wife and children, constructed a little shanty, which could have been but little more than a hunter's camp. He could not lift solid logs to build a substantial house. The hard-trodden ground was the only floor of the single room which he enclosed. It was roofed with bark of trees piled heavily on, which afforded quite effectual protection from the rain. A hole cut through the slender logs was the only window. A fire was built in one corner, and the smoke eddied through a hole left in the roof. The skins of bears, buffaloes, and wolves provided couches, all sufficient for weary ones, who needed no artificial opiate to promote sleep. Such, in general, were the primitive homes of many of those bold emigrants who abandoned the comforts of civilized life for the solitudes of the wilderness.

They did not want for most of what are called the necessaries of life. The river and the forest furnished a great variety of fish and game. Their hut, humble as it was, effectually protected them from the deluging tempest and the inclement cold. The climate was genial in a very high degree, and the soil, in its wonderful fertility, abundantly supplied them with corn and other simple vegetables. But the silence and solitude which reigned are represented, by those who experienced them, as at times something dreadful.

One principal motive which led these people to cross the mountains, was the prospect of an ultimate fortune in the rise of land. Every man who built a cabin and raised a crop of grain, however small, was entitled to four hundred acres of land, and a preemption right to one thousand more adjoining, to be secured by a land-office warrant.

1. What type of nonfiction is this passage?

   a. biography
   b. autobiography
   c. essay
   d. personal narrative

2. What is the purpose of this passage?

   a. to persuade the audience that emigration is difficult
   b. to inform the audience about the Crocketts' journey.
   c. to give an opinion on how to survive in the wild.
   d. to express emotions about the Crocketts' journey.

3. How does the author organize the passage?

   a. cause and effect organization
   b. problem and solution organization
   c. spatial organization
   d. chronological organization

4. The author feels that the Crockett's immigration to the New World was

   a. a very successful voyage.
   b. basically a painless journey.
   c. *a hard and challenging journey.*
   d. a totally unsuccessful voyage.

5. "The campfire, cheering the darkness of the night, drying their often wet garments, and warming their chilled limbs with its genial glow . . ." This quote contains an example of

   a. *personification.*
   b. onomatopoeia.
   c. hyperbole.
   d. metaphor.

6. The fattest of turkeys and the most tender steaks of venison, roasted upon forked sticks, which they held in their hands over the coals, feasted their voracious appetites. This, to them, was almost sumptuous food." This quote indicates that the family

   a. was used to this type of food.
   b. needed to eat more vegetables.
   c. wasted the food they acquired.
   d. *had rarely eaten this type of food.*

7. If in the Crockett's situation, the author probably would **not** have

   a. traveled from Ireland to the New World.
   b. *traveled so far from civilization.*
   c. stayed so long in one location.
   d. built a home near the Hawkins River.

8. Which of these problems does the author identify as the greatest challenge for the family?

   a. deciding where to live
   b. *handling the solitude*
   c. building a shelter
   d. acquiring food to eat

9. What causes does the author give for emigrants traveling farther into the uninhabited New World?

The author lists two main causes for emigration into the New World: to escape the limitations and poverty of civilization and to acquire property and, therefore, wealth. The author first suggests the need to escape society when he describes the Crocketts' living conditions in Pennsylvania, noting, " The family probably landed in Philadelphia, and dwelt somewhere in Pennsylvania, for a year or two, in one of those slab shanties, with which all are familiar as the abodes of the poorest class of Irish emigrants." Assuming the family wanted to better their living environment, the author later comments that descendants of emigrants "who, weary of the restraints of civilization, were ever ready to plunge into the wildest depths of the wilderness." This escape to a more hopeful and peaceful life is again suggested as the author describing the travelers as abandoning "the comforts of civilized life for the solitudes of the wilderness." In addition the author suggests the promise of land and possibly fortune as a second cause for the hard journey: "Every man who built a cabin and raised a crop of grain, however small, was entitled to four hundred acres of land, and a preemption right to one thousand more adjoining, to be secured by a land-office warrant." The promise of a greater freedom brought on by the unrestrained wilderness and the opportunity for wealth are two causes the author cites for the emigration.

10. How does the author's description of nature illustrate his attitude towards it? Carefully consider the author's diction when describing nature. Use specific evidence from the text to support your answer.

One possible answer:

The author's diction reveals his profound respect for nature's magnificence. The author first comments, "This stream takes its rise among the western ravines of the Alleghanies, in Southwestern Virginia. Flowing hundreds of miles through one of the most solitary and romantic regions upon the globe, it finally unites with the Clinch River, thus forming the majestic Tennessee." Words such as "romantic" and "majestic" connote a reverence for nature. This is further emphasized as he describes the Crockett's new home: "But then, for leagues in every direction, the solemn forest stood in all its grandeur." Again words such as "solemn" and "grandeur," suggesting a formality and stateliness, depict nature as something deserving deference. The author realizes that part of nature's magnificence is its strength, noting those that settle in the deepest wilderness face "perils, privations, and hardships" as they learn how to live in nature's grand realm.

11. How credible and reliable is the author of this passage? Use specific evidence from the text to support your answer.

Students should note that the author's biography loses both credibility and reliability in the way that the information is presented. The author presents a biased view of the Indian culture: he comments they hunt "wild beasts scarcely more savage than themselves." In addition to this bias, he speculates for the benefit of sensationalism, noting, "Probably a single pack-horse conveyed their few household goods." In addition, he assumes that the campfires "enabled them to enjoy that almost greatest of earthly luxuries, peaceful sleep." While he tries to identify those facts that are not known—"In this lonely home, Mr. Crockett, with his wife and children, dwelt for some months, perhaps years—we know not how long"—these comments are sandwiched between opinionated remarks such as "The family probably landed in Philadelphia, and dwelt somewhere in Pennsylvania, for a year or two, in one of those slab shanties, with which all are familiar as the abodes of the poorest class of Irish emigrants." The author's bias and assumptions lead readers to question both the reliability and the credibility of the text.

"The Darkling Thrush"

by Thomas Hardy

I leant upon a coppice gate   1
    When Frost was spectre-gray,
And Winter's dregs made desolate
    The weakening eye of day.
The tangled bine-stems scored the sky   5
    Like strings from broken lyres,
And all mankind that haunted nigh
    Had sought their household fires.

The land's sharp features seemed to be
    The Century's corpse outleant,   10
His crypt the cloudy canopy,
    The wind his death-lament.
The ancient pulse of germ and birth
    Was shrunken hard and dry,
And every spirit upon earth   15
    Seemed fervourless as I.

At once a voice outburst among
    The bleak twigs overhead
In a full-hearted evensong
    Of joy illimited;   20
An aged thrush, frail, gaunt, and small,
    In blast-beruffled plume,
Had chosen thus to fling his soul
    Upon the growing gloom.

So little cause for carollings   25
    Of such ecstatic sound
Was written on terrestrial things
    Afar or nigh around,
That I could think there trembled through
    His happy good-night air   30
Some blessed Hope, whereof he knew
    And I was unaware.

December 1900

1. The simile in lines 5–6 emphasizes the

    a. coldness of the land.
    b. music of the land.
    c. *ruin of the land.*
    d. strong bond of the land.

2. What does "The ancient pulse of germ and birth/Was shrunken hard and dry" mean?

    a. Disease is all around the land.
    b. *The seeds of rebirth are dead.*
    c. The people are all mean now.
    d. The people are all getting older.

3. The narrator of the poem can be described as

    a. *depressed.*
    b. angry.
    c. evil.
    d. cold.

4. The darkling thrush can be described as

    a. *weak.*
    b. depressed.
    c. beautiful.
    d. calming.

5. "Had chosen thus to fling his soul/Upon the growing gloom." The words in this passage connote

    a. hope.
    b. anger.
    c. *desperation.*
    d. joy.

6. Lines 25–30 suggest that the cause for caroling is the

    a. surrounding land.
    b. beautiful night air.
    c. distant landscape.
    d. *hope inside the bird.*

161

7. How does the first stanza set the tone for the rest of the poem?

The first stanza helps create the cold, depressing tone found throughout much of the poem. Hardy first achieves this effect through the recurring imagery of death; he uses words associated with ghosts such as "spectre" and "haunted." The idea of ghosts insinuates that people and objects are only shadows of what they once had been, an idea that continues throughout the poem after Hardy expresses his hopelessness for the future of the world in the second stanza. He continues to build this tone with a simile comparing the trees to broken strings from lyres. This nonfunctional and broken image is strengthened as the narrator describes himself as "leaning" on the coppice gate rather than having the strength to stand on his own or to be actively moving. He also achieves the gloomy tone with the setting, commenting that it is close to the end of the day—"the weakening eye of day" as a metaphor for the sun—during wintertime. Winter is described as leaving its deposit on the last moments of daylight, causing frost to form on most the land. Both the death of the day and the season of death and coldness achieve the desolate tone. In fact, the only hint of warmth comes from the household fires for which the townspeople searched. However the reader will note that Hardy merely claims they "sought" their fires but does not confirm that they actually found warmth. The setting, diction, and figurative language all create the dismal tone found in the rest of the poem.

8. How does the author use sound devices and rhythm to create an effect in the poem? Use specific evidence from the text to support your answer.

The author uses sound devices to illustrate the bird's interruption of the dreary nature of the poem. The author repeats hard sounds to emphasize the harshness of the land using alliteration: "dregs made desolate," "crypt the cloudy canopy," "stems scored the sky," and "growing gloom." Also, the consonance in "Winter's dregs" as the narrator describes the depressing view creates a slow, tired feeling. In addition, Hardy's rhythm highlights the brief interruption in the gloom caused by the little bird. The reader notices that a very steady rhythm and rhyme characterizes the first two stanzas. However, the rhythm is disrupted in the third stanza when the bird appears; this is particularly evident in line 21: "An aged thrush, frail, gaunt, and small." Just as the small bird causes the narrator to stop and think, the reader has to slow down and pay special attention to the bird.

9. What is the significance of the date at the bottom of the poem? What effect does this have on the poem? Use specific evidence from the text to support your answer.

One possible answer:
The date at the bottom of the poem indicates that not only is it about to be a new year but also a new century. This helps the reader to make sense of Hardy's comparison of the end of the century and a corpse. In this extended metaphor, the landscape becomes the century's body while the sky becomes a tomb. This further accentuates the narrator's gloom; normally the sky seems a limitless entity; however, here it becomes something very restricting and suffocating. In addition, the wind becomes the song grieving the century's death. This contrasts sharply to the song that is introduced in the next stanza. The date at the end of the poem and the metaphor help to develop the narrator's outlook: instead of being excited about the new century and possible rebirth, the narrator can only concentrate on death, gloom, and hopelessness.

10. Is this an optimistic or a pessimistic poem? What evidence exists to support the view opposite your own view? Provide specific evidence from the text when examining the poem from these critical perspectives.

Some students will say that the poem is an overwhelmingly pessimistic poem. These students will comment on the tone and mood of the first two stanzas as discussed above. They will also focus on the state of the bird that is developed as a symbol of hope in this poem. The bird is described as an "aged thrush, frail, gaunt, and small," illustrating that this last symbol of hope will soon perish, perhaps after "flinging his soul" in a final act of desperation. Finally students will comment on the narrator's closing lines. While the bird seems to see some reason for hope (and even this is described as "trembling"), the narrator who ultimately cannot — will continue into the new century hopeless about the possibility of rebirth.

Other students will say that, despite the bleak tone, the poem is still optimistic. Students may note that the bird's song is strong: "In a full-hearted evensong / Of joy illimited." The song is mentioned before the bird, suggesting that while the bird itself is tired and has taken a beating (blast-beruffled plume) perhaps from the lamenting winds, the bird's spirit and hope remain strong and infinite. Students may note that the winter is almost over as suggested by the "dregs," or final remnants, of winter; students may comment that while the narrator cannot fully comprehend that rebirth is still possible, the upcoming spring, or the new century, may bring a change. This is also evident in the final lines when the narrator mentions that the bird has no reason to sing when looking around the physical ground. The narrator does acknowledge that he might be missing something: "That I could think there trembled through / His happy good-night air / Some blessed Hope." The word, "could," suggests a hope that he is missing something. The poet acknowledges — when he capitalizes Hope and describes it as "blessed" — that perhaps hope is not in the physical land that he focuses on for most of the poem but in something more spiritual.

Question 1	Analyzing Figurative Language
Question 2	Summarizing and Paraphrasing
Question 3	Drawing Conclusions
Question 4	Making Inferences
Question 5	Analyzing Diction
Question 6	Making Inferences
Question 7	Analyzing Development of Tone/Mood
Question 8	Analyzing Sound Devices/Rhythm
Question 9	Evaluating Historical Periods in Literature
Question 10	Examining Literature from Several Critical Perspectives

164

THE CELEBRATED JUMPING FROG OF CALAVERAS COUNTY

by Mark Twain

In compliance with the request of a friend of mine, who wrote me from the East, I called on good-natured, garrulous old Simon Wheeler, and inquired after my friend's friend, Leonidas W. Smiley, as requested to do, and I hereunto append the result. I have a lurking suspicion that Leonidas W. Smiley is a myth; and that my friend never knew such a personage; and that he only conjectured that if I asked old Wheeler about him, it would remind him of his infamous Jim Smiley, and he would go to work and bore me to death with some exasperating reminiscence of him as long and as tedious as it should be useless to me. If that was the design, it succeeded.

I found Simon Wheeler dozing comfortably by the barroom stove of the dilapidated tavern in the decayed mining camp of Angel's, and I noticed that he was fat and bald-headed, and had an expression of winning gentleness and simplicity upon his tranquil countenance. He roused up, and gave me good-day. I told him a friend had commissioned me to make some inquiries about a cherished companion of his boyhood named Leonidas W. Smiley— Rev. Leonidas W. Smiley, a young minister of the Gospel, who he had heard was at one time a resident of Angel's Camp. I added that if Mr. Wheeler could tell me anything about this Rev. Leonidas W. Smiley, I would feel under many obligations to him.

Simon Wheeler backed me into a corner and blockaded me there with his chair, and then sat down and reeled off the monotonous narrative which follows this paragraph. He never smiled, he never frowned, he never changed his voice from the gentle-flowing key to which he tuned his initial sentence, he never betrayed the slightest suspicion of enthusiasm; but all through the interminable narrative there ran a vein of impressive earnestness and sincerity, which showed me plainly that, so far from his imagining that there was anything ridiculous or funny about his story, he regarded it as a really important matter, and admired its two heroes as men of transcendent genius in finesse.

I let him go on in his own way, and never interrupted him once.

"Rev. Leonidas W. H'm, Reverend Le— well, there was a feller here once by the name of Jim Smiley, in the winter of '49—or may be it was the spring of '50—I don't recollect exactly, somehow, though what makes me think it was one or the other is because I remember the big flume warn't finished when he first came to the camp; but any way, he was the curiousest man about always betting on anything that turned up you ever see, if he could get anybody to bet on the other side; and if he couldn't he'd change sides. Any way that suited the other man would suit him—any way just so's he got a bet, he was satisfied. But still he was lucky, uncommon lucky; he most always come out winner. He was always ready and laying for a chance; there couldn't be no solit'ry thing mentioned but that feller'd offer to bet on it, and take any side you please, as I was just telling you. If there was a horse-race, you'd find him flush or you'd find him busted at the end of it; if there was a dog-fight, he'd bet on it; if there was a cat-fight, he'd bet on it; if there was a chicken-fight, he'd bet on it; why, if there was two birds setting on a fence, he would bet you which one would fly first; or if there was a camp-meeting, he would be there reg'lar to bet on Parson Walker, which he judged to be the best exhorter about here, and he was, too, and a good man. If he even see a straddle-bug start to go anywheres, he would bet you how long it would take him to get to—to wherever he was going to, and if you took him up, he would foller that straddle-bug to Mexico but what he would find out where he was bound for and how long he was on the road. Lots of the boys here has seen that Smiley and can tell you about him. Why, it never made no difference to him—he'd bet on any thing—the dangest feller. Parson Walker's wife laid very sick once, for a good while, and it seemed as if they warn't going to save her; but one morning he come in, and Smiley up and asked him how she was, and he said she was considerable better—thank the Lord for his inf'nit' mercy—and coming on so smart that with the blessing of Prov'dence she'd get well yet; and Smiley, before he thought, says, 'Well, I'll risk two-and-a-half she don't anyway.'"

Thish-yer Smiley had a mare—the boys called her the fifteen-minute nag, but that was only in fun, you know, because, of course, she was faster than that—and he used to win money on that horse, for all she was so slow and always had the asthma, or the distemper, or the consumption, or something of that kind. They used to give her two or three hundred yards start, and then pass her under way; but always at the fag-end of the race she'd get excited and desperate-like, and come cavorting and straddling up, and scattering her legs around limber, sometimes in the air, and sometimes out to one side amongst the fences, and kicking up m-o-r-e dust and raising m-o-r-e racket with her coughing and sneezing and blowing her nose—and always fetch up at the stand just about a neck ahead, as near as you could cipher it down.

And he had a little small bull-pup, that to look at him you'd think he warn't worth a cent but to set around and look ornery and lay for a chance to steal something. But as soon as money was up on him he was a different dog; his under-jaw'd begin to stick out like the fo'-castle of a steamboat, and

his teeth would uncover and shine like the furnaces. And a dog might tackle him and bully-rag him, and bite him, and throw him over his shoulder two or three times, and Andrew Jackson—which was the name of the pup—Andrew Jackson would never let on but what he was satisfied, and hadn't expected nothing else—and the bets being doubled and doubled on the other side all the time, till the money was all up; and then all of a sudden he would grab that other dog jest by the j'int of his hind leg and freeze to it—not chaw, you understand, but only just grip and hang on till they throwed up the sponge, if it was a year. Smiley always come out winner on that pup, till he harnessed a dog once that didn't have no hind legs, because they'd been sawed off in a circular saw, and when the thing had gone along far enough, and the money was all up, and he come to make a snatch for his pet holt, he see in a minute how he'd been imposed on, and how the other dog had him in the door, so to speak, and he 'peared surprised, and then he looked sorter discouraged-like, and didn't try no more to win the fight, and so he got shucked out bad. He gave Smiley a look, as much as to say his heart was broke, and it was his fault, for putting up a dog that hadn't no hind legs for him to take holt of, which was his main dependence in a fight, and then he limped off a piece and laid down and died. It was a good pup, was that Andrew Jackson, and would have made a name for hisself if he'd lived, for the stuff was in him and he had genius—I know it, because he hadn't no opportunities to speak of, and it don't stand to reason that a dog could make such a fight as he could under them circumstances if he hadn't no talent. It always makes me feel sorry when I think of that last fight of his'n, and the way it turned out.

Well, thish-yer Smiley had rat-tarriers, and chicken cocks, and tom-cats and all of them kind of things, till you couldn't rest, and you couldn't fetch nothing for him to bet on but he'd match you. He ketched a frog one day, and took him home, and said he cal'lated to educate him; and so he never done nothing for three months but set in his back yard and learn that frog to jump. And you bet you he did learn him, too. He'd give him a little punch behind, and the next minute you'd see that frog whirling in the air like a doughnut—see him turn one summerset, or may be a couple, if he got a good start, and come down flat-footed and all right, like a cat. He got him up so in the matter of ketching flies, and kep' him in practice so constant, that he'd nail a fly every time as fur as he could see him. Smiley said all a frog wanted was education, and he could do 'most anything—and I believe him. Why, I've seen him set Dan'l Webster down here on this floor—Dan'l Webster was the name of the frog—and sing out, "Flies, Dan'l, flies!" and quicker'n you could wink he'd spring straight up and snake a fly off'n the counter there, and flop down on the floor ag'in as solid as a gob of mud, and fall to scratching the side of his head with his hind foot as indifferent as if he hadn't no idea he'd been doin' any more'n any frog might do. You never see a frog so modest and straightfor'ard as he was, for all he was so gifted. And when it come to fair and square jumping on a dead level, he could get over more ground at one straddle than any animal of his breed you ever see. Jumping on a dead level was his strong suit, you understand; and when it come to that, Smiley would ante up money on him as long as he had a red. Smiley was monstrous proud of his frog, and well he might be, for fellers that had traveled and been everywheres, all said he laid over any frog that ever they see.

Well, Smiley kep' the beast in a little lattice box, and he used to fetch him downtown sometimes and lay for a bet. One day a feller—a stranger in the camp, he was—come across him with his box, and says:

"What might be that you've got in the box?"

And Smiley says, sorter indifferent-like, "It might be a parrot, or it might be a canary, maybe, but it ain't—it's only just a frog."

And the feller took it, and looked at it careful, and turned it round this way and that, and says, "H'm—so 'tis. Well, what's he good for?"

"Well," Smiley says, easy and careless, "he's good enough for one thing, I should judge—he can outjump any frog in Calaveras county."

The feller took the box again, and took another long, particular look, and give it back to Smiley, and says, very deliberate, "Well," he says, "I don't see no p'ints about that frog that's any better'n any other frog."

"Maybe you don't," Smiley says. "Maybe you understand frogs and maybe you don't understand 'em; maybe you've had experience, and maybe you ain't only a amature, as it were. Anyways, I've got my opinion and I'll risk forty dollars that he can outjump any frog in Calaveras County."

And the feller studied a minute, and then says, kinder sad like, "Well, I'm only a stranger here, and I ain't got no frog; but if I had a frog, I'd bet you."

And then Smiley says, "That's all right—that's all right—if you'll hold my box a minute, I'll go and get you a frog." And so the feller took the box, and put up his forty dollars along with Smiley's, and set down to wait.

So he set there a good while thinking and thinking to his-self, and then he got the frog out and prized his mouth open and took a teaspoon and filled him full of quail shot—filled! him pretty near up to his chin—and set him on the floor. Smiley he went to the swamp and slopped around in the mud for a long time, and finally he ketched a frog, and fetched him in, and give him to this feller, and says:

"Now, if you're ready, set him alongside of Dan'l, with his forepaws just even with Dan'l's, and I'll give the word." Then he says, "One—two—three—git!" and him and the feller touched up the frogs from behind, and the new frog hopped off lively, but Dan'l give a heave, and hysted up his shoulders—so—like a Frenchman, but it warn't no use—he couldn't budge; he was planted as solid as a church, and he couldn't no more stir than if he was anchored out. Smiley was a good deal surprised, and he was disgusted too, but he didn't have no idea what the matter was, of course.

The feller took the money and started away; and when he was going out at the door, he sorter jerked his thumb over his shoulder—so—at Dan'l, and says again, very deliberate, "Well," he says, "I don't see no p'ints about that frog that's any better'n any other frog."

Smiley he stood scratching his head and looking down at Dan'l a long time, and at last says, "I do wonder what in the nation that frog throwed off for—I wonder if there ain't something the matter with him—he 'pears to look mighty baggy, somehow." And

he ketched Dan'l up by the nap of the neck, and hefted him, and says, "Why blame my cats if he don't weigh five pounds!" and turned him upside down and he belched out a double handful of shot. And then he see how it was, and he was the maddest man—he set the frog down and took out after that feller, but he never ketched him. And—

(Here Simon Wheeler heard his name called from the front yard, and got up to see what was wanted.) And turning to me as he moved away, he said: "Just set where you are, stranger, and rest easy—I ain't going to be gone a second."

But, by your leave, I did not think that a continuation of the history of the enterprising vagabond Jim Smiley would be likely to afford me much information concerning the Rev. Leonidas W. Smiley, and so I started away.

At the door I met the sociable Wheeler returning, and he buttonholed me and recommenced:

"Well, thish-yer Smiley had a yaller, one-eyed cow that didn't have no tail, only jest a short stump like a bannanner, and—"

However, lacking both time and inclination, I did not wait to hear about the afflicted cow, but took my leave.

1. Twain's story takes the form of

   a. fairy tale.
   b. myth.
   c. legend.
   d. *tall tale.*

2. The narrator believes his friend's intention was to

   a. gain information.
   b. find Leonidas Smiley.
   c. *trick the narrator.*
   d. locate Simon Wheeler.

3. The word, "scattering," used to describe the horse's legs, connotes

   a. quickness.
   b. hazard.
   c. length.
   d. sturdiness.

4. The setting of the story is most likely

   a. the old west.
   b. northern states.
   c. the east coast.
   d. Mexico.

5. "If he even see a straddle-bug start to go anywheres, he would bet you how long it would take him to get to—to wherever he was going to, and if you took him up, he would foller that straddle-bug to Mexico but what he would find out where he was bound for and how long he was on the road." This passage contains an example of

   a. simile.
   b. metaphor.
   c. personification.
   d. hyperbole.

6. " . . . his under-jaw'd begin to stick out like the fo'-castle of a steamboat, and his teeth would uncover and shine like the furnaces . . . " These similes emphasize the bull-pup's

   a. mean demeanor during a bet.
   b. funny-looking features.
   c. meanness towards his owner.
   d. aggravation towards fighting.

7. Jim Smiley can **best** be characterized as

   a. honest.
   b. angry.
   c. offensive.
   d. sly.

8. How does Simon Wheeler feel about Jim Smiley?

   a. He thinks Jim needs help for his gambling.
   b. He thinks Jim is a cheater and a sneak.
   c. He really admires and respects Jim.
   d. He thinks Jim has too many animals.

169

9. How does the story's point of view and text organization add to the overall effect of the text? Use specific evidence from the text to support your point.

The story's first person point of view and story-within-a-story framing help to develop Simon Wheeler's tall-tale tendencies and the narrator's annoyance with this style. The first person point of view immediately portrays the narrator's feelings toward Wheeler's story as he comments, "he would go to work and bore me to death with some exasperating reminiscence of him as long and as tedious as it should be useless to me." Even before hearing the story, the audience has already been warned of its monotonous nature. If the author had just started with Wheeler's story, the audience would have lost the dimension that separates the narrator from Simon. The two clearly come from different backgrounds. The reader imagines (and maybe even identifies with) the narrator as he is trapped ("blockaded") into listening to this story. It also helps students to get to know Simon Wheeler better. Although the narrator first notes that Wheeler is fat, bald, and snoozing, he quickly realizes that Wheeler is also gentle, simplistic, and serious. It was Wheeler's serious telling of such an outrageous story that created humor and made Smiley and his animals appear more heroic and amazing than they actually could have been.

10. Explain how irony helps to develop humor in the text. Use specific examples from the text to support your answer.

The author uses situational and dramatic irony to create humor within the text. The first example is when Wheeler describes the bull-pup's final fight. Since the pup's opponent is missing his two hind legs, the audience would assume that the pup could easily win the fight. However, since the pup's strategy is to bite on the back two legs, the pup has no idea how to win the fight and ends up losing and dying. The unexpected nature of the pup's loss combined with Wheeler's overly-sentimental reaction—"It was a good pup, was that Andrew Jackson, and would have made a name for hisself if he'd lived, for the stuff was in him and he had genius"—creates humor.

The second example of irony comes at the end when Smiley is perplexed about his frog's performance: ". . . he was planted as solid as a church, and he couldn't no more stir than if he was anchored out. Smiley was a good deal surprised, and he was disgusted too, but he didn't have no idea what the matter was, of course." The audience realizes the reason for the frog's performance, finding descriptions of the frog as "anchored" and Smiley's confusion funny. This humor is further developed as Smiley "stood scratching his head and looking down at Dan'l a long time, and at last says, 'I do wonder what in the nation that frog throwed off for—I wonder if there ain't something the matter with him—he 'pears to look mighty baggy, somehow'." His description of the frog as "baggy" creates humor since the audience knows before Smiley does that the frog has literally become a bag of quail shot.

11. How does figurative language help to develop Smiley's frog? Use specific evidence from the text to support your answer.

Twain uses similes and hyperbole to develop Wheeler's admiration of the frog. Wheeler comments, "He'd give him a little punch behind, and the next minute you'd see that frog whirling in the air like a doughnut — see him turn one summerset, or may be a couple, if he got a good start, and come down flat-footed and all right, like a cat." Comparing the frog to a doughnut emphasizes the frog's perfect circle as it is flying through the air. This simile also develops the next simile in which the frog is described as landing with a cat's grace. In addition, Wheeler exaggerates the frog's skills: "Why, I've seen him set Dan'l Webster down here on this floor — Dan'l Webster was the name of the frog — and sing out, 'Flies, Dan'l, flies!' and quicker'n you could wink he'd spring straight up and snake a fly off'n the counter there, and flop down on the floor ag'in as solid as a gob of mud, and fall to scratching the side of his head with his hind foot as indifferent as if he hadn't no idea he'd been doin' any more'n any frog might do." The exaggeration of both the frog's obedience and his ability to catch flies works with the similes to develop the frog as a superhero-type animal.

12. How is Simon Wheeler characterized? Provide examples of direct and/or indirect characterization to support your point.

One possible answer:
Simon Wheeler is characterized as pushy. As soon as the narrator mentions Rev. Leonidas W. Smiley, Wheeler backs the narrator into a corner and blockades him with a chair. Simon's character is again indirectly developed at the end of the text when the narrator describes himself as buttonholed by Wheeler. These actions were also alluded to in the beginning when the narrator noted that this had probably been some trick his friend was trying to play on him, knowing that Wheeler would trap him into listening to the long and tedious story. In addition, the reader may note that Wheeler does not stop for questions or comments from the narrator; in fact, he only pauses for a moment when interrupted by someone calling his name. Wheeler would rather control the conversation, telling his outrageous stories of Jim Smiley.

13. Evaluate the use of dialect within the text. How effective is it in the development of the overall text?

One possible answer:

Twain's use of dialect establishes the tone of the text as well as the differences between the narrator and Simon Wheeler. The dialect creates an informal tone necessary to capture the oral storytelling that takes place in the text. It brings the reader into the old west and makes Simon Wheeler's personality more believable as he goes off on tangents—"Rev. Leonidas W. H'm, Reverend Le—well, there was a feller here once by the name of Jim Smiley, in the winter of '49—or may be it was the spring of '50—I don't recollect exactly, somehow, though what makes me think it was one or the other is because I remember the big flume warn't finished." The reader actually hears his voice instead of just reading his words. In addition, the reader notices that while the narrator speaks formally using correct grammar, Simon frequently speaks ungrammatically with informal diction. Twain creates a notable difference between the two characters, developing the narrator's reasons for his rude exit and sharp criticism of Wheeler's story. They are two people from very dissimilar backgrounds and very dissimilar values. The refined narrator does not appreciate the tall tales of the rugged, old western miner.

Question 1	Distinguishing Among Genres of Fiction
Question 2	Summarizing and Paraphrasing
Question 3	Analyzing Diction
Question 4	Analyzing Conflict, Plot, and Setting
Question 5	Analyzing Figurative Language
Question 6	Analyzing Figurative Language
Question 7	Analyzing Character
Question 8	Analyzing Character
Question 9	Analyzing Point of View/Analyzing Text Organization
Question 10	Analyzing Irony
Question 11	Analyzing Figurative Language
Question 12	Analyzing Character
Question 13	Evaluating Author's Craft/Style

FROM *PRIDE AND PREJUDICE*

by Jane Austen

Mr. Bennet was among the earliest of those who waited on Mr. Bingley. He had always intended to visit him, though to the last always assuring his wife that he should not go; and till the evening after the visit was paid she had no knowledge of it. It was then disclosed in the following manner. Observing his second daughter employed in trimming a hat, he suddenly addressed her with:

"I hope Mr. Bingley will like it, Lizzy."

"We are not in a way to know what Mr. Bingley likes," said her mother resentfully, "since we are not to visit."

"But you forget, mamma," said Elizabeth, "that we shall meet him at the assemblies, and that Mrs. Long promised to introduce him."

"I do not believe Mrs. Long will do any such thing. She has two nieces of her own. She is a selfish, hypocritical woman, and I have no opinion of her."

"No more have I," said Mr. Bennet; "and I am glad to find that you do not depend on her serving you."

Mrs. Bennet deigned not to make any reply, but, unable to contain herself, began scolding one of her daughters.

"Don't keep coughing so, Kitty, for Heaven's sake! Have a little compassion on my nerves. You tear them to pieces."

"Kitty has no discretion in her coughs," said her father; "she times them ill."

"I do not cough for my own amusement," replied Kitty fretfully. "When is your next ball to be, Lizzy?"

"To-morrow fortnight."

"Aye, so it is," cried her mother, "and Mrs. Long does not come back till the day before; so it will be impossible for her to introduce him, for she will not know him herself."

"Then, my dear, you may have the advantage of your friend, and introduce Mr. Bingley to her."

"Impossible, Mr. Bennet, impossible, when I am not acquainted with him myself; how can you be so teasing?"

"I honor your circumspection. A fortnight's acquaintance is certainly very little. One cannot know what a man really is by the end of a fortnight. But if we do not venture somebody else will; and after all, Mrs. Long and her daughters must stand their chance; and, therefore, as she will think it an act of kindness, if you decline the office, I will take it on myself."

The girls stared at their father. Mrs. Bennet said only, "Nonsense, nonsense!"

"What can be the meaning of that emphatic exclamation?" cried he. "Do you consider the forms of introduction, and the stress that is laid on them, as nonsense? I cannot quite agree with you there. What say you, Mary? For you are a young lady of deep reflection, I know, and read great books and make extracts."

Mary wished to say something sensible, but knew not how.

"While Mary is adjusting her ideas," he continued, "let us return to Mr. Bingley."

"I am sick of Mr. Bingley," cried his wife.

"I am sorry to hear that; but why did not you tell me that before? If I had known as much this morning I certainly would not have called on him. It is very unlucky; but as I have actually paid the visit, we cannot escape the acquaintance now."

The astonishment of the ladies was just what he wished; that of Mrs. Bennet perhaps surpassing the rest; though, when the first tumult of joy was over, she began to declare that it was what she had expected all the while.

"How good it was in you, my dear Mr. Bennet! But I knew I should persuade you at last. I was sure you loved your girls too well to neglect such an acquaintance. Well, how pleased I am! and it is such a good joke, too, that you should have gone this morning and never said a word about it till now."

"Now, Kitty, you may cough as much as you choose," said Mr. Bennet; and, as he spoke, he left the room, fatigued with the raptures of his wife.

"What an excellent father you have, girls!" said she, when the door was shut. "I do not know how you will ever make him amends for his kindness; or me, either, for that matter. At our time of life it is not so pleasant, I can tell you, to be making new acquaintances every day; but for your sakes, we would do anything. Lydia, my love, though you are the youngest, I dare say Mr. Bingley will dance with you at the next ball."

"Oh!" said Lydia stoutly, "I am not afraid; for though I am the youngest, I'm the tallest."

The rest of the evening was spent in conjecturing how soon he would return Mr. Bennet's visit, and determining when they should ask him to dinner.

1. In what point of view is the story written?

   a. first person
   b. third person limited
   c. ***third person omniscient***
   d. objective

2. Mr. Bennet can **best** be described as

   a. ***teasing.***
   b. mean.
   c. honest.
   d. tired.

3. "She is a selfish, hypocritical woman, and I have no opinion of her." This statement contains an example of

   a. situational irony.
   b. dramatic irony.
   c. ***verbal irony.***
   d. no irony at all.

4. In this passage, the word, "raptures," most nearly means

   a. yelling.
   b. ecstasy.
   c. questions.
   d. ideas.

5. Why do the girls want to meet Mr. Bingley?

   a. They hear he throws lavish and spectacular parties.
   b. They need to ask him for an important favor.
   c. They need to know everyone Mrs. Long knows.
   d. They want to pursue their romantic interests.

6. Why are the girls quiet when Mr. Bennet says he should introduce Mrs. Long and her nieces to Mr. Bingley?

   a. The girls agree with their fathers' remarks.
   b. The girls don't want them to meet Mr. Bingley.
   c. The girls don't understand what their father said.
   d. The girls were not paying attention to their father.

7. What causes Mrs. Bennet to say that she is sick of Mr. Bingley?

   a. She is flustered and angered by her husband's comments.
   b. She no longer thinks Mr. Bingley is a worthy man to meet.
   c. She has started to feel ill from too much conversation.
   d. She doesn't like it when they talk about Mrs. Long.

8. Why does Mr. Bennet say, "Now, Kitty, you may cough as much as you choose," after he tells the ladies he has visited Mr. Bingley?

   a. He knows that she really wants to cough.
   b. He has to give her permission to cough.
   c. He knows his wife will no longer yell at Kitty.
   d. He knows that it will annoy his wife terribly.

9. Which of these is **not** an effect of Mr. Bennet's announcement that he visited Mr. Bingley?

   a. The women talk about Mr. Bingley all evening.
   b. Lizzy trims her hat to prepare for the ball.
   c. Mrs. Bennet thinks her husband is fantastic.
   d. The ladies are astonished and overjoyed.

10. "Kitty has no discretion in her coughs," said her father; "she times them ill." What device does Austen use in this sentence? What is its effect on the overall passage? Use specific evidence from the text to support your answer.

One possible answer:

Austen uses a pun to illustrate Mrs. Bennet's ridiculous nature and Mr. Bennet's cleverness. After Mrs. Bennet yells at Kitty for coughing, claiming that she needs to "have a little compassion on my nerves. You tear them to pieces," Mr. Bennet returns with this comment. In one sense it could be taken that Kitty is ill, and that is why she is coughing so much. In another sense it could be taken that Kitty has poor timing with her cough; she shouldn't cough when Mrs. Bennet is so agitated. In either case, Mr. Bennet's ambiguous statement illustrates his cleverness and Mrs. Bennet's selfish nature. She only cares that Kitty's cough is bothering her, not that her daughter might actually be sick and require attention. Mr. Bennet's comment indicates that he recognizes his wife's egocentric behavior.

11. How is Mrs. Bennet characterized in this passage? Use specific evidence from the text to support your answer.

Mrs. Bennet is characterized as an emotional and selfish character. Austen's use of dramatic irony helps to illustrate this point. At the beginning of the passage, the reader finds out that Mr. Bennet has already talked to Mr. Bingley; however, Mrs. Bennet does not know this. This allows the reader to see Mrs. Bennet's true nature when she doesn't get what she wants. She resentfully makes snide comments when her husband asks Lizzy about her hat. In addition, not only is she nasty to her husband, but she also takes her anger out on Kitty who is simply coughing. Both her actions and what she says continue to indirectly characterize her as when she claims that introducing Mrs. Long and her nieces to Mr. Bingley would be nonsense. However, this statement echoes earlier text when she declared that Mrs. Long was a "selfish, hypocritical woman" because she would probably break her promise to introduce Mrs. Bennet and the girls to Mr. Bingley. In fact, she herself is the selfish, hypocritical woman. She further shows her emotional, self-centered nature by her quick change in demeanor after she knows that Mr. Bennet had met with Mr. Bingley. She calls her husband an "excellent father" but then quickly gives herself credit as well saying, "At our time of life it is not so pleasant, I can tell you, to be making new acquaintances every day; but for your sakes, we would do anything." Through dramatic irony and indirect characterization, Austen creates Mrs. Bennet's egotistical nature.

12. What do the women characters in the passage seem to value most? Use specific evidence from the text to support your answer.

The women in the passage seem most concerned with physical appearances. In the beginning of the passage, Lizzy is described as trimming a hat, trying to improve her appearance. This emphasis on appearance is furthered as Mrs. Bennet and the girls worry about how they will be introduced to Mr. Bingley while following the strict code of conduct for the time period. Mr. Bennet reminds them, "Do you consider the forms of introduction, and the stress that is laid on them, as nonsense?" in response to their negative reaction toward his idea to introduce Mrs. Long and her nieces to Mrs. Bingley. Even Mary, who is described by Mr. Bennet as well read (presumably in code-of-conduct books) cannot argue against her father. Instead she is described as wishing to "say something sensible, but knew not how." At the end emphasis is again put on appearances with Lydia's remark that her confidence resides in the fact that she is tall. The women spend the evening determining the right way to invite Mr. Bingley to dinner.

Question 1	Analyzing Point of View
Question 2	Analyzing Character
Question 3	Analyzing Irony
Question 4	Analyzing Diction
Question 5	Drawing Conclusions
Question 6	Making Inferences
Question 7	Analyzing Cause and Effect
Question 8	Making Inferences
Question 9	Analyzing Cause and Effect
Question 10	Analyzing Pun
Question 11	Analyzing Character
Question 12	Analyzing Character/ Drawing Conclusions

PASSAGE I: "OUT, OUT—"

by Robert Frost

The buzz-saw snarled and rattled in the yard	1
And made dust and dropped stove-length sticks of wood,	
Sweet-scented stuff when the breeze drew across it.	
And from there those that lifted eyes could count	
Five mountain ranges one behind the other	5
Under the sunset far into Vermont.	
And the saw snarled and rattled, snarled and rattled,	
As it ran light, or had to bear a load.	
And nothing happened: day was all but done.	
Call it a day, I wish they might have said	10
To please the boy by giving him the half hour	
That a boy counts so much when saved from work.	
His sister stood beside them in her apron	
To tell them "Supper." At the word, the saw,	
As if to prove saws knew what supper meant,	15
Leaped out at the boy's hand, or seemed to leap—	
He must have given the hand. However it was,	
Neither refused the meeting. But the hand!	
The boy's first outcry was a rueful laugh,	
As he swung toward them holding up the hand	20
Half in appeal, but half as if to keep	
The life from spilling. Then the boy saw all—	
Since he was old enough to know, big boy	
Doing a man's work, though a child at heart—	
He saw all spoiled. "Don't let him cut my hand off—	25
The doctor, when he comes. Don't let him, sister!"	
So. But the hand was gone already.	
The doctor put him in the dark of ether.	
He lay and puffed his lips out with his breath.	
And then—the watcher at his pulse took fright.	30
No one believed. They listened at his heart.	
Little—less—nothing!—and that ended it.	
No more to build on there. And they, since they	
Were not the one dead, turned to their affairs.	

179

PASSAGE II: FROM ACT V, SCENE V OF *MACBETH*

by William Shakespeare

Seyton.
The Queen, my lord, is dead.   1

Macbeth.
She should have died hereafter;
There would have been a time for such a word.
Tomorrow, and tomorrow, and tomorrow
Creeps in this petty pace from day to day   5
To the last syllable of recorded time;
And all our yesterdays have lighted fools
The way to dusty death. Out, out, brief candle!
Life's but a walking shadow, a poor player
That struts and frets his hour upon the stage   10
And then is heard no more. It is a tale
Told by an idiot, full of sound and fury,
Signifying nothing.

Passage I

1. In which genre(s) of poetry is this poem?

   a. dramatic poetry
   b. narrative poetry
   c. lyric poetry
   d. dramatic and lyric poetry

2. Line 1 contains an example of

   a. simile.
   b. metaphor.
   c. onomatopoeia.
   d. hyperbole.

3. Which line foreshadows that something might go wrong?

   a. line 2
   b. line 4
   c. line 8
   d. line 10

4. "Life" in Line 22 stands for

   a. blood.
   b. wood.
   c. the hand.
   d. his spirit.

5. What causes the boy to lose his hand?

   a. He loses concentration for a moment.
   b. The buzz-saw malfunctions and breaks.
   c. He becomes lightheaded from lack of food.
   d. The buzz-saw comes to life in his hands.

6. Why is the boy's first reaction a "rueful laugh"?

   a. He thinks that the event is funny.
   b. He thinks that it is all a game.
   c. He is in sorry disbelief of the event.
   d. He is mad at his sister for yelling.

7. The overall tone of the poem can **best** be described as

   a. angry.
   b. sentimental.
   c. sympathetic.
   d. confused.

Passage II

8. The overall tone of this passage can **best** be described as

   a. depressed.
   b. factual.
   c. angry.
   d. apologetic.

9. Lines 9 contains an example of

   a. simile.
   b. metaphor.
   c. personification.
   d. hyperbole.

10. In this passage, the word, "creeps," most nearly means

    a. shifts gradually.
    b. spreads along a surface.
    c. proceeds cautiously.
    d. moves slowly.

181

11. Line 10 contains an example of

    a. simile.
    b. alliteration.
    c. consonance.
    d. hyperbole.

Passages I and II

12. Frost published "Out, Out—" during World War I. How might this event and time period have affected his writing? Use specific evidence from the text to support your answer.

Readers may recognize the emphasis on the boy who seems to have had to grow up too quickly. The boy's youth is first emphasized by the mere repetition of the word, "boy," throughout the poem. While the boy is deemed young, he is not treated this way in the text: "Call it a day, I wish they might have said / To please the boy by giving him the half hour / That a boy counts so much when saved from work." The boy appears to have been overworked and unable to revel in the play of typical youth. His lost youth is again referenced after the accident: "Since he was old enough to know, big boy / Doing a man's work, though a child at heart — / He saw all spoiled." Again the boy is described as going beyond his years in his work; however, the narrator notes that he was experienced enough (perhaps from having to do a man's work) to know that his life would never be the same. While he understands that all is "spoiled" he is not mature enough to understand the gravity of the moment; he is worried about saving his hand rather than his life. From the beginning the boy seemed overworked; he seemed too tired to fight the saw, and the narrator comments that the boy seemed to have given up his hand to the saw, perhaps in exhaustion. Immediately after the accident occurs, he almost apologetically puts up his hand as if he knows he will no longer be able to work as he needs to do. These references may be tied either to the young boys who had to go to battle or to the young boys left to do the work of a men as fathers were sent off to war.

13. How does the setting of Frost's poem help to develop the overall effect of the poem? Use specific evidence from the text to support your answer.

One possible answer:

Frost's pleasant picture of the rural landscape masks the horrible tragedy soon to occur, surprising the audience with situational irony. Frost uses imagery to describe the sights, smells, and sounds of the work on the farm. He mentions the smell of the "sweet-scented stuff" as the aroma of freshly-cut wood is carried on the breeze. He also mentions the "five mountain ranges one behind the other / Under the sunset far into Vermont," emphasizing the beauty of the land. These observations of the land sharply contrast with the misfortune soon to occur and hint at the truth readers must realize at the end of the poem: Not all things (or people) will be as affected by the boy's death as some may think they should be. The one interruption to the peaceful landscape is the snarling saw. While at first it may be seen as evidence of the hard work of the farmers, the saw becomes increasingly ominous as the snarling and rattling is repeated throughout the text, finally leading to the narrator's disturbing wish to "call it a day, I wish they might have said." The setting makes the boy's death more of a surprise and also shows the detachment between the land and the boy's fate.

14. How does personification help to develop Frost's poem? Use specific evidence from the text to support your answer.

Personification presents the buzz-saw as a live, savage beast that attacks the boy, emphasizing the danger in everyday items in our ordinary lives. The buzz-saw is the one thing in the very beginning that contrasts with the pleasant setting of the poem. Frost describes the saw as snarling; this lifelike quality is further emphasized by the repetition of the onomatopoeic word two additional times in the text. The narrator also describes the saw as attacking the boy: "At the word, the saw, / As if to prove saws knew what supper meant, / Leaped out at the boy's hand, or seemed to leap— / He must have given the hand. However it was, / Neither refused the meeting." Describing the contact between the saw and the boy as a savage beast attacking his helpless prey makes the saw seem much more dangerous and the boy much more helpless than if the event had just been presented as an accident. The boy and, therefore, his life seems to be so very fragile when compared to the beastlike qualities of the saw, and the meeting of the two emphasizes the fragility and brevity of life in general.

15. Why does Frost entitle his poem "Out, Out—"? What connections can be made between the two passages? Use specific evidence from both texts to support your answer.

In the title, Frost alludes to Shakespeare's line—"Out, out brief candle"—in order to emphasize the brevity and unpredictability of life which both passages address. Shakespeare addresses life, referring to it as a metaphorical candle. Just as the flame of a candle is easily and sometimes accidentally put out, Shakespeare makes the point that life is fragile, brief, and somewhat unpredictable. This idea is reinforced in Frost's poem as the boy dies young and unexpectedly. Connections can also be made to Shakespeare's comparison of life to a "walking shadow, a poor player / That struts and frets his hour upon the stage / And then is heard no more." "Heard no more" echoes in Frost's poem. The boy is described as puffing his lips out with his breath, and the people gather to listen until the boy's pulse drops to nothing. The poem then chills the audience with, "that ended it." Just as people would leave the theatre after the show, the gatherers are described as turning to their affairs. Since their candles have not yet been put out, they may feel they can waste no more time on the dead boy. Unfortunately, Shakespeare's final words "signifying nothing" reverberate in Frost's poem as well: his sharp comment "that ended it" in combination with "No more to build on there" seem surprisingly unemotional at the time of a young boy's death. While the narrator is mostly sympathetic in the poem, he seems to mirror the aloofness of the others in these lines. With the onlookers coldly turning to their own business, the reader is left wondering what the significance of the boy's life had been to anyone.

16. Evaluate the quality of Frost's poem. What is it that makes it largely effective or ineffective for you as a reader? Use specific evidence from the text to support your answer.

Students who favorably evaluate the poem may comment on the use of personification in the text or the allusion to Macbeth. *Others may note Frost's rhythm; the rhythm flows smoothly in the first lines while he paints a pleasant setting through his use of run-on lines. However, when things start to go wrong in the poem, the rhythm is no longer as smooth. Beginning in line 9, Frost uses caesura (pauses within the lines created with punctuation) to interrupt the smooth rhythm of the first lines. Whether presenting a favorable or an unfavorable evaluation, students should provide specific evidence from the text in their evaluation.*

"I Fall Into Disgrace" from *David Copperfield*

by Charles Dickens

We dined alone, we three together. He seemed to be very fond of my mother—I am afraid I liked him none the better for that—and she was very fond of him. I gathered from what they said, that an elder sister of his was coming to stay with them, and that she was expected that evening. I am not certain whether I found out then, or afterwards, that, without being actively concerned in any business, he had some share in, or some annual charge upon the profits of, a wine-merchant's house in London, with which his family had been connected from his great-grandfather's time, and in which his sister had a similar interest; but I may mention it in this place, whether or no.

After dinner, when we were sitting by the fire, and I was meditating an escape to Peggotty without having the hardihood to slip away, lest it should offend the master of the house, a coach drove up to the garden-gate and he went out to receive the visitor. My mother followed him. I was timidly following her, when she turned round at the parlor door, in the dusk, and taking me in her embrace as she had been used to do, whispered me to love my new father and be obedient to him. She did this hurriedly and secretly, as if it were wrong, but tenderly; and, putting out her hand behind her, held mine in it, until we came near to where he was standing in the garden, where she let mine go, and drew hers through his arm.

It was Miss Murdstone who was arrived, and a gloomy-looking lady she was; dark, like her brother, whom she greatly resembled in face and voice; and with very heavy eyebrows, nearly meeting over her large nose, as if, being disabled by the wrongs of her sex from wearing whiskers, she had carried them to that account. She brought with her two uncompromising hard black boxes, with her initials on the lids in hard brass nails. When she paid the coachman she took her money out of a hard steel purse, and she kept the purse in a very jail of a bag which hung upon her arm by a heavy chain, and shut up like a bite. I had never, at that time, seen such a metallic lady altogether as Miss Murdstone was.

She was brought into the parlor with many tokens of welcome, and there formally recognized my mother as a new and near relation. Then she looked at me, and said:

'Is that your boy, sister-in-law?'

My mother acknowledged me.

'Generally speaking,' said Miss Murdstone, 'I don't like boys. How d'ye do, boy?'

Under these encouraging circumstances, I replied that I was very well, and that I hoped she was the same; with such an indifferent grace, that Miss Murdstone disposed of me in two words:

'Wants manner!'

Having uttered which, with great distinctness, she begged the favor of being shown to her room, which became to me from that time forth a place of awe and dread, wherein the two black boxes were never seen open or known to be left unlocked, and where (for I peeped in once or twice when she was out) numerous little steel fetters and rivets, with which Miss Murdstone embellished herself when she was dressed, generally hung upon the looking-glass in formidable array.

As well as I could make out, she had come for good, and had no intention of ever going again. She began to 'help' my mother next morning, and was in and out of the store-closet all day, putting things to rights, and making havoc in the old arrangements. Almost the first remarkable thing I observed in Miss Murdstone was, her being constantly haunted by a suspicion that the servants had a man secreted somewhere on the premises. Under the influence of this delusion, she dived into the coal-cellar at the most untimely hours, and scarcely ever opened the door of a dark cupboard without clapping it to again, in the belief that she had got him.

Though there was nothing very airy about Miss Murdstone, she was a perfect Lark in point of getting up. She was up (and, as I believe to this hour, looking for that man) before anybody in the house was stirring. Peggotty gave it as her opinion that she even slept with one eye open; but I could not concur in this idea; for I tried it myself after hearing the suggestion thrown out, and found it couldn't be done.

On the very first morning after her arrival she was up and ringing her bell at cock-crow. When my mother came down to breakfast and was going to make the tea, Miss Murdstone gave her a kind of peck on the cheek, which was her nearest approach to a kiss, and said:

'Now, Clara, my dear, I am come here, you know, to relieve you of all the trouble I can. You're much too pretty and thoughtless' —my mother blushed but laughed, and seemed not to dislike this character— 'to have any duties imposed upon you that can be undertaken by me. If you'll be so good as give me your keys, my dear, I'll attend to all this sort of thing in future.'

From that time, Miss Murdstone kept the keys in her own little jail all day, and under her pillow all night, and my mother had no more to do with them than I had.

My mother did not suffer her authority to pass from her without a shadow of protest. One night when Miss Murdstone had been developing certain household plans to her brother, of which he signified his approbation, my mother suddenly began to cry, and said she thought she might have been consulted.

'Clara!' said Mr. Murdstone sternly. 'Clara! I wonder at you.'

'Oh, it's very well to say you wonder, Edward!' cried my mother, 'and it's very well for you to talk about firmness, but you wouldn't like it yourself.'

Firmness, I may observe, was the grand quality on which both Mr. and Miss Murdstone took their stand. However I might have expressed my comprehension of it at that time, if I had been called upon, I nevertheless did clearly comprehend in my own way, that it was another name for tyranny; and for a certain gloomy, arrogant, devil's humor, that was in them both. The creed, as I should state it now, was this. Mr. Murdstone was firm; nobody in his world was to be so firm as Mr. Murdstone; nobody else in his world was to be firm at all, for everybody was to be bent to his firmness. Miss Murdstone was an exception. She might be firm, but only by relationship, and in an inferior and tributary degree. My mother was another exception. She might be firm, and must be; but only in bearing their firmness, and firmly believing there was no other firmness upon earth.

'It's very hard,' said my mother, 'that in my own house—'

'My own house?' repeated Mr. Murdstone. 'Clara!'

'OUR own house, I mean,' faltered my mother, evidently frightened- 'I hope you must know what I mean, Edward — it's very hard that in YOUR own house I may not have a word to say about domestic matters. I am sure I managed very well before we were married. There's evidence,' said my mother, sobbing; 'ask Peggotty if I didn't do very well when I wasn't interfered with!'

'Edward,' said Miss Murdstone, 'let there be an end of this. I go tomorrow.'

'Jane Murdstone,' said her brother, 'be silent! How dare you to insinuate that you don't know my character better than your words imply?'

'I am sure,' my poor mother went on, at a grievous disadvantage, and with many tears, 'I don't want anybody to go. I should be very miserable and unhappy if anybody was to go. I don't ask much. I am not unreasonable. I only want to be consulted sometimes. I am very much obliged to anybody who assists me, and I only want to be consulted as a mere form, sometimes. I thought you were pleased, once, with my being a little inexperienced and girlish, Edward – I am sure you said so - but you seem to hate me for it now, you are so severe.'

'Edward,' said Miss Murdstone, again, 'let there be an end of this. I go tomorrow.'

'Jane Murdstone,' thundered Mr. Murdstone. 'Will you be silent? How dare you?'

Miss Murdstone made a jail-delivery of her pocket-handkerchief, and held it before her eyes.

'Clara,' he continued, looking at my mother, 'you surprise me! You astound me! Yes, I had a satisfaction in the thought of marrying an inexperienced and artless person, and forming her character, and infusing into it some amount of that firmness and decision of which it stood in need. But when Jane Murdstone is kind enough to come to my assistance in this endeavor, and to assume, for my sake, a condition something like a housekeeper's, and when she meets with a base return—'

'Oh, pray, pray, Edward,' cried my mother, 'don't accuse me of being ungrateful. I am sure I am not ungrateful. No one ever said I was before. I have many faults, but not that. Oh, don't, my dear!'

'When Jane Murdstone meets, I say,' he went on, after waiting until my mother was silent, 'with a base return, that feeling of mine is chilled and altered.'

'Don't, my love, say that!' implored my mother very piteously. 'Oh, don't, Edward! I can't bear to hear it. Whatever I am, I am affectionate. I know I am affectionate. I wouldn't say it, if I wasn't sure that I am. Ask Peggotty. I am sure she'll tell you I'm affectionate.'

1. In what point of view is the story written?

   a. *first person*
   b. third person limited
   c. third person omniscient
   d. objective

2. The narrator can **best** be described as

   a. angry.
   b. depressed.
   c. *humorous.*
   d. happy.

188

3. Which of the following is a fact about Mr. Murdstone?

   a. He is very fond of the narrator's mother.
   b. He is not nice to the narrator's mother.
   c. He has a sister named Jane Murdstone.
   d. He likes to be in charge of the home.

4. Clara's behavior as Mr. Murdstone first goes out to meet his sister illustrates that

   a. she cares if her son likes her husband.
   b. he really wants to meet Miss Murdstone.
   c. he loves her son more than anything.
   d. she worries about pleasing her husband.

5. "She kept the purse in a very jail of a bag which hung upon her arm by a heavy chain, and shut up like a bite" The simile emphasizes that her purse appears

   a. large.
   b. new.
   c. hostile.
   d. expensive.

6. Why has Miss Murdstone come to the house?

   a. to visit the family
   b. to control the house
   c. to negotiate business
   d. to find a husband

7. "My mother did not suffer her authority to pass from her without a shadow of protest." In this passage, the word, "shadow," insinuates

   a. an aggressive protest.
   b. an upsetting protest.
   c. a long protest.
   d. a weak protest.

8. "We dined alone, we three together." What literary device is Dickens using in this passage, and what effect does it have on the passage? Use specific examples from the text to support your answer.

One possible answer:

Dickens uses a paradox to immediately establish the divided nature of the family. At first the audience wonders how they could be eating alone when they are together; however, later the audience understands that while they are not physically alone, they are emotionally and mentally disconnected from each other. This is further developed in the passage when the narrator comments that he was "meditating an escape" from dinner and when the narrator's mother pleads with him to obey his new father. Clara and her husband's dissatisfaction is also emphasized later in the text when she asks for some say in the household, and he denies her request, accusing her of being ungrateful.

9. How is Miss Murdstone characterized using direct and indirect characterization? Use specific examples from the text to support your answer.

One possible answer:

Miss Murdstone is depicted as a cold, hard woman. The narrator blatantly comments on her characteristics when he says, "I had never, at that time, seen such a metallic lady." This is further emphasized indirectly through her looks, actions, and spoken words. She is described as a person with "heavy eyebrows" who was carrying "uncompromising hard black boxes, with her initials on the lids in hard brass nails" as well as a "hard steel purse." In addition, the narrator describes her jewelry as "numerous little steel fetters and rivets." All of these physical elements create a very serious, cold woman who seems interested in keeping control. As with her physical description, her comments and action also define her. She quickly says, "I don't like boys" upon meeting the narrator. Also, she merely pecks Clara when greeting her and keeps the keys to the house "in her own little jail all day." Everything about her seems harsh and restrictive. From this description, the audience knows that Miss Murdstone is just faking sadness and tears when Clara asks for her opinion to be considered; it is only a ploy to keep control of the household.

10. Predict what will happen next in the argument involving Mr. Murdstone, Miss Murdstone, and Clara. Use specific examples from the text to support your answer.

Most students will agree that Clara will give in to the argument and allow Mr. and Miss Murdstone to make all of the future decisions. Clara wants to please her husband, which is shown when she pleads with her son to accept and obey his new father. In addition, Clara's concern is presented as only a "shadow of a protest," only an imitation of a genuine argument. Upon the threat from Miss Murdstone to leave, Clara immediately recoils, saying that she only wants to be "consulted sometimes" and later conceding to "consulted as a mere form, sometimes." In addition, she backs down from her comments about having an opinion in her house; she quickly corrects herself saying "our house" and finally "your house." By the end of the passage, Clara no longer focuses on earning back some authority in the house but rather on defending her character. Clara will continue to lose influence in the household, probably to the narrator's detriment.

11. Charles Dickens is known for his satires of society. What does he seem to be making fun of in the passage? Use specific examples from the text to support your answer.

One possible answer:
Dickens criticizes the roles of most women during the Victorian time period. Clara is presented as a senseless, weak character under the oppressive thumb of the hostile patriarch of the family. At one point in their argument Clara comments, "I thought you were pleased, once, with my being a little inexperienced and girlish, Edward—I am sure you said so—but you seem to hate me for it now, you are so severe." Mr. Murdstone responds, "I had a satisfaction in the thought of marrying an inexperienced and artless person, and forming her character, and infusing into it some amount of that firmness and decision of which it stood in need." The relationship is not presented as a partnership but rather one in which he tries to determine her character. Clara cannot even stand up for her qualities on her own, and instead turns to Peggotty to defend her character. Even Miss Murdstone, whom the reader notices is depicted as "like her brother . . . in face and voice," describes Clara as "much too pretty and thoughtless" to take care of the house. Dickens satirizes the women of the time who acted and were treated like fragile creatures who couldn't handle responsibility or power.

192

FROM ACT I OF
THE IMPORTANCE OF BEING EARNEST
by Oscar Wilde

Algernon. Bring me that cigarette case Mr. Worthing left in the smoking-room the last time he dined here.

Lane. Yes, sir.

[**Lane** goes out.]

Jack. Do you mean to say you have had my cigarette case all this time? I wish to goodness you had let me know. I have been writing frantic letters to Scotland Yard about it. I was very nearly offering a large reward.

Algernon. Well, I wish you would offer one. I happen to be more than usually hard up.

Jack. There is no good offering a large reward now that the thing is found.

[Enter **Lane** with the cigarette case on a salver. **Algernon** takes it at once. **Lane** goes out.]

Algernon. I think that is rather mean of you, Ernest, I must say. [Opens case and examines it.] However, it makes no matter, for, now that I look at the inscription inside, I find that the thing isn't yours after all.

Jack. Of course it's mine. [Moving to him.] You have seen me with it a hundred times, and you have no right whatsoever to read what is written inside. It is a very ungentlemanly thing to read a private cigarette case.

Algernon. Oh! it is absurd to have a hard and fast rule about what one should read and what one shouldn't. More than half of modern culture depends on what one shouldn't read.

Jack. I am quite aware of the fact, and I don't propose to discuss modern culture. It isn't the sort of thing one should talk of in private. I simply want my cigarette case back.

Algernon. Yes; but this isn't your cigarette case. This cigarette case is a present from some one of the name of Cecily, and you said you didn't know any one of that name.

Jack. Well, if you want to know, Cecily happens to be my aunt.

Algernon. Your aunt!

Jack. Yes. Charming old lady she is, too. Lives at Tunbridge Wells. Just give it back to me, Algy.

Algernon. [Retreating to back of sofa.] But why does she call herself little Cecily if she is your aunt and lives at Tunbridge Wells? [Reading.] 'From little Cecily with her fondest love.'

Jack. [Moving to sofa and kneeling upon it.] My dear fellow, what on earth is there in that? Some aunts are tall, some aunts are not tall. That is a matter that surely an aunt may be allowed to decide for herself. You seem to think that every aunt should be

193

exactly like your aunt! That is absurd! For Heaven's sake give me back my cigarette case. [Follows **Algernon** round the room.]

Algernon. Yes. But why does your aunt call you her uncle? 'From little Cecily, with her fondest love to her dear Uncle Jack.' There is no objection, I admit, to an aunt being a small aunt, but why an aunt, no matter what her size may be, should call her own nephew her uncle, I can't quite make out. Besides, your name isn't Jack at all; it is Ernest.

Jack. It isn't Ernest; it's Jack.

Algernon. You have always told me it was Ernest. I have introduced you to every one as Ernest. You answer to the name of Ernest. You look as if your name was Ernest. You are the most earnest-looking person I ever saw in my life. It is perfectly absurd your saying that your name isn't Ernest. It's on your cards. Here is one of them. [Taking it from case.] 'Mr. Ernest Worthing, B. 4, The Albany.' I'll keep this as a proof that your name is Ernest if ever you attempt to deny it to me, or to Gwendolen, or to any one else. [Puts the card in his pocket.]

Jack. Well, my name is Ernest in town and Jack in the country, and the cigarette case was given to me in the country.

Algernon. Yes, but that does not account for the fact that your small Aunt Cecily, who lives at Tunbridge Wells, calls you her dear uncle. Come, old boy, you had much better have the thing out at once.

Jack. My dear Algy, you talk exactly as if you were a dentist. It is very vulgar to talk like a dentist when one isn't a dentist. It produces a false impression.

Algernon. Well, that is exactly what dentists always do. Now, go on! Tell me the whole thing. I may mention that I have always suspected you of being a confirmed and secret Bunburyist; and I am quite sure of it now.

Jack. Bunburyist? What on earth do you mean by a Bunburyist?

Algernon. I'll reveal to you the meaning of that incomparable expression as soon as you are kind enough to inform me why you are Ernest in town and Jack in the country.

Jack. Well, produce my cigarette case first.

Algernon. Here it is. [Hands cigarette case.] Now produce your explanation, and pray make it improbable. [Sits on sofa.]

Jack. My dear fellow, there is nothing improbable about my explanation at all. In fact it's perfectly ordinary. Old Mr. Thomas Cardew, who adopted me when I was a little boy, made me in his will guardian to his grand-daughter, Miss Cecily Cardew. Cecily, who addresses me as her uncle from motives of respect that you could not possibly appreciate, lives at my place in the country under the charge of her admirable governess, Miss Prism.

Algernon. Where is that place in the country, by the way?

Jack. That is nothing to you, dear boy. You are not going to be invited . . . I may tell you candidly that the place is not in Shropshire.

Algernon. I suspected that, my dear fellow! I have Bunburyed all over Shropshire on two separate occasions. Now, go on. Why are you Ernest in town and Jack in the country?

Jack. My dear Algy, I don't know whether you will be able to understand my real motives. You are hardly serious enough. When one is placed in the position of guardian, one has to adopt a very high moral tone on all subjects. It's one's duty to do so. And as a high moral tone can hardly be said to conduce very much to either one's health or one's happiness, in order to get up to town I have always pretended to have a younger brother of the name of Ernest, who lives in the Albany, and gets into the most dreadful scrapes. That, my dear Algy, is the whole truth pure and simple.

Algernon. The truth is rarely pure and never simple. Modern life would be very tedious if it were either, and modern literature a complete impossibility!

Jack. That wouldn't be at all a bad thing.

Algernon. Literary criticism is not your forte, my dear fellow. Don't try it. You should leave that to people who haven't been at a University. They do it so well in the daily papers. What you really are is a Bunburyist. I was quite right in saying you were a Bunburyist. You are one of the most advanced Bunburyists I know.

Jack. What on earth do you mean?

Algernon. You have invented a very useful younger brother called Ernest, in order that you may be able to come up to town as often as you like. I have invented an invaluable permanent invalid called Bunbury, in order that I may be able to go down into the country whenever I choose. Bunbury is perfectly invaluable. If it wasn't for Bunbury's extraordinary bad health, for instance, I wouldn't be able to dine with you at Willis's tonight, for I have been really engaged to Aunt Augusta for more than a week.

Jack. I haven't asked you to dine with me anywhere tonight.

Algernon. I know. You are absurdly careless about sending out invitations. It is very foolish of you. Nothing annoys people so much as not receiving invitations.

Jack. You had much better dine with your Aunt Augusta.

Algernon. I haven't the smallest intention of doing anything of the kind. To begin with, I dined there on Monday, and once a week is quite enough to dine with one's own relations. In the second place, whenever I do dine there I am always treated as a member of the family, and sent down with either no woman at all, or two. In the third place, I know perfectly well whom she will place me next to, tonight. She will place me next Mary Farquhar, who always flirts with her own husband across the dinner-table. That is not very pleasant. Indeed, it is not even decent . . . and that sort of thing is enormously on the increase. The amount of women in London who flirt with their own husbands is perfectly scandalous. It looks so bad. It is simply washing one's clean linen in public. Besides, now that I know you to be a confirmed Bunburyist I naturally want to talk to you about Bunburying. I want to tell you the rules.

1. Who is Lane?

    a. a friend
    b. a coworker
    c. a servant
    d. a relative

2. Why does Algernon claim, ". . . now that I look at the inscription inside, I find that the thing isn't yours after all"?

    a. He believes that he mistakenly thought the case was Jack's.
    b. He doesn't think that Lane brought the right case.
    c. He believes that Jack stole the case from someone.
    d. He wants Jack to tell the story behind the case.

3. What is a Bunburyist?

    a. one who deceives
    b. one who travels
    c. one with two names
    d. one who smokes

4. Why does Jack feel the need to Bunbury?

    a. He can't stand the countryside.
    b. He loves his apartment in the city.
    c. He wants more fun and excitement.
    d. He wants to see Algernon more often.

5. How does Algernon's Bunbury help him get out of social engagements?

    a. Algernon pretends he already has plans with Bunbury.
    b. Algernon pretends that Bunbury's health is failing.
    c. Algernon pretends he has caught a cold from Bunbury.
    d. Algernon pretends Bunbury has dropped in unexpectedly.

6. "It is simply washing one's clean linen in public." What does Algernon mean by this statement?

    a. The couple demonstrates how happy they are together.
    b. The couple puts all of their problems out there to see.
    c. The couple talks too much about having to do laundry.
    d. The couple talks too much about business matters.

7. The tone of the overall passage is **best** described as

    a. serious.
    b. sympathetic.
    c. frivolous.
    d. joyful.

8. How does Wilde use puns to create an effect in the text? Use specific evidence from the text to support your answer.

Wilde uses puns to create humor and develop the characters' emphasis on appearances. The first example comes when Algernon comments, "You look as if your name was Ernest. You are the most earnest-looking person I ever saw in my life." As the passage is a drama meant to be heard, the audience would not be sure whether or not Algernon meant that he looked "Ernest" or "earnest." Algernon says that Jack is a most serious, sincere-looking person; however, he has been lying about his name in order to have more fun. This emphasis on appearances again comes up when Jack notes, "My dear Algy, you talk exactly as if you were a dentist. It is very vulgar to talk like a dentist when one isn't a dentist. It produces a false impression." Using a play on the word, "impression," Wilde once again creates humor and brings to light the idea of pretending to be something one is not.

9. From the given passage, would Algernon be considered a round or flat character? Use specific evidence from the text to support your answer.

Algernon is developed as a flat character. The audience only sees the irresponsible and trivial side of the character. He prompts Jack to give him a reward for finding his cigarette case, remarking that he is "more than usually hard up" for money. He also has created a fictitious friend to get out of any engagement that he does not want to fulfill and invites himself to go out with Jack. While he seems to lack responsibility in social situations, he also desires to revel in only those things scandalous. He sees couples that only flirt with each other as indecent and comments, "More than half of modern culture depends on what one shouldn't read." Algernon's flat character is important in the development of the story as Wilde satirizes the superficiality of the people of his time.

197

10. Wilde wrote *The Importance of Being Earnest* during the Victorian Era. Judging from Wilde's satire of the time, what can you determine about his opinion of the people in that time period?

One possible answer:

Wilde believes the people of his time to be hypocritical beings obsessed with proper decorum. Both characters use deception to get out of social expectations: Jack wants some freedom from being Cecily's guardian, and Algernon wants to be able to come and go as he pleases. However, Jack comments that Algernon would not understand his reasons because Algernon is "hardly serious enough." Even though Jack and Algernon are essentially doing the same thing, Jack feels that he is more noble. Wilde also addresses the idea of proper decorum; Jack states, "I don't propose to discuss modern culture. It isn't the sort of thing one should talk of in private." Later Algernon remarks, "You are absurdly careless about sending out invitations. It is very foolish of you. Nothing annoys people so much as not receiving invitations." Wilde presents the people of his time as people who create such social rules and then find ways to get around them. Oscar Wilde recognized that the most important thing of the time was creating a façade of sincerity and social responsibility in which to hide all indiscretions.

Question 1	Analyzing Character
Question 2	Drawing Conclusions
Question 3	Drawing Conclusions
Question 4	Drawing Conclusions
Question 5	Making Inferences
Question 6	Making Inferences/ Analyzing Figurative Language
Question 7	Analyzing Development of Tone and Mood
Question 8	Analyzing Pun
Question 9	Analyzing Character
Question 10	Examining Cultures and Historical Periods in Literature

198

A WAGNER MATINEE

by Willa Cather

I received one morning a letter, written in pale ink on glassy, blue-lined notepaper, and bearing the postmark of a little Nebraska village. This communication, worn and rubbed, looking as though it had been carried for some days in a coat pocket that was none too clean, was from my Uncle Howard and informed me that his wife had been left a small legacy by a bachelor relative who had recently died, and that it would be necessary for her to go to Boston to attend to the settling of the estate. He requested me to meet her at the station and render her whatever services might be necessary. On examining the date indicated as that of her arrival I found it no later than tomorrow. He had characteristically delayed writing until, had I been away from home for a day, I must have missed the good woman altogether.

The name of my Aunt Georgiana called up not alone her own figure, at once pathetic and grotesque, but opened before my feet a gulf of recollection so wide and deep that, as the letter dropped from my hand, I felt suddenly a stranger to all the present conditions of my existence, wholly ill at ease and out of place amid the familiar surroundings of my study. I became, in short, the gangling farm boy my aunt had known, scourged with chilblains and bashfulness, my hands cracked and sore from the corn husking. I felt the knuckles of my thumb tentatively, as though they were raw again. I sat again before her parlor organ, fumbling the scales with my stiff, red hands, while she, beside me, made canvas mittens for the huskers.

The next morning, after preparing my landlady somewhat, I set out for the station. When the train arrived I had some difficulty in finding my aunt. She was the last of the passengers to alight, and it was not until I got her into the carriage that she seemed really to recognize me. She had come all the way in a day coach; her linen duster had become black with soot, and her black bonnet gray with dust, during the journey. When we arrived at my boardinghouse the landlady put her to bed at once and I did not see her again until the next morning.

Whatever shock Mrs. Springer experienced at my aunt's appearance she considerately concealed. As for myself, I saw my aunt's misshapen figure with that feeling of awe and respect with which we behold explorers who have left their ears and fingers north of Franz Josef Land, or their health somewhere along the Upper Congo. My Aunt Georgiana had been a music teacher at the Boston Conservatory, somewhere back in the latter sixties. One summer, while visiting in the little village among the Green Mountains where her ancestors had dwelt for generations, she had kindled the callow fancy of the most idle and shiftless of all the village lads, and had conceived for this Howard Carpenter one of those extravagant passions which a handsome country boy of twenty-one sometimes inspires in an angular, spectacled woman of thirty. When she returned to her duties in Boston, Howard followed her, and the upshot of this inexplicable infatuation was that she eloped with him, eluding the reproaches of her family and the criticisms of her friends by going with him to the Nebraska frontier. Carpenter, who, of course, had no money, had taken a homestead in Red Willow County, fifty miles from the railroad. There they had measured off their quarter section themselves by driving across the prairie in a wagon, to the wheel of which they had tied a red cotton handkerchief, and counting off its revolutions. They built a dugout in the red hillside, one of those cave dwellings whose inmates so often reverted to primitive conditions. Their water they

199

got from the lagoons where the buffalo drank, and their slender stock of provisions was always at the mercy of bands of roving Indians. For thirty years my aunt had not been further than fifty miles from the homestead.

But Mrs. Springer knew nothing of all this, and must have been considerably shocked at what was left of my kinswoman. Beneath the soiled linen duster which, on her arrival, was the most conspicuous feature of her costume, she wore a black stuff dress, whose ornamentation showed that she had surrendered herself unquestioningly into the hands of a country dressmaker. My poor aunt's figure, however, would have presented astonishing difficulties to any dressmaker. Originally stooped, her shoulders were now almost bent together over her sunken chest. She wore no stays, and her gown, which trailed unevenly behind, rose in a sort of peak over her abdomen. She wore ill-fitting false teeth, and her skin was as yellow as a Mongolian's from constant exposure to a pitiless wind and to the alkaline water which hardens the most transparent cuticle into a sort of flexible leather.

I owed to this woman most of the good that ever came my way in my boyhood, and had a reverential affection for her. During the years when I was riding herd for my uncle, my aunt, after cooking the three meals—the first of which was ready at six o'clock in the morning—and putting the six children to bed, would often stand until midnight at her ironing board, with me at the kitchen table beside her, hearing me recite Latin declensions and conjugations, gently shaking me when my drowsy head sank down over a page of irregular verbs. It was to her, at her ironing or mending, that I read my first Shakespeare, and her old textbook on mythology was the first that ever came into my empty hands. She taught me my scales and exercises, too—on

the little parlor organ, which her husband had bought her after fifteen years, during which she had not so much as seen any instrument, but an accordion that belonged to one of the Norwegian farmhands. She would sit beside me by the hour, darning and counting while I struggled with the "Joyous Farmer," but she seldom talked to me about music, and I understood why. She was a pious woman; she had the consolations of religion and, to her at least, her martyrdom was not wholly sordid. Once when I had been doggedly beating out some easy passages from an old score of *Euryanthe* I had found among her music books, she came up to me and, putting her hands over my eyes, gently drew my head back upon her shoulder, saying tremulously, "Don't love it so well, Clark, or it may be taken from you. Oh, dear boy, pray that whatever your sacrifice may be, it be not that."

When my aunt appeared on the morning after her arrival she was still in a semi-somnambulant state. She seemed not to realize that she was in the city where she had spent her youth, the place longed for hungrily half a lifetime. She had been so wretchedly train-sick throughout the journey that she had no recollection of anything but her discomfort, and, to all intents and purposes, there were but a few hours of nightmare between the farm in Red Willow County and my study on Newbury Street. I had planned a little pleasure for her that afternoon, to repay her for some of the glorious moments she had given me when we used to milk together in the straw-thatched cowshed and she, because I was more than usually tired, or because her husband had spoken sharply to me, would tell me of the splendid performance of the *Huguenots* she had seen in Paris, in her youth. At two o'clock the Symphony Orchestra was to give a Wagner program, and I intended to take my aunt; though, as I conversed with her I grew doubtful about her enjoyment of it. Indeed, for her own sake, I could only wish her taste for such things quite dead, and the long struggle mercifully ended at last. I suggested our visiting the Conservatory and the Common before lunch, but she seemed altogether too timid to wish to venture out. She questioned me absently about various changes in the city, but she was chiefly concerned that she had forgotten to leave instructions about feeding half-skimmed milk to a certain weakling calf, "old Maggie's calf, you know, Clark," she explained, evidently having forgotten how long I had been away. She was further troubled because she had neglected to tell her daughter about the freshly opened kit of mackerel in the cellar, which would spoil if it were not used directly.

I asked her whether she had ever heard any of the Wagnerian operas and found that she had not, though she was perfectly familiar with their respective situations, and had once possessed the piano score of *The Flying Dutchman*. I began to think it would have been best to get her back to Red Willow County without waking her, and regretted having suggested the concert.

1. What is Willa Cather's purpose in writing "A Wagner Matinee"?

   a. **to entertain readers with a good tale**
   b. to inform readers about Wagner's music
   c. to persuade readers to live in cities
   d. to persuade readers to become farmers

2. What is the author inferring in the following sentence?

   "He had characteristically delayed writing until, had I been away from home for a day, I must have missed the good woman altogether."

   a. **The uncle was a person who often put off doing things into the future.**
   b. The uncle was an extremely tidy and punctual person.
   c. The uncle did not want the narrator to meet her aunt.
   d. The uncle did not realize how far it was to Boston.

3. Which genre of fiction is this piece?

   a. **historical**
   b. science fiction
   c. fantasy
   d. mystery

4. What effect did corn husking have on the narrator?

   a. It caused him to be a gangling boy.
   b. It helped him to play the parlor organ.
   c. **His hands became stiff, raw, and red.**
   d. It made him pursue the life of a farmer.

5. The narrator says, "The next morning, after preparing my landlady somewhat, I set out for the station." When he says "preparing my landlady somewhat," he means that

   a. he knows nothing about his aunt so can only prepare his landlady somewhat about her arrival.
   b. he doesn't think that his landlady will allow his aunt to stay with him where he lived.
   c. ***he wants his landlady to know that he will have a visitor, but he doesn't tell her all the details.***
   d. he wants to be sure that his landlady knows everything about his aunt who is coming to visit.

6. How does the author describe the narrator's reaction to his Aunt Georgiana's misshapen figure?

   a. ***To describe his reaction she uses similes about explorers who have met with disaster.***
   b. She uses metaphors about explorers who have met with disaster to describe his reaction.
   c. To describe his reaction she personifies explorers who have met with disaster.
   d. She uses the symbols of explorers who have met with disaster to describe his reaction.

7. How did Aunt Georgiana end up moving from Boston to Nebraska?

   a. She did not like living in Boston and had always wanted to move away.
   b. Her family forced her move to Nebraska in order to find a husband.
   c. She fell in love with a man who had grown up in Nebraska and who always wanted to return to his home.
   d. ***She had fallen in love with a man whom her family did not accept, so the couple avoided the criticisms by moving far away.***

8. Which of the following **best** describes Aunt Georgiana's husband when they first met?

   a. hardworking
   b. ***lazy***
   c. dishonest
   d. useful

9. What can you infer from the text in paragraph 4 about the homestead?

   a. It was very good farmland.
   b. It was very expensive.
   c. ***It was free.***
   d. It belonged to Howard's father.

10. The narrator says, "I owed to this woman most of the good that ever came my way in my boyhood, and had a reverential affection for her." This is a surprising statement because the narrator

    a. seemed to strongly dislike his aunt.
    b. had just finished describing his aunt as a wonderful person.
    c. obviously did not care for anyone who had such dirty clothes.
    d. *had just finished describing his aunt as a grotesque-looking person.*

11. It is clear from the story that Aunt Georgiana had

    a. *had profound and important effects on the narrator.*
    b. had little or no impact on the life of the narrator.
    c. made the narrator's life miserable in Nebraska.
    d. insisted that the narrator stay in Nebraska.

12. When she says the following, what does Aunt Georgiana mean?

"Don't love it so well, Clark, or it may be taken from you. Oh, dear boy, pray that whatever your sacrifice may be, it be not that."

One possible answer:

Aunt Georgiana is speaking from her own very disappointing experience. Having been a music teacher in Boston, she had to give all that up (She had no instrument for 15 years and then, after that, she had only a parlor organ) and pursue the very difficult life of a farmer in Nebraska. It is clear from this statement that she wants to try to protect Clark from experiencing a similar loss. She is also cautioning him not to love anything too much because it might be taken away, advice that could dissuade him from fully experiencing life. The second part of her statement shows that she cared very deeply about music and, of all things, feels that that sacrifice was the greatest of all the ones she had made. It is clear that she still felt the pain of giving that up a great deal.

Students should understand that this is one of the most important themes in the story. They should be able to describe how the loss of music had been devastating to Aunt Georgiana and why she hoped to protect Clark from a similar fate.

13. Describe what happens to the narrator when he first remembers his Aunt Georgiana. What does he mean by a "gulf of recollection so wide and deep . . ."?

The narrator is deeply shocked when he thinks about his aunt because remembering her brings back his past life, which was so very different from his present circumstances. The wide and deep gulf of recollection is his way of describing the power of his memories from the past, saying that they are very strong. By his recollections the narrator is transformed from a mature and self-confident adult living in Boston into a Nebraska farm boy who is both bashful and fumbling.

Students should describe the narrator's reaction when he thinks about his aunt. They be able to express an understanding that the memories had brought back feelings that he probably had not felt since he was a young farm boy in Nebraska.

14. How does the author use the description of the letter in the first paragraph to tell the reader about the uncle?

The author states that the letter was "worn and rubbed" and appeared to have been carried around for some time before it was mailed; it looked as if the pocket it was carried in was "none too clean." The latter indicates that the uncle is probably someone who has dirt on his hands or who does not keep his coat clean. This could indicate that the uncle works on a farm or does some kind of labor that involves getting dirty.

Students should discuss details from the letter to describe the character of the uncle.

15. How do you think the narrator, the nephew, feels about Howard and Georgiana's home in Nebraska? What words tell you how he feels?

One possible answer:

The narrator thinks that the Carpenter home is horrible and not really a fit place to live. He used the terms "cave dwellings", "inmates," and "primitive conditions," all of which imply that the home was unfit. He also described that they had gotten their water from the same lagoons where buffalo drank and that they had been at the mercy of bands of Indians.

Students should describe what they think the narrator feels about the homestead. They should support their ideas with words and sentences from the text.

16. Clark says that "he began to think it would have been best to get her back to Red Willow County without waking her, and regretted having suggested the concert." What would you have predicted would happen to Aunt Georgiana when Clark took her to listen to the Wagner program?

One possible answer:

Though it seemed from what Clark has said that his aunt might not enjoy or even be able to go to the concert, there was another possibility. Having longed for years for Boston and for her past life in music, the music in itself might impact her as much as thinking back to his childhood in Nebraska had impacted Clark. From the story, it seems that Aunt Georgiana still feels very deeply about music. It is possible that she would be filled with emotion and gratitude to be listening to a concert once again. It is also possible that this experience could make her deeply regret her decision to live far from Boston and could arouse the feeling in her that she did not want to return to her husband and home.

Students should make predictions and then support them with information from the story. They should base their ideas on what they have already learned about Aunt Georgiana and apply this to predicting how Aunt Georgiana will react to the concert.

Journey of the Beagle

by Charles Darwin

ST. JAGO—CAPE DE VERD ISLANDS

The scenery of St. Domingo possesses a beauty totally unexpected, from the prevalent gloomy character of the rest of the island. The village is situated at the bottom of a valley, bounded by lofty and jagged walls of stratified lava. The black rocks afford a most striking contrast with the bright green vegetation, which follows the banks of a little stream of clear water. It happened to be a grand feast-day, and the village was full of people. On our return we overtook a party of about twenty young black girls, dressed in excellent taste; their black skins and snow-white linen being set off by coloured turbans and large shawls. As soon as we approached near, they suddenly all turned round, and covering the path with their shawls, sung with great energy a wild song, beating time with their hands upon their legs. We threw them some vintems, which were received with screams of laughter, and we left them redoubling the noise of their song.

One morning the view was singularly clear; the distant mountains being projected with the sharpest outline on a heavy bank of dark blue clouds. Judging from the appearance, and from similar cases in England, I supposed that the air was saturated with moisture. The fact, however, turned out quite the contrary. The hygrometer gave a difference of 29.6 degrees, between the temperature of the air, and the point at which dew was precipitated. This difference was nearly double that which I had observed on the previous mornings. This unusual degree of atmospheric dryness was accompanied by continual flashes of lightning. Is it not an uncommon case, thus to find a remarkable degree of aerial transparency with such a state of weather?

Generally the atmosphere is hazy; and this is caused by the falling of impalpably fine dust, which was found to have slightly injured the astronomical instruments. The morning before we anchored at Porto Praya, I collected a little packet of this brown-coloured fine dust, which appeared to have been filtered from the wind by the gauze of the vane at the mast-head. Mr. Lyell has also given me four packets of dust which fell on a vessel a few hundred miles northward of these islands. Professor Ehrenberg finds that this dust consists in great part of infusoria with siliceous shields, and of the siliceous tissue of plants. In five little packets which I sent him, he has ascertained no less than sixty-seven different organic forms! The infusoria, with the exception of two marine species, are all inhabitants of fresh-water. I have found no less than fifteen different accounts of dust having fallen on vessels when far out in the Atlantic. From the direction of the wind whenever it has fallen, and from its having always fallen during those months when the harmattan is known to raise clouds of dust high into the atmosphere, we may feel sure that it all comes from Africa. It is, however, a very singular fact, that, although Professor Ehrenberg knows many species of infusoria peculiar to Africa, he finds none of these in the dust which I sent him. On the other hand, he finds in it two species which hitherto he knows as living only in South America. The dust falls in such quantities as to dirty everything on board, and to hurt people's eyes; vessels even have run on shore owing to the obscurity of the atmosphere. It has often fallen on ships when several hundred, and even more than a thousand miles from the coast of Africa, and at points sixteen hundred miles distant in a north and south direction. In some dust which was collected on a vessel three hundred miles from the

207

land, I was much surprised to find particles of stone above the thousandth of an inch square, mixed with finer matter. After this fact one need not be surprised at the diffusion of the far lighter and smaller sporules of cryptogamic plants.

The geology of this island is the most interesting part of its natural history. On entering the harbour, a perfectly horizontal white band, in the face of the sea cliff, may be seen running for some miles along the coast, and at the height of about forty-five feet above the water. Upon examination this white stratum is found to consist of calcareous matter with numerous shells embedded, most or all of which now exist on the neighbouring coast. It rests on ancient volcanic rocks, and has been covered by a stream of basalt, which must have entered the sea when the white shelly bed was lying at the bottom. It is interesting to trace the changes produced by the heat of the overlying lava, on the friable mass, which in parts has been converted into a crystalline limestone, and in other parts into a compact spotted stone Where the lime has been caught up by the scoriaceous fragments of the lower surface of the stream, it is converted into groups of beautifully radiated fibres resembling arragonite. The beds of lava rise in successive gently-sloping plains, towards the interior, whence the deluges of melted stone have originally proceeded. Within historical times, no signs of volcanic activity have, I believe, been manifested in any part of St. Jago. Even the form of a crater can but rarely be discovered on the summits of the many red cindery hills; yet the more recent streams can be distinguished on the coast, forming lines of cliffs of less height, but stretching out in advance of those belonging to an older series: the height of the cliffs thus affording a rude measure of the age of the streams.

During our stay, I observed the habits of some marine animals. A large Aplysia is very common. This sea-slug is about five inches long; and is of a dirty yellowish colour veined with purple. On each side of the lower surface, or foot, there is a broad membrane, which appears sometimes to act as a ventilator, in causing a current of water to flow over the dorsal branchiae or lungs. It feeds on the delicate sea-weeds which grow among the stones in muddy and shallow water; and I found in its stomach several small pebbles, as in the gizzard of a bird. This slug, when disturbed, emits a very fine purplish-red fluid, which stains the water for the space of a foot around. Besides this means of defense, an acrid secretion, which is spread over its body, causes a sharp, stinging sensation, similar to that produced by the Physalia, or Portuguese man-of-war.

I was much interested, on several occasions, by watching the habits of an Octopus, or cuttle-fish. Although common in the pools of water left by the retiring tide, these animals were not easily caught. By means of their long arms and suckers, they could drag their bodies into very narrow crevices; and when thus fixed, it required great force to remove them. At other times they darted tail first, with the rapidity of an arrow, from one side of the pool to the other, at the same instant discolouring the water with a dark chestnut-brown ink. These animals also escape detection by a very extraordinary, chameleon-like power of changing their colour. They appear to vary their tints according to the nature of the ground over which they pass: when in deep water, their general shade was brownish purple, but when placed on the land, or in shallow water, this dark tint changed into one of a yellowish green. The colour, examined more carefully, was a French grey, with numerous minute spots of bright yellow: the former of these varied in intensity; the latter entirely disappeared and appeared again by turns. These changes were effected in such a manner, that clouds, varying in tint between a hyacinth red and a chestnut-brown, were continually passing over the body. Any part, being subjected to a slight shock of galvanism, became almost black: a similar effect, but in a less degree, was produced by scratching the skin with a needle. These clouds, or blushes as they may be called, are said to be produced by the alternate expansion and contraction of minute vesicles containing variously coloured fluids.

This cuttle-fish displayed its chameleon-like power both during the act of swimming and whilst remaining stationary at the bottom. I was much amused by the various arts to escape detection used by one individual, which seemed fully aware that I was watching it. Remaining for a time motionless, it would then stealthily advance an inch or two, like a cat after a mouse; sometimes changing its colour: it thus proceeded, till having gained a deeper part, it darted away, leaving a dusky train of ink to hide the hole into which it had crawled.

While looking for marine animals, with my head about two feet above the rocky shore, I was more than once saluted by a jet of water, accompanied by a slight grating noise. At first I could not think what it was, but afterwards I found out that it was this cuttle-fish, which, though concealed in a hole, thus often led me to its discovery. That it possesses the power of ejecting water there is no doubt, and it appeared to me that it could certainly take good aim by directing the tube or siphon on the under side of its body. From the difficulty which these animals have in carrying their heads, they cannot crawl with ease when placed on the ground. I observed that one which I kept in the cabin was slightly phosphorescent in the dark.

1. What is the purpose of this piece?

   a. *to inform readers about the places that Darwin is visting*
   b. to entertain readers with a story about people from another culture
   c. to persuade readers to visit St. Domingo and the other islands.
   d. to explain the customs and rituals of the people of Cape De Verd.

2. What effect does Darwin say took place when he and his group threw the vintems to the girls?

   a. They were offended and ran away.
   b. *They thought it was very funny.*
   c. They were pleased and asked for more.
   d. They were offended and became angry.

3. What does Darwin infer in the second paragraph by the appearance of the clouds?

    a. He infers that the air will be quite dry based on his experience in England.

    b. Based on his experience in England he infers that the air will be full of moisture.

    c. He infers that there is a heavy bank of dark blue clouds near the mountains.

    d. He infers that the lightning he sees is the result of the very dry conditions.

4. Darwin states, "Professor Ehrenberg finds that this dust consists in great part of infusoria with siliceous shields, and of the siliceous tissue of plants." After reading paragraph three, it is possible to conclude that "infusoria" are mostly

    a. living forms that live in fresh water.

    b. fine particles of dirt and debris.

    c. caused by the motion of the ship.

    d. particles that have come from clouds.

5. What genre of nonfiction is this piece?

    a. biography

    b. letter

    c. science article

    d. criticism

6. Darwin says, "The dust falls in such quantities as to dirty everything on board, and to hurt people's eyes; vessels even have run on shore owing to the obscurity of the atmosphere. It has often fallen on ships when several hundred, and even more than a thousand miles from the coast of Africa, and at points sixteen hundred miles distant in a north and south direction." What does Darwin say is particularly unusual about the infusoria that Professor Ehrenberg found in the dust samples he received from Darwin?

    a. None of the infusoria were familiar so they must have been from South America.

    b. None of the infusoria were familiar so they must have been from Africa.

    c. All the infusoria were familiar because they had come from Africa.

    d. The infusoria were not familiar species from Africa but from South America.

7. To what cause does Darwin attribute the horizontal white band in the face of the sea cliff and why does he think this?

    a. It was probably formed by volcanic activity because of the absence of sea shells.

    b. Because it includes many seashells it had once been part of a seabed.

    c. It was created by atmospheric activity because of its height on the cliff.

    d. It was formed by the droppings of millions of sea birds that live there.

8. Darwin states, "Where the lime has been caught up by the scoriaceous fragments of the lower surface of the stream, it is converted into groups of beautifully radiated fibres resembling arragonite." This statement is

   a. a fact because he thinks that the fibers are beautiful.
   b. an opinion because he is saying that the fibers are beautiful.
   c. an opinion because he says that the fibers resemble arrogonite.
   d. an opinion because he says that the lime has been converted.

9. What is the most likely meaning of the word, "rude," in the following phrase?

   . . . the height of the cliffs thus affording a rude measure of the age of the streams.

   a. obnoxious
   b. angry
   c. not very accurate
   d. very accurate

10. Which of the following **best** describes Darwin's style of writing?

    a. informative and scientific
    b. simple and humorous
    c. complex and exciting
    d. dull and uninformative

11. What conclusion can you draw from Darwin's description of the cuttle-fish?

    a. The cuttle-fish spends all of its life submerged under the water.
    b. The cuttle-fish lives part of the time in the water and part of the time on land.
    c. The cuttle-fish does not need to spend time in the water in order to survive.
    d. The cuttle-fish stays the same color because it does not need protection.

12. Based on his writing, what generalizations can you make about Darwin's writing, research, and methods? What is the primary way that Darwin writes about the places he visits? What impact do you think he had on the animals he studied? Use examples from the text to support your ideas.

    One possible answer:

    Darwin's writing is generally descriptive; he goes into great detail about each thing that he describes. He is clearly trying to keep an accurate and thorough record of the landscape, the animals, and the plants wherever he visits. He has a scientific style of writing and uses many words—including such words as "siliceous," "cryptogamic," and "scoriaceous"—that only other scientists would probably know.

Darwin in some cases must have captured and killed some animals that he was studying. For example, he says that he discovered pebbles in the stomach of sea-slug, much as could be found in the gizzard of a bird. He must have killed the sea-slug in order to find this out. He also refers to the color of a cuttle-fish on land, which probably means he put it on land and to a cuttle-fish that he kept in his cabin on board the ship.

Students' responses to this three-part question should be thoughtful, accurate, and well supported with examples from the text.

13. Write a summary of Darwin's description of the cuttle-fish.

One possible answer:

The cuttle-fish is also called an octopus. It has long arms and suckers and can hide in tight crevices in the rock. It moves in pools of water, tail first, in a rapid motion and leaves a trail of ink behind. The cuttle-fish changes its color depending on where it is and what color is below it. The changes of color are caused by the expanding and contracting of small vesicles that contain colored fluids. Darwin observed one cuttle-fish that tried to escape detection by changing colors, moving slowly, and then darting away leaving ink behind it. Some of the cuttle-fish squirt water out into the air when they are in midst of rocks. One specimen appeared to be slightly phosphorescent in the dark.

In their own words, students should write concise and clear summaries of Darwin's description of the cuttle-fish. Look for accuracy, completeness, and clear expression.

14. What does this piece tell you about the beliefs of the author about science?

It is clear from the piece that Darwin believes in scientific observation and the importance of recording what he sees. He must feel that his observations will be useful to other scientists and to people in general. He keeps a detailed and careful record, one that most likely he plans to share with others.

Students should state what they understand about Darwin's beliefs about science and give convincing explanations for the reasoning behind them.

15. Describe how Darwin organizes his writing. Use examples from the text to support your ideas.

One possible answer:
Darwin has two basic ways of organizing his writing. First of all, he writes about a particular location. In this passage he is writing about St. Domingo and Porto Praya. When he is in a particular location, Darwin then organizes his writing around specific topics. For example, in this case he begins by describing meeting some local girls who are part of a feast day. Then he goes into a detailed description of the atmosphere and the dust that is present in the air. He moves from that topic to discussing the geology of the area, and after that he describes two types of marine animals: a sea slug and the cuttle-fish.

Students should show how Darwin organizes his writing and include several examples from the text.

214

John F. Kennedy's Inaugural Address

We observe today not a victory of party but a celebration of freedom . . . symbolizing an end as well as a beginning . . . signifying renewal as well as change for I have sworn before you and Almighty God the same solemn oath our forbears prescribed nearly a century and three-quarters ago.

The world is very different now, for man holds in his mortal hands the power to abolish all forms of human poverty and all forms of human life. And yet the same revolutionary beliefs for which our forbears fought are still at issue around the globe . . . the belief that the rights of man come not from the generosity of the state but from the hand of God. We dare not forget today that we are the heirs of that first revolution.

Let the word go forth from this time and place . . . to friend and foe alike . . . that the torch has been passed to a new generation of Americans . . . born in this century, tempered by war, disciplined by a hard and bitter peace, proud of our ancient heritage . . . and unwilling to witness or permit the slow undoing of those human rights to which this nation has always been committed, and to which we are committed today . . . at home and around the world.

Let every nation know . . . whether it wishes us well or ill . . . that we shall pay any price, bear any burden, meet any hardship, support any friend, oppose any foe, to assure the survival and the success of liberty. This much we pledge . . . and more.

To those old allies whose cultural and spiritual origins we share: we pledge the loyalty of faithful friends. United . . . there is little we cannot do in a host of co-operative ventures. Divided . . . there is little we can do . . . for we dare not meet a powerful challenge, at odds, and split asunder. To those new states whom we welcome to the ranks of the free: we pledge our word that one form of colonial control shall not have passed away merely to be replaced by a far more iron tyranny. We shall not always expect to find them supporting our view. But we shall always hope to find them strongly supporting their own freedom . . . and to remember that . . . in the past . . . those who foolishly sought power by riding the back of the tiger ended up inside. To those people in the huts and villages of half the globe struggling to break the bonds of mass misery: we pledge our best efforts to help them help themselves, for whatever period is required . . . not because the Communists may be doing it, not because we seek their votes, but because it is right. If a free society cannot help the many who are poor, it cannot save the few who are rich.

To our sister republics south of our border: we offer a special pledge . . . to convert our good words into good deeds . . . in a new alliance for progress . . . to assist free men and free governments in casting off the chains of poverty. But this peaceful revolution of hope cannot become the prey of hostile powers. Let all our neighbors know that we shall join with them to oppose aggression or subversion anywhere in the Americas . . . and let every other power know that this hemisphere intends to remain the master of its own house.

To that world assembly of sovereign states: the United Nations . . . our last best hope in an age where the instruments of war have far outpaced the instruments of peace, we renew our pledge of support . . . to prevent it from becoming merely a forum for invective . . . to strengthen its shield of the new and the weak . . . and to enlarge the area in which its writ may run.

Finally, to those nations who would make themselves our adversaries, we offer not a pledge but a request: that both sides begin anew the quest for peace; before the dark powers of destruction unleashed by science engulf all humanity in planned or accidental self-destruction. We dare not tempt them with weakness. For only when our arms are sufficient beyond doubt can we be certain beyond doubt that they will never be employed. But neither can two great and powerful groups of nations take comfort from our present course . . . both sides overburdened by the cost of modern weapons, both rightly alarmed by the steady spread of the deadly atom, yet both racing to alter that uncertain balance of terror that stays the hand of Mankind's final war.

So let us begin anew . . . remembering on both sides that civility is not a sign of weakness, and sincerity is always subject to proof. Let us never negotiate out of fear, but let us never fear to negotiate. Let both sides explore what problems unite us instead of belaboring those problems which divide us. Let both sides, for the first time, formulate serious and precise proposals for the inspection and control of arms . . . and bring the absolute power to destroy other nations under the absolute control of all nations. Let both sides seek to invoke the wonders of science instead of its terrors. Together let us explore the stars, conquer the deserts, eradicate disease, tap the ocean depths, and encourage the arts and commerce. Let both sides unite to heed in all corners of the earth the command of Isaiah . . . to "undo the heavy burdens . . . let the oppressed go free."

And if a beachhead of co-operation may push back the jungle of suspicion . . . let both sides join in creating not a new balance of power . . . but a new world of law . . . where the strong are just . . . and the weak secure . . . and the peace preserved. . . . All this will not be finished in the first one hundred days. Nor will it be finished in the first one thousand days . . . nor in the life of this administration, nor even perhaps in our lifetime on this planet. But let us begin.

In your hands, my fellow citizens . . . more than mine . . . will rest the final success or failure of our course. Since this country was founded, each generation of Americans has been summoned to give testimony to its national loyalty. The graves of young Americans who answered the call to service surround the globe. Now the trumpet summons us again . . . not as a call to bear arms, though arms we need . . . not as a call to battle . . . though embattled we are . . . but a call to bear the burden of a long twilight struggle . . . year in and year out, rejoicing in hope, patient in tribulation . . . a struggle against the common enemies of man: tyranny . . . poverty . . . disease . . . and war itself. Can we forge against these enemies a grand and global alliance . . . North and South . . . East and West . . . that can assure a more fruitful life for all mankind? Will you join in that historic effort?

In the long history of the world, only a few generations have been granted the role of defending freedom in its hour of maximum danger; I do not shrink from this responsibility . . . I welcome it. I do not believe that any of us would exchange places with any other people or any other generation. The energy, the faith, the devotion which we bring to this endeavor will light our country and all who serve it . . . and the glow from that fire can truly light the world.

And so, my fellow Americans . . . ask not what your country can do for you . . . ask what you can do for your country. My fellow citizens of the world . . . ask not what America will do for you, but what together we can do for the Freedom of Man.

Finally, whether you are citizens of America or citizens of the world, ask of us here the same high standards of strength and sacrifice which we ask of you. With a good conscience our only sure reward, with history the final judge of our deeds; let us go forth to lead the land we love, asking His blessing and His help, but knowing that here on earth God's work must truly be our own.

1. Who is the speaker's audience?

   a. *people throughout the world*
   b. only people in the United States of America
   c. only people in communist countries
   d. the Senate and House of Representatives

2. Why does the speaker use the phrase, "We observe today not a victory of party but a celebration of freedom"?

   a. to downplay the role of elections
   b. *to unite the winners and losers*
   c. to rub in the speaker's victory
   d. to deride those who are not free

3. In paragraphs 1 and 2, which of the following are **not** appeals to tradition?

   a. The speaker gives the same oath that the forbearers prescribed.
   b. The speaker and his audience are the heirs of the revolution.
   c. Their revolutionary beliefs are still being tested around the world.
   d. *The revolution must be defended at any and all cost.*

4. In paragraphs 1 and 2, what does the speaker say is different about his time period from the time of his forbears?

   a. the revolution
   b. *the power to aid or destroy humanity*
   c. the ideals of man
   d. the growth of communist systems

5. To ensure liberty throughout the world, the speaker says that his country will do all of the following **except**

   a. make sacrifices.
   b. take responsibility.
   c. *defend any enemy*.
   d. endure hardships.

6. What is the speaker saying in paragraph 5?

   a. *It is right to help people in need to help themselves.*
   b. One who tries to ride a tiger will fall off its back.
   c. Colonial control is often replaced by tyranny.
   d. He expects unconditional support from his allies.

7. In paragraph 7, what does the speaker say about the United Nations?

   a. It should be systematically dismantled and forgotten.
   b. *It is the world's final hope in a dangerous world.*
   c. Its power should be maintained, though restructured.
   d. It should work to ban all nuclear activity in the world.

8. In paragraph 8, what does the word, "adversaries," mean?

   a. friends
   b. *enemies*
   c. challenges
   d. acquaintances

9. In paragraph 8, what is the meaning of the phrase, "deadly atom"?

   a. nuclear power
   b. atomic engines
   c. *nuclear weapons*
   d. the space race

10. Which of the following effects of amassing nuclear weaponry does the speaker **not** staate in paragraph 8?

    a. enormous cost
    b. threat to humans
    c. *certain destruction*
    d. weapons stockpiles

11. Which of the following is a fact?

    a. To assure . . . the success of liberty, " . . . we shall pay any price, bear any burden . . . "
    b. *"Each generation of Americans" will have to serve . . .*
    c. "If a free society cannot help the many who are poor it cannot save . . . the rich.
    d. Those who have tried to abuse power have ". . . ended up inside" the tiger.

12. In paragraph 9, what is the speaker's purpose?

    a. *to call on all nations to join to make a better world*
    b. to describe the world situation during his time period
    c. to point out what is right and what is wrong
    d. to persuade his enemies that a free world is inevitable

13. In paragraph 10, what does the speaker say about his policies?

    a. They will be carried out during his first one hundred days.
    b. They will be carried out by the end of his first term in office.
    c. They will be implemented by the coming generations.
    d. They may never be completed, but they must be begun.

14. What is the purpose of the first sentence in paragraph 12?

    a. to underscore the importance of the endeavor and to show the speaker's conviction
    b. to define the responsibilities of a generation and to prepare them for their challenges
    c. to respond to criticism from conservatives who believe in policies of isolation
    d. to show how freedom spreads from place to place like a light warming a room

15. The tone of this speech is

    a. light and comical.
    b. angry, yet troubled.
    c. urgent and scientific.
    d. confident and firm.

16. Describe some of the many "audiences" this speaker addresses. Note how he communicates with each.

Because the speaker believes the whole world is his audience, John Fitzgerald Kennedy takes time to address people in the United States and people in other nations around the world, friendly and hostile countries, countries in the eastern and western hemispheres, as well as the rich and the poor. He uses the word, "to," so that each respective audience will know he is directly acknowledging them. Kennedy also reviews the issues of the day as seen by different cultures and countries and, in doing so, acknowledges how others see the world. He both confronts and challenges these viewpoints and offers his own way of seeking peace and prosperity in the world.

17. An inaugural address is a launching point for four years of service. What did this president hope to accomplish with this speech in 1961 and how did he attempt to set other goals for his administration?

The inaugural address is a new president's first formal policy statement to the nation and the world at large. It is delivered immediately after taking the oath of office. In his speech, Kennedy outlined a broad set of policies, first to show that he had a grand vision for his presidency, and second to indicate some of the issues he would be addressing during his time as president. In speaking about these things, the president challenged both his critics and his administration to attempt to solve some of the most vexing stalemated problems of that time.

18. How does the speaker try to persuade his audience that his country's ideals are right while others are wrong?

The speaker divides the world into two categories: those people who are free and those who are not. He says that his side is just, caring, and rational, while those who oppose him are not. He also argues that his side has been empowered by God because God has created us all free. He advances the correctness of the traditions he will uphold and asserts the moral high ground by promising not to replace tyranny with a different form of tyranny. Kennedy's call for a moral society also rebuked those who had wanted the United States to control the world after World War II, without regard to right or wrong.

19. What paragraphs constitute the introduction, body, and conclusion respectively? What is the function of each of these parts?

One possible answer:

The introduction comes in paragraphs 1–4 where the speaker gives his analysis of the times and throws out a direct challenge to the world at large. The body of the essay, paragraphs 5–10, is where the speaker addresses his audience and analyzes his country's foreign policy. In a time of cold war paralysis, he asks for change, a daring political move. He could have been accused of being weak or of giving his enemies an opening to exploit. In the conclusion, paragraphs 11–13, the speaker addresses the people in the U.S., informing them about their responsibilities. He pinpoints the end results his policies will achieve. His final challenge of what Americans can do for their country signals a fresh approach to traditional problems.

20. How is your world different from the one represented in the speech?

Students should discuss the downfall of the Soviet Union and the end of the Cold War. They could talk about instability in the Middle East and the threat of terrorism. They should also note how many issues not only have not changed but have actually gotten worse. The plight of the world's poor and the destruction of the planet are two examples. Kennedy's United States had just emerged from two punishing world wars and was ready to apply fresh energy to remake the power struggles of old. Students could also mention the health threat of AIDS and the continued threat of nuclear powers in secondary nations. Science's role in the arms race has now turned more to stem cell research and technological advancement.

Question 1	Analyzing the Author's Purpose
Question 2	Evaluating Author's Style
Question 3	Analyzing Persuasion and Propaganda Techniques
Question 4	Comparing and Contrasting
Question 5	Analyzing Predictions
Question 6	Evaluating Author's Style
Question 7	Summarizing and Paraphrasing Information
Question 8	Analyzing Diction: Denotation
Question 9	Analyzing Diction: Connotation
Question 10	Analyzing Cause and Effect
Question 11	Distinguishing Fact and Opinion
Question 12	Making Generalizations
Question 13	Analyzing Point of View
Question 14	Interpreting the Theme and Main Idea
Question 15	Analyzing Development of Tone and Mood
Question 16	Evaluating Author's Craft
Question 17	Drawing Conclusions
Question 18	Making Inferences
Question 19	Analyzing Text Structure and Organization
Question 20	Using Prior Knowledge

"SPLENDOR FALLS" FROM *THE PRINCESS*

by Alfred, Lord Tennyson

The splendor falls on castle walls   1
    And snowy summits old in story;
The long light shakes across the lakes,
    And the wild cataract leaps in glory.
Blow, bugle, blow, set the wild echoes flying,   5
Blow, bugle; answer, echoes, dying. dying, dying.

    O, hark, O, hear! how thin and clear,
    And thinner, clearer, farther going!
O, sweet and far from cliff and scar
    The horns of Elfland faintly blowing!   10
Blow, let us hear the purple glens replying,
Blow, bugle; answer, echoes, dying, dying, dying.

    O love, they die in yon rich sky,
    They faint on hill or field or river;
Our echoes roll from soul to soul,   15
    And grow for ever and for ever.
Blow, bugle, blow, set the wild echoes flying,
And answer, echoes, answer, dying, dying, dying.

1. What is the setting of this poem?

    a. a dark cavern
    b. a city center
    c. a mountainside
    d. a rocky shoreline

2. With whom is speaker of this poem communicating?

    a. his deceased father
    b. a loved one
    c. his belief in God
    d. people in the valley

3. What is the meter of the poem?

    a. seven syllable lines, iambic
    b. eight syllable lines, iambic
    c. eight syllable lines, trochee
    d. nine syllable lines, trochee

4. What is the effect of the repetition at the end of each stanza?

   a. ***It imitates the dying of the echoes.***
   b. It accentuates death through duplication.
   c. It reminds the reader that sounds fade.
   d. It underscores the dangers of mountain climbing.

5. In line 4, what is the meaning of the word, "cataract"?

   a. ***lofty waterfall***
   b. herd of deer
   c. young man
   d. eye problem

6. The first stanza utilizes all of the following literary devices **except**

   a. internal rhyme.
   b. ***understatement.***
   c. personification.
   d. repetition.

7. What is the genre of this poem?

   a. epic poetry
   b. narrative poetry
   c. ***lyrical poetry***
   d. limerick poetry

8. All of the following are personified in the poem **except**

   a. "light" (line 3).
   b. "cataract" (line 4).
   c. "glens" (line 11).
   d. ***"walls" (line 1).***

9. What is the meaning of lines 15 and 16?

   a. The echoes of bugles pass from ear to ear.
   b. The echoes return to the sender and die.
   c. ***Human legacies never die.***
   d. He commands the bugles to keep blowing.

10. What is the tone of the passage? What words in this passage help to establish the tone? How does it contribute to the overall mood conveyed to the reader?

One possible answer:

Words like "glory," "sweet," "Elfland," and "flying" give the poem a grandiose and magical tone, which serves as a contrast to the somber mortality of words like "die" and "dying." The poet paints a rich portrait of an old castle nestled in snowbound mountains. The reader can easily sense and imagine the mysteries that lurk within this setting. The idea of long rolling sounds through deep purple valleys adds an air of wonderment and hidden epic tales. The description of that dying call makes a reader ponder if it is a love cry or one of doom and destruction, a death knell perhaps to a lost era or lost love. The words, "for ever" and "soul to soul," also suggest a timelessness that matches the stately mountains and ancient civilizations lost to ruins.

11. What is the style of this poem and when do you think it was written? Why?

The poem has a Romantic feeling to it because it deals with the nature of mortality as seen in nature. This would suggest that it is either from the Romantic or Victorian era, which seems fitting because the poem also has a set rhyme scheme and strict meter, characteristic of these eras. It avoids realism or any epic storytelling, which would also place it in another era and another style of poetry.

12. What are the two types of echoes that are compared in this passage? How does the structure of the poem mirror the poet's emphasis on these images?

This poem compares the echoes made by sound waves to the figurative echoes made by the human souls. The repeating chorus at the end of each stanza calls out like sounds echoing and fading. This matches the calls of "O," in lines 7, 9, and 13. This cry could be the lost plea of human souls or the poet replying. Even the body of the poem is offset like the lyrics to a song or chant. The sounds described by the poet function as both songs and cries hidden in the lonesome wail of a bugle.

13. Paraphrase lines 13–16. Explain your reasoning for paraphrasing it the way you did.

One possible answer:
The bugle's echoes die, but the echoes made by humanity will never die. These echoes could have many interpretations. The legacy an individual leaves carries on like an echo of that person's existence into the generations after death. An echo of a life would also be seen as the effect someone would have on others who live on. The poet may also be specifically referring to a lost love and to the repercussions of that loss. The afterlife, the unknown of death, has long been seen as a bridge to life and the poet is toying with the connection between the two through the concept of the sounds of life rolling from soul to soul.

14. How does the alliteration of "b-" and "d-" and "-ing" sounds affect the reader in the last two lines of most stanzas?

The alliteration of "b-" in "blow" and "bugle" provides a trumpeting sound to reinforce the imagery. "B-" is an explosive, forceful expression, while "d-" is a quiet, grieving, suppressing sound. The repeat of "-ing" gives a sense of the sound carrying onward in an active motion. This propels the reader to the next stanza and gives the poem a rolling, continuous, carrying-on feel. This matches the imagery as well and mimics a song-like chant.

Question 1   Analyzing Conflict, Plot, and Setting
Question 2   Drawing Conclusions
Question 3   Analyzing Sound Devices and Rhythm
Question 4   Evaluating Author's Craft
Question 5   Analyzing Diction: Connotation and Denotation
Question 6   Evaluating Author's Style
Question 7   Distinguishing Among Different Genres of Fiction
Question 8   Analyzing Figurative Language
Question 9   Making Inferences
Question 10   Analyzing Development of Tone and Mood
Question 11   Distinguishing Among Different Genres of Poetry
Question 12   Comparing and Contrasting
Question 13   Summarizing and Paraphrasing Information
Question 14   Examining Literature from Several Critical Perspectives

THE STORY OF AN HOUR

by Kate Chopin

Knowing that Mrs. Mallard was afflicted with a heart trouble, great care was taken to break to her as gently as possible the news of her husband's death.

It was her sister Josephine who told her, in broken sentences; veiled hints that revealed in half concealing. Her husband's friend Richards was there, too, near her. It was he who had been in the newspaper office when intelligence of the railroad disaster was received, with Brently Mallard's name leading the list of "killed." He had only taken the time to assure himself of its truth by a second telegram, and had hastened to forestall any less careful, less tender friend in bearing the sad message.

She did not hear the story as many women have heard the same, with a paralyzed inability to accept its significance. She wept at once, with sudden, wild abandonment, in her sister's arms. When the storm of grief had spent itself she went away to her room alone. She would have no one follow her.

There stood, facing the open window, a comfortable, roomy armchair. Into this she sank, pressed down by a physical exhaustion that haunted her body and seemed to reach into her soul.

She could see in the open square before her house the tops of trees that were all aquiver with the new spring life. The delicious breath of rain was in the air. In the street below a peddler was crying his wares. The notes of a distant song which some one was singing reached her faintly, and countless sparrows were twittering in the eaves.

There were patches of blue sky showing here and there through the clouds that had met and piled one above the other in the west facing her window.

She sat with her head thrown back upon the cushion of the chair, quite motionless, except when a sob came up into her throat and shook her, as a child who has cried itself to sleep continues to sob in its dreams.

She was young, with a fair, calm face, whose lines bespoke repression and even a certain strength. But now there was a dull stare in her eyes, whose gaze was fixed away off yonder on one of those patches of blue sky. It was not a glance of reflection, but rather indicated a suspension of intelligent thought.

There was something coming to her and she was waiting for it, fearfully. What was it? She did not know; it was too subtle and elusive to name. But she felt it, creeping out of the sky, reaching toward her through the sounds, the scents, the color that filled the air.

Now her bosom rose and fell tumultuously. She was beginning to recognize this thing that was approaching to possess her, and she was striving to beat it back with her will—as powerless as her two white slender hands would have been.

When she abandoned herself a little whispered word escaped her slightly parted lips. She said it over and over under her breath: "free, free, free!" The vacant stare and the look of terror that had followed it went from her eyes. They stayed keen and bright. Her pulses beat fast, and the coursing blood warmed and relaxed every inch of her body.

She did not stop to ask if it were or were not a monstrous joy that held her. A clear and exalted perception enabled her to dismiss the suggestion as trivial.

She knew that she would weep again when she saw the kind, tender hands folded in death; the face that had never looked save with love upon her, fixed and gray and dead. But she saw beyond that bitter moment a long procession of years to come that would belong to her absolutely. And she opened and spread her arms out to them in welcome. There would be no one to live for during those coming years; she would live for herself. There would be no powerful will bending hers in that blind persistence with which men and women believe they have a right to impose a private will upon a fellow-creature. A kind intention or a cruel intention made the act seem no less a crime as she looked upon it in that brief moment of illumination.

And yet she had loved him—sometimes. Often she had not. What did it matter! What could love, the unsolved mystery, count for in face of this possession of self-assertion which she suddenly recognized as the strongest impulse of her being!

"Free! Body and soul free!" she kept whispering.

Josephine was kneeling before the closed door with her lips to the keyhole, imploring for admission. "Louise, open the door! I beg, open the door—you will make yourself ill. What are you doing Louise? For heaven's sake open the door."

"Go away. I am not making myself ill." No; she was drinking in a very elixir of life through that open window. Her fancy was running riot along those days ahead of her. Spring days, and summer days, and all sorts of days that would be her own. She breathed a quick prayer that life might be long. It was only yesterday she had thought with a shudder that life might be long.

She arose at length and opened the door to her sister's importunities. There was a feverish triumph in her eyes, and she carried herself unwittingly like a goddess of Victory. She clasped her sister's waist, and together they descended the stairs. Richards stood waiting for them at the bottom.

Some one was opening the front door with a latchkey. It was Brently Mallard who entered, a little travel-stained, composedly carrying his grip-sack and umbrella. He had been far from the scene of accident, and did not even know there had been one. He stood amazed at Josephine's piercing cry; at Richards' quick motion to screen him from the view of his wife.

But Richards was too late.

When the doctors came they said she had died of heart disease — of joy that kills.

1. Where does this story take place?

    a. St. Louis
    b. *Mrs. Mallard's home*
    c. Richard's office
    d. Josephine's home

2. Upon hearing that her husband has died in paragraph 3, in what way does the author say that Mrs. Mallard reacts differently than most women would have?

    a. She denies the fact of her husband's passing.
    b. *All at once, she weeps uncontrollably.*
    c. She blames her husband for the accident.
    d. She is skeptical of her husband's passing.

3. What is the story's point of view?

   a. first person
   b. second person
   c. **_third person limited_**
   d. third person omniscient

4. Why is so much care given in telling Mrs. Mallard about the accident?

   a. Mrs. Mallard is very aggressive.
   b. **_Mrs. Mallard has a heart condition._**
   c. Mrs. Mallard is away from her support group.
   d. Mrs. Mallard has already predicted this event.

5. What do the subjects described in paragraph 5 symbolize?

   a. **_beauty, life, renewal_**
   b. birds, peddler, nature
   c. death, failure, phobia
   d. love, sleep, warmth

6. In paragraph 8, what word victimizes Mrs. Mallard?

   a. **_"repression"_**
   b. "dull"
   c. "suspension"
   d. "intelligent"

7. What is the tone of paragraph 9?

   a. sorrowful and pathetic
   b. curious and mischievous
   c. **_fearful, yet anticipatory_**
   d. giddy and expectant

8. An "epiphany" is a moment of realization, understanding, or insight. In what paragraph does Mrs. Mallard experience her epiphany?

   a. 2
   b. **_11_**
   c. 14
   d. 16

9. In paragraph 14, what does the author says is Mrs. Mallard's strongest impulse?

   a. love
   b. **_self-assertion_**
   c. mystery
   d. indifference

10. All of the following happen in paragraph 17 **except**

   a. Mrs. Mallard permits her sister's entrance.
   b. Mrs. Mallard opens a window.
   c. Mrs. Mallard dreams of the days ahead of her.
   d. Mrs. Mallard prays that she might live a long life.

11. Mrs. Mallard is to independence as

   a. water is to evaporation.
   b. freedom is to prisoner.
   c. a patient is to sickness.
   d. an insomniac is to sleep.

12. Among other places, in what type of anthology would this story most likely appear?

   a. science fiction
   b. speculative fiction
   c. persuasive nonfiction
   d. feminist fiction

13. In paragraph 18, what is the meaning of the word, "importunities"?

   a. pleadings
   b. imports
   c. insults
   d. criticisms

14. What can the reader infer about Mr. and Mrs. Mallard's relationship? What evidence from the passage reveals both past problems and issues they might have in the future if they stay together?

Though the author indicates that Mrs. Mallard loved her husband (sometimes), she gives the impression that Mrs. Mallard is largely unhappy in her marriage. In describing her, the author writes that in her appearance there is evidence of "repression" (par. 8). Her husband has obviously tried to control her life (par. 13), the effect being that Mrs. Mallard feels like less of a person. Yet she obviously feels that there was some love in the marriage, even if this is her fantasy in grief (par. 13) when she thinks ahead to his funeral and "the face that had never looked save with love upon her". In paragraph 14, she notes, "And yet she had loved him—sometimes." Clearly, theirs was a marriage that mostly likely would have endured with some love and they would have remained rather distant toward one another into their old age.

231

15. **What is the cause of Mrs. Mallard's death?**

One possible answer:

Mrs. Mallard dies from the shock of seeing her husband walk through the door. We can infer that, upon seeing her husband, Mrs. Mallard is devastated because her hopes for the future have been dashed. The author also mentions a heart condition which may have been a convenient excuse for her sudden attack. The cause, however, could be as much shock in seeing a dead man walk in as dread in having this burden return. Nor can simple surprise be discounted.

16. **What is ironic about the ending and which kind of irony does it represent?**

One possible answer:

Mr. Mallard's entrance at the close of the story is an example of situational irony because the reader thinks this person is dead. The perception by the other characters that Mrs. Mallard has died of joy is dramatic irony because we as readers are aware that she has been made unhappy by the entrance of her husband. It could be argued that the fact that Mrs. Mallard prays for a long life, but dies shortly after is an example of situational irony. It could also have been merely a coincidence that the two events happened so closely in time. The act of Mrs. Mallard praying does not prove that she herself believes that she will live a long life. If Mrs. Mallard had believed that she would live a long life, then this situation would have been ironic.

17. Feminist critics analyze literature from different time periods looking at how political, social, and cultural elements influence how a female character perceives herself and how she is perceived by others. Why might this work appeal to feminist critics?

This literature has been analyzed by feminist critics who have noted that Mrs. Mallard felt powerless due to her relationship with her husband. Their relationship is obviously more complex than simply domination by the husband. She had stayed with her husband for hidden reasons, and so her friends seem unaware of her disaffection. Their problems could not have been obvious. This repression of her dissatisfaction could be cited by feminists as one of her husband's many powers over her—that it may have increased her shock through dread in seeing her torturer alive after she thinks she has escaped his abuse. Still, his presumed death seems to allow her to analyze her station in life and, in doing so, she seems well aware of the limitations of her marriage, proving her to hardly be a cowed victim.

"OLD IRONSIDES"

by Oliver Wendell Holmes

AY, tear her tattered ensign down   1
Long has it waved on high,
And many an eye has danced to see
That banner in the sky;
Beneath it rung the battle shout,   5
And burst the cannon's roar;—
The meteor of the ocean air
Shall sweep the clouds no more.

Her deck, once red with heroes' blood,
Where knelt the vanquished foe,   10
When winds were hurrying o'er the flood,
And waves were white below,
No more shall feel the victor's tread,
Or know the conquered knee;—
The harpies of the shore shall pluck   15
The eagle of the sea!

Oh better that her shattered hulk
Should sink beneath the wave;
Her thunders shook the mighty deep,
And there should be her grave;   20
Nail to the mast her holy flag,
Set every threadbare sail,
And give her to the god of storms,
The lightning and the gale!

1. What is the subject of this poem?

   a. a woman
   b. a ship
   c. a harpy
   d. a flag

2. What is the poem's meter?

   a. 7–5 iambic
   b. 7–6 trochaic
   c. 8–6 iambic
   d. 9–6 trochaic

3. In line 1, why is the word, "AY," capitalized?

    a. It is a negative denunciation of "No!"
    b. It is a positive cry of "Yes!"
    c. It is a friendly introduction of "Hello!"
    d. It is a annoyed admission of "I am speaking to you!"

4. Which line uses figurative language?

    a. Line 2
    b. Line 3
    c. Line 10
    d. Line 9

5. In the context of line 7, what is the meaning of the word, "meteor"?

    a. fast passage
    b. cold stone
    c. smoking cannonball
    d. extraterrestrial object

6. In line 10, what is the meaning of the word, "vanquished"?

    a. victorious
    b. drowned
    c. defeated
    d. heroic

7. Line 12 uses which sound device?

    a. alliteration
    b. assonance
    c. consonance
    d. onomatopoeia

8. With what does the speaker compare the subject?

    a. an eagle
    b. a whale
    c. a storm
    d. a harpy

9. What does the speaker argue in stanza 3?

    a. Tear the ensign down because it is too old.
    b. The harpies of the shore will tear it apart.
    c. It would be better if the ship sunk into the ocean.
    d. The ship should be completely burnt to the ground.

10. What is the genre of this poem?

    a. epic
    b. *lyrical*
    c. discursive
    d. elegiac

11. Which of the following is an oxymoron?

    a. "tattered ensign" (line 1)
    b. "battle shout" (line 5)
    c. *"shattered hulk" (line 17)*
    d. "thunders shook" (line 19)

12. What effect does the meter have on the last word in every line? How does the poet use rhyme and meter to advance the cause the poem triumphs?

Meter stresses the word, accentuating the rhyme and the word choice. The poem takes on a singsong quality, which matches its purpose as a chant calling for the preservation of this old grand ship. The song recalls its glory, and the neat, ordered rhythms of the meter turn that history into a chant of lore – almost as if it were a tribute repeated by generation after generation to honor this tradition.

13. What kinds of struggles has the ship had to endure? How does the poet use this past to honor the ship?

The ship has endured storms, time, and conflict. The poet's call for preserving the ship evokes its long and varied history and reminds the readers (as well as the authorities) that this ship has seen too much history to merely be cast aside as a wreck that needs replacing. The poet even mockingly notes that it would be better for this historic ship to be sunk in battle than to be neglected by those who won't preserve it.

14. In line 15, who are the "harpies" of the land? How does the poet display his attitude towards these harpies?

The "harpies" are people who do not wish to preserve the ship as a historical monument. The poet suggests that these people are tearing the ship apart. This adds further meaning to the metaphor and evokes comparison to the harpies of myth, who were giant birds that tore apart human prey. The term has since come to mean anyone who pecks or attacks continuously (to harp on a subject, for example) and the poet uses this sense to belittle anyone who fails to preserve the ship he loves.

15. What is the tone of the poem? What kinds of words help to establish it?

The tone of the poem is part heroic with words like "long," "rung," "shout," "heroes," and "cannon." Contrastingly the author uses words like "tear," "tattered," "harpies," and "pluck" to show the lack of regard some people have for the ship. A holier-than-thou tone also helps to place the poet's call for preservation on a higher plane than any practical use or scuttling of this ship. The language used imparts a lofty air and pushes the history of the ship into myth and legend, strengthening any argument that it is just another ship ready to retire.

Question 1	Interpreting the Theme and Main Idea
Question 2	Analyzing Rhythm
Question 3	Interpreting Text Features
Question 4	Analyzing Figurative Language
Question 5	Analyzing Diction: Connotation
Question 6	Analyzing Diction: Denotation
Question 7	Analyzing Sound Devices
Question 8	Drawing Conclusions
Question 9	Making Generalizations
Question 10	Distinguishing Among Different Genres of Poetry
Question 11	Analyzing Oxymoron
Question 12	Analyzing Sound Devices and Rhythm
Question 13	Analyzing Conflict, Plot, and Setting
Question 14	Analyzing Character
Question 15	Analyzing Development of Tone and Mood

"LETTER 4" FROM FRANKENSTEIN

by Mary Shelley

To Mrs. Saville, England

August 5th, 17–

So strange an accident has happened to us that I cannot forbear recording it, although it is very probable that you will see me before these papers can come into your possession.

Last Monday (July 31st) we were nearly surrounded by ice, which closed in the ship on all sides, scarcely leaving her the sea-room in which she floated. Our situation was somewhat dangerous, especially as we were compassed round by a very thick fog. We accordingly lay to, hoping that some change would take place in the atmosphere and weather.

About two o'clock the mist cleared away, and we beheld, stretched out in every direction, vast and irregular plains of ice, which seemed to have no end. Some of my comrades groaned, and my own mind began to grow watchful with anxious thoughts, when a strange sight suddenly attracted our attention and diverted our solicitude from our own situation. We perceived a low carriage, fixed on a sledge and drawn by dogs, pass on towards the north, at the distance of half a mile; a being which had the shape of a man, but apparently of gigantic stature, sat in the sledge and guided the dogs. We watched the rapid progress of the traveller with our telescopes until he was lost among the distant inequalities of the ice. This appearance excited our unqualified wonder. We were, as we believed, many hundred miles from any land; but this apparition seemed to denote that it was not, in reality, so distant as we had supposed. Shut in, however, by ice, it was impossible to follow his track, which we had observed with the greatest attention.

About two hours after this occurrence we heard the ground sea, and before night the ice broke and freed our ship. We, however, lay to until the morning, fearing to encounter in the dark those large loose masses which float about after the breaking up of the ice. I profited of this time to rest for a few hours.

In the morning, however, as soon as it was light, I went upon deck and found all the sailors busy on one side of the vessel, apparently talking to someone in the sea. It was, in fact, a sledge, like that we had seen before, which had drifted towards us in the night on a large fragment of ice. Only one dog remained alive; but there was a human being within it whom the sailors were persuading to enter the vessel. He was not, as the other traveller seemed to be, a savage inhabitant of some undiscovered island, but a European. When I appeared on deck the master said, "Here is our captain, and he will not allow you to perish on the open sea."

On perceiving me, the stranger addressed me in English, although with a foreign accent. "Before I come on board your vessel," said he, "will you have the kindness to inform me whither you are bound?"

You may conceive my astonishment on hearing such a question addressed to me from a man on the brink of destruction and to whom I should have supposed that my vessel would have been a resource which he would not have exchanged for the most precious wealth the earth can afford. I replied, however, that we were on a voyage of discovery towards the northern pole.

Upon hearing this he appeared satisfied and consented to come on board. Good God! Margaret, if you had seen the man who thus capitulated for his safety, your surprise would have been boundless. His limbs were nearly frozen, and his body dreadfully emaciated by fatigue and suffering. I never

239

saw a man in so wretched a condition. We attempted to carry him into the cabin, but as soon as he had quitted the fresh air he fainted. We accordingly brought him back to the deck and restored him to animation by rubbing him with brandy and forcing him to swallow a small quantity. As soon as he showed signs of life we wrapped him up in blankets and placed him near the chimney of the kitchen stove. By slow degrees he recovered and ate a little soup, which restored him wonderfully.

Two days passed in this manner before he was able to speak, and I often feared that his sufferings had deprived him of understanding. When he had in some measure recovered, I removed him to my own cabin and attended on him as much as my duty would permit. I never saw a more interesting creature: his eyes have generally an expression of wildness, and even madness, but there are moments when, if anyone performs an act of kindness towards him or does him the most trifling service, his whole countenance is lighted up, as it were, with a beam of benevolence and sweetness that I never saw equalled. But he is generally melancholy and despairing, and sometimes he gnashes his teeth, as if impatient of the weight of woes that oppresses him.

When my guest was a little recovered I had great trouble to keep off the men, who wished to ask him a thousand questions; but I would not allow him to be tormented by their idle curiosity, in a state of body and mind whose restoration evidently depended upon entire repose. Once, however, the lieutenant asked why he had come so far upon the ice in so strange a vehicle.

His countenance instantly assumed an aspect of the deepest gloom, and he replied, "To seek one who fled from me."

"And did the man whom you pursued travel in the same fashion?"

"Yes."

"Then I fancy we have seen him, for the day before we picked you up we saw some dogs drawing a sledge, with a man in it, across the ice."

This aroused the stranger's attention, and he asked a multitude of questions concerning the route which the demon, as he called him, had pursued. Soon after, when he was alone with me, he said, "I have, doubtless, excited your curiosity, as well as that of these good people; but you are too considerate to make inquiries."

"Certainly; it would indeed be very impertinent and inhuman in me to trouble you with any inquisitiveness of mine."

"And yet you rescued me from a strange and perilous situation; you have benevolently restored me to life."

Soon after this he inquired if I thought that the breaking up of the ice had destroyed the other sledge. I replied that I could not answer with any degree of certainty, for the ice had not broken until near midnight, and the traveller might have arrived at a place of safety before that time; but of this I could not judge. From this time a new spirit of life animated the decaying frame of the stranger. He manifested the greatest eagerness to be upon deck to watch for the sledge which had before appeared; but I have persuaded him to remain in the cabin, for he is far too weak to sustain the rawness of the atmosphere. I have promised that someone should watch for him and give him instant notice if any new object should appear in sight.

Such is my journal of what relates to this strange occurrence up to the present day. The stranger has gradually improved in health but is very silent and appears uneasy when anyone except myself enters his cabin. Yet his manners are so conciliating and gentle that the sailors are all interested in him, although they have had very little communication with him. For my own part, I begin to love him as a brother, and his constant and deep grief fills me with sympathy and compassion. He must have been a noble creature in his better days, being even now in wreck so attractive and amiable. I said in one of my letters, my dear Margaret, that I should find no friend on the wide ocean; yet I have found a man who, before his spirit had been broken by misery, I should have been happy to have possessed as the brother of my heart.

I shall continue my journal concerning the stranger at intervals, should I have any fresh incidents to record.

1. Which of the following does the first paragraph do?

    a. It introduces the writer of the letter by her first name.
    b. It tells the reader the whereabouts of the writer of the letter.
    c. **It adds suspense through an air of mystery.**
    d. It extends kind salutations to Mrs. Saville.

2. In paragraph 2, what is the meaning of the word, "compassed"?

    a. circles
    b. directions
    c. **encircled**
    d. directly

3. What does the appearance of the dog team and sledge seem to prove to the writer?

    a. Help is not all that far off.
    b. **They are not too far from land.**
    c. Men live within the Arctic Circle.
    d. The crew can survive severe weather.

4. Who is the writer of the letter in this passage?

    a. a crew member
    b. the ship's cook
    c. **the ship's captain**
    d. a passenger

5. Where is the ship bound?

    a. back to London, England
    b. to Archangel, Russia
    c. Antarctica
    d. **towards the North Pole**

6. All of the following can be inferred about the rescued man **except** that

    a. he was traveling by dogsled and was quite worried.
    b. the people in his native country do not speak English.
    c. he had only recently been out on the ice.
    d. he was being pursued by the gigantic man.

7. In paragraph 8, how does the writer of the letter describe the rescued man?

    a. wicked
    b. mad
    c. despairing
    d. trifling

8. From what point of view was this letter written?

    a. first person
    b. second person
    c. third person limited
    d. third person omniscient

9. With what is the rescued man mainly concerned?

    a. the ice around the ship
    b. the man he is pursuing
    c. his own state of health
    d. how he can repay the writer of the letter

10. What can we infer about the writer of the letter by examining his style?

    a. He is a common man.
    b. He is well educated.
    c. He is extremely wealthy.
    d. He was educated at Oxford.

11. In paragraphs 4–6, what does the writer of the letter find ironic about the rescue of the man? Why does the author include these details?

One possible answer:

The writer of the letter finds it ironic that the rescued man is contemplating not boarding the vessel because he would rather pursue the demon northward instead of returning southward. One would normally expect someone lost on the ice flows far from land to be grateful to see any ship at all but this gentleman is obsessed and doesn't want to think of himself; his single-minded pursuit is all he cares about. The author adds this strange twist to increase the disconcerting nature of the tale being told. First, an odd sight, some sort of creature passes, and then shortly thereafter, another strange encounter—all caused the reader to wonder just what is going on here.

12. The writer of the letter says to Mrs. Saville in the opening paragraph that it is more likely that he will see her before the letters come into her possession. How can this be? Why does he write these letters if this is true?

One possible answer:

The writer of the letter is on a ship in the icy Arctic Circle. There is no possible way for the letters to be delivered to Mrs. Saville until the writer of the letter returns to warmer waters. The writer of the letter writes the letters to record what has happened, like a running diary, so that when he finally does mail them, the reader will have an account of this strange affair. With mail service very slow and patchy in this era, there was hardly any reason to hurry and mail these letters. They would be carried on a ship to England, so they would probably take as long as it would take the writer to return home.

243

13. In paragraph 16, what reasoning does the rescued man give for answering the writer of the letter's questions? Why wouldn't the rescued man want to answer the writer of the letter's questions? How does this add to the tension of the story?

In paragraph 16, the rescued man believes that he must answer the writer of the letter's questions because the writer of the letter rescued him and restored him to health. He doesn't deny that the writer of the letter is "impertinent and inhuman" to trouble him with questions, he merely admits that, because he owes his life to the writer of the letter, he will submit to questions. Clearly, he doesn't want to explain the strange circumstances that brought him out on the ice and he doesn't even begin to explain the other strange creature he is pursuing. The author shows the rescued man to be hiding a secret which will, of course, intrigue the reader who wants to know what is happening. The secrets will be revealed slowly to keep the reader reading.

14. The writer of the letter protects the rescued man from having to answer too many questions. What does this reveal about the writer of the letter? How does this device help the writer of a mystery story to maintain tension and build the mystery?

One possible answer:

This shows that the writer of the letter is a kind man who is more concerned about the well being of his passenger than about satisfying his own personal curiosities. It also reveals the custom of the time to show civility and politeness towards a stranger. As much as he would like to pepper him with questions, he holds off out of politeness. The author uses this custom to only slowly reveal bits and pieces of the mystery. Of course, the man who was rescued also doesn't want to start a panic by revealing that a monster is on the loose, nor does he wish to admit his fault in the release of this creature. But the author gives enough hints of this to increase the reader's sense of foreboding.

15. How does the writer of the letter describe the rescued man in paragraphs 8–9?

The writer of the letter describes the rescued man as being wild-eyed, sad, and longing for something. Interestingly, he also describes him as extremely gracious whenever someone performs an act of kindness towards him. The writer's description of the rescued man's physical condition also reveals hints about how long he had been out on the ice and the desperation that had driven him to hunt the monster past any point of reasonable effort. The man is emaciated and fatigued and yet doesn't want to give up, even though he knows he needs rest and recovery. This reveals his obsession.

16. How reliable is the narrator? Give evidence for or against.

One possible answer:

The reader can assume that the narrator in this passage is fairly reliable because he is telling the story in the first person to Mrs. Saville. His writing is effective because it clearly describes events, leaving no room for confusion. On the other hand, the writer of the letter may be embellishing the tale to amaze his reader back home. He adds flourishes and goes so far as to say he loves the rescued man as a brother, revealing a somewhat melancholic streak. This calls some of his narrative into question.

17. *Frankenstein*, like many early novels, is known as epistolary literature because it is a story told through a series of letters. After reading this passage, what do you believe are some of the benefits and drawbacks of epistolary writing as compared to writing in the third person?

One possible answer:

The epistolary novel is interesting to read because it is confessional in that the writer of the letter is recording his or her thoughts for a confidant or for personal use. It is always amusing to read the private letters or the journal of someone because they may reveal a great deal about the nature of the writer. This insight makes for fascinating literature with an almost eye-at-the-keyhole insight into character. One drawback is that the narrator cannot always be reliable. A third-person novel gives a story more credibility, because the narrator is separated from the main character, which makes it easier to see a character's flaws. The narrator isn't directly involved in the action and thus maintains a perspective. Epistolary writing maintains objectivity because the intended reader of the letter is basically a surrogate for the reader of the novel. The tale retold in letter form maintains the familiar personal insight of first person perspective but distances itself from the action by being an afterward account passed along to an interested party.

Street Scenes in Washington

by Louisa May Alcott

The mules were my especial delight; and an hour's study of a constant succession of them introduced me to many of their characteristics; for six of these odd little beasts drew each army wagon, and went hopping like frogs through the stream of mud that gently rolled along the street.

The coquettish mule had small feet, a nicely trimmed tassel of a tail, perked-up ears, and seemed much given to little tosses of the head, affected skips and prances; and, if he wore the bells, or were bedizened with a bit of finery, put on as many airs as any belle.

The moral mule was a stout, hardworking creature, always tugging with all his might; often pulling away after the rest had stopped, laboring under the conscientious delusion that food for the entire army depended upon his private exertions. I respected this style of mule; and, had I possessed a juicy cabbage, would have pressed it upon him, with thanks for his excellent example.

The histrionic mule was a melodramatic quadruped, prone to startling humanity by erratic leaps, and wild plunges, much shaking of his stubborn head, and lashing out of his vicious heels; now and then falling flat, and apparently dying a la Forrest; a gasp—a squirm—a flop, and so on, till the street was well blocked up, the drivers all swearing like demons in bad hats, and the chief actor's circulation decidedly quickened by every variety of kick, cuff, jerk, and haul. When the last breath seemed to have left his body, and "doctors were in vain," a sudden resurrection took place; and if ever a mule laughed with scornful triumph, that was the beast, as he leisurely rose, gave a comfortable shake, and, calmly regarding the excited crowd seemed to say—"A hit! a decided hit! for the stupidest of animals has bamboozled a dozen men. Now, then! what are you stopping the way for?"

The pathetic mule was, perhaps, the most interesting of all; for, though he always seemed to be the smallest, thinnest, weakest of the six, the postillion, with big boots, long-tailed coat, and heavy whip, was sure to bestride this one, who struggled feebly along, head down, coat muddy and rough, eye spiritless and sad, his very tail a mortified stump, and the whole beast a picture of meek misery, fit to touch a heart of stone.

The jovial mule was a roly poly, happy-go-lucky little piece of horse-flesh, taking every thing easily, from cudgeling to caressing; strolling along with a roguish twinkle of the eye, and, if the thing were possible, would have had his hands in his pockets, and whistled as he went. If there ever chanced to be an apple core, a stray turnip, or wisp of hay, in the gutter, this Mark Tapley was sure to find it, and none of his mates seemed to begrudge him his bite. I suspected this fellow was the peacemaker, confidant, and friend of all the others, for he had a sort of "Cheer—up,—old—boy,—I'll—pull—you—through" look, which was exceedingly engaging.

Pigs also possessed attractions for me, never having had an opportunity of observing their graces of mind and manner, till I came to Washington, whose porcine citizens appeared to enjoy a larger liberty than many of its human ones. Stout, sedate-looking pigs, hurried by each morning to their places of business, with a preoccupied air, and sonorous greeting to their friends.

Genteel pigs, with an extra curl to their tails, promenaded in pairs, lunching here and there, like gentlemen of leisure. Rowdy pigs pushed the passers-by off the sidewalk;

tipsy pigs hiccoughed their version of "We won't go home till morning," from the gutter; and delicate young pigs tripped daintily through the mud, as if they plumed themselves upon their ankles, and kept themselves particularly neat in point of stockings. Maternal pigs, with their interesting families, strolled by in the sun; and often the pink, baby-like squealers lay down for a nap, with a trust in Providence worthy of human imitation.

1. What is the method the author uses to write this passage?

    a. persuasion
    b. personal narrative
    c. description
    d. narration

2. What is the purpose of this essay?

    a. to complain about the unreliability of animals
    b. to compare animals to human beings
    c. to compare and contrast mules with pigs
    d. to show the shortcomings of animal labor

3. What is the tone of this passage?

    a. satiric and candid
    b. urgent and confident
    c. disdainful and rude
    d. moralistic and sentimental

4. What is the genre of the passage?

    a. social commentary
    b. biographical detail
    c. scientific study
    d. parody of fiction

5. How much time does the author say she spent observing her topic?

    a. five minutes
    b. one half-hour
    c. one hour
    d. a season

6. All of the following are true of the histrionic mule **except** that he

    a. tends to be very melodramatic.
    b. has a tendency to scare people.
    c. interests the author the most.
    d. enjoys a good practical joke.

7. Which two mules show the greatest contrast?

    a. the moral mule and the coquettish mule
    b. the jovial mule and the pathetic mule
    c. the jovial mule and the coquettish mule
    d. the good mule and the bad mule

8. Which mule does the author say she most respects?

    a. the coquettish mule
    b. the moral mule
    c. the histrionic mule
    d. the jovial mule

9. Which of the following is a type of pig that the author does **not** discuss?

    a. genteel.
    b. rowdy.
    c. maternal.
    d. intelligent.

10. Mules are to the working class as

    a. mules are to animals.
    b. politicians are to pigs.
    c. pigs are to the upper class.
    d. pigs are to happiness.

11. What makes this work humorous? What other functions might it serve?

The author is humorous in that she uses satire by comparing animals to humans. She goes to great lengths to describe the unique personalities of each type of mule, which makes her writing both witty and humorous. She also used lofty vocabulary to create her portraits of these animals that scarcely match their lowly stature. This juxtaposition also adds an absurd note to the trouble she undertakes to describe a street scene most citizens of Washington would walk right past. She also is accurately describing the world around her. In doing this, she provides a record of the times.

12. What qualities might the author find most attractive, or least attractive, in humanity?

The author probably respects the qualities that are seen in the moral mule. This mule is hardworking and dependable. It works when others refuse, and it is not afraid to take personal responsibility for its work. The description of the other types of mules pokes fun at human failings, such as acting the coquette, being a pathetic type to attract attention, or being the histrionic type who is given to extremes. Like the humans Alcott satirizes, these personalities can be both charming and / or obnoxious.

250

13. What qualities might the author find most disgusting in humanity?

One possible answer:

The author probably least respects the qualities seen in the histrionic mule because has the opposite character of the moral mule. While the moral mule wants to work, the histrionic mule wants to lie down, and while the moral mule is conscious of its responsibility, the histrionic mule is not. She also seems to loathe the injustice of the moral mule who labors tirelessly setting an example followed by few. She wants to reward that creature for his effort but knows that he, like most humans, will go unrewarded. She is also not very fond of the way the pathetic mule is treated, implying that humans of the same type are often treated the same way.

14. How biased is the writing in this passage?

One possible answer:

The writing is a statement of the author's opinions, which clearly show her likes and dislikes. This is meant to be humorous rather than descriptive and educational. Readers may find her descriptions of animals as prejudiced because she is interpreting animal behavior in human terms. A student of the natural world could probably more accurately ascertain why these mules act the way they do, but it wouldn't be half as intriguing or entertaining. Here bias gives the piece a personality and a dash of spice.

Question 1	Evaluating Author's Craft
Question 2	Analyzing the Author's Purpose
Question 3	Analyzing Development of Tone and Mood
Question 4	Distinguishing Among Different Genres of Nonfiction
Question 5	Analyzing Point of View
Question 6	Analyzing Character
Question 7	Comparing and Contrasting
Question 8	Analyzing Cause and Effect
Question 9	Analyzing Diction: Connotation and Denotation
Question 10	Drawing Conclusions
Question 11	Evaluating Author's Style
Question 12	Making Generalizations
Question 13	Making Inferences
Question 14	Recognizing the Author's Bias and Beliefs

From *Narrative of the Life of a Slave*

by Frederick Douglass

I was born in Tuckahoe, near Hillsborough, and about twelve miles from Easton, in Talbot county, Maryland. I have no accurate knowledge of my age, never having seen any authentic record containing it. By far the larger part of the slaves know as little of their ages as horses know of theirs, and it is the wish of most masters within my knowledge to keep their slaves thus ignorant. I do not remember to have ever met a slave who could tell of his birthday. They seldom come nearer to it than planting-time, harvest-time, cherry-time, spring-time, or fall-time. A want of information concerning my own was a source of unhappiness to me even during childhood. The white children could tell their ages. I could not tell why I ought to be deprived of the same privilege. I was not allowed to make any inquiries of my master concerning it. He deemed all such inquiries on the part of a slave improper and impertinent, and evidence of a restless spirit. The nearest estimate I can give makes me now between twenty-seven and twenty-eight years of age. I come to this, from hearing my master say, some time during 1835, I was about seventeen years old.

My mother was named Harriet Bailey. She was the daughter of Isaac and Betsey Bailey, both colored, and quite dark. My mother was of a darker complexion than either my grandmother or grandfather.

My father was a white man. He was admitted to be such by all I ever heard speak of my parentage. The opinion was also whispered that my master was my father; but of the correctness of this opinion, I know nothing; the means of knowing was withheld from me. My mother and I were separated when I was but an infant—before I knew her as my mother. It is a common custom, in the part of Maryland from which I ran away, to part children from their mothers at a very early age. Frequently, before the child has reached its twelfth month, its mother is taken from it, and hired out on some farm a considerable distance off, and the child is placed under the care of an old woman, too old for field labor. For what this separation is done, I do not know, unless it be to hinder the development of the child's affection toward its mother, and to blunt and destroy the natural affection of the mother for the child. This is the inevitable result.

I never saw my mother, to know her as such, more than four or five times in my life; and each of these times was very short in duration, and at night. She was hired by a Mr. Stewart, who lived about twelve miles from my home. She made her journeys to see me in the night, traveling the whole distance on foot, after the performance of her day's work. She was a field hand, and a whipping is the penalty of not being in the field at sunrise, unless a slave has special permission from his or her master to the contrary—a permission which they seldom get, and one that gives to him that gives it the proud name of being a kind master. I do not recollect of ever seeing my mother by the light of day. She was with me in the night. She would lie down with me, and get me to sleep, but long before I waked she was gone. Very little communication ever took place between us.

Death soon ended what little we could have while she lived, and with it her hardships and suffering. She died when I was about seven years old, on one of my master's farms, near Lee's Mill. I was not allowed to be present during her illness, at her death, or burial. She was gone long before I knew any thing about it. Never having enjoyed, to any considerable extent, her soothing presence, her tender and watchful care, I received the tidings of her death with much the same emotions I should have probably felt at the death of a stranger.

1. What is the main point of this passage?

    a. **Slavery broke up families.**
    b. Slaves did not know their ages.
    c. Slavery had lasting effects.
    d. Escaping slavery was difficult.

2. What analogy does the writer use?

    a. He compares mothers to fathers.
    b. He compares masters to slaves.
    c. **He compares slaves to horses.**
    d. He compares white and slave boys.

3. How does not knowing his own age affect the narrator?

    a. He is unmoved and mellow.
    b. **He is envious and sad.**
    c. He is enlightened and respectful.
    d. He is timid and reclusive.

4. Because she walks so far to see him, what can we infer about the narrator's mother?

    a. She did not like work very much.
    b. She enjoyed traveling the countryside.
    c. **She loved her son very much.**
    d. She was not afraid of being punished.

5. Which of the following is a fact?

    a. The narrator's father was his master.
    b. The narrator's master was fairly kind.
    c. **The narrator's mother was very dark.**
    d. The narrator was seventeen in 1835.

6. Slaves who inquire about their age are seen as all of the following **except**

    a. rude.
    b. restless.
    c. impudent.
    d. **attentive.**

7. Which of the following predictions can we make about the narrator?

    a. He will be kept in ignorance until the day he dies.
    b. He will escape to the North and work as a farm hand.
    c. **He will become a free man able to look back on his experience.**
    d. He will live an unhappy life working in the fields.

8. What can be concluded about the narrator?

   a. He was a loving son to his poor, sick mother.
   b. ***He had little emotional connection with his mother.***
   c. He felt an unbreakable bond with his mother.
   d. He was heartbroken when he heard of his mother's death.

9. What is the tone of this narrative?

   a. angry and vengeful
   b. sentimental and moralistic
   c. ***informative and penetrating***
   d. nostalgic and playful

10. According to this narrative, which of the following is **not** true about slaves in Maryland?

    a. They were not allowed to celebrate their birthdays.
    b. Slaves in Maryland were punished for not working from dawn to dusk.
    c. ***They were taught to read and write by their parents if the master was their father.***
    d. Slaves did not have everyday contact with their parents but kept in touch.

11. What is the narrator's purpose?

One possible answer:

The narrator's purpose is to persuade people that slavery is evil but he doesn't just come right out and say this. He is careful to keep a measured tone and to avoid the anger that he obviously feels. Part of his point is that slavery dehumanizes those caught in its trap. His lack of feeling about the death of his own mother is proof that the master's attempt to remove family connections so that slaves could be kept docile was part of a system that worked in its evil efficiency. Douglass is also educating the reader, describing conditions that were not widely known at the time this was written. His work put a face on a cruel economic system that persisted because it provided free labor and increased profits. His detailed description of slave life showed that nothing had been free. The slaves had paid many times over in their blood and in their endurance of inhumane working conditions. No reader could experience this narrative without calling for an end to slavery.

12. The narrator provides examples to strengthen his writing by making a generalization, and then giving an example, or vice versa. Discuss this persuasive technique and judge its effectiveness.

The narrator provides an example first by saying that he doesn't know how old he is. He then generalizes by claiming that most of the slaves were unsure of their ages. He qualifies this statement by noting that he hadn't met any slave who knew his or her age, implying that some might have, but he hadn't had any personal experience with this phenomenon. This adds power to this simple example of slavery's inhumanity. He doesn't make a sweeping statement that every slave suffered the same thing. He sticks with what he personally knows and lets the reader judge his generalization. The narrator also says that he was separated from his mother at an early age, and then goes on to say that this practice is common. He claims that separating a mother from her son destroys the bond between them, and then he gives his own personal account, proving his claim true. Here again, the technique is effective because the example gives a human face to the general observation about a slaving practice. If the author had merely listed ten things slave owners did to disorient and dehumanize their slaves so they were easier to control, it would not have had the same power as a story about a mother walking all night just to touch her lost son.

13. How does the narrator reveal his level of education and use it as an effective element of his composition?

We can infer from the writing that the narrator is well educated. Clearly Fredrick Douglass advanced well beyond his beginnings as a common field hand. Not only could he write at all (this skill, like reading, was usually denied most slaves) but he writes well, both describing his horror with power and control. The reader can also assume that his master didn't impart these talents to the writer. He obviously had someone help him tell his story. The grace and dignity in his prose, however, seems natural, something that education alone wouldn't produce. His gifts as a writer also appear to stem from his understanding of the ways of the world, and how his story must be told to reach a wider audience and convey this evil existence he has endured. His education helps his story to be appreciated while not distracting from the subject matter, which took place when he lacked any formal schooling.

14. Why is the author's style so effective?

The images the author provides are concrete and emotional. The image of the narrator upset at not knowing his age or unmoved upon hearing about his mother's death are effective in this manner. His tone is informative and collected. His sentence variety and precise wording paint him as a well educated, focused, and clear-thinking man, which adds to his ability to persuade. He avoids discussing the larger implications of the slave trade, nor does he spend much effort portraying his masters. His focus on the intimate life of a slave forces the reader to focus on the effects, and not on the torturers or the faulty reasons advanced for maintaining this cruel economic imprisonment.

15. Why were personal slave narratives such powerful weapons for those who wanted to end enslavement?

One possible answer:

The slave narrative not only exposes the evils of slavery; it shows the humanity and intelligence of those who are unjustly enslaved. The narrative's greatest power also is inherent in the format of an eyewitness account. Proponents of slavery were always quick to point out that many slaves were treated well and they were happy simple folk who knew no better. However, after these narratives began to appear, the inhumane aspect of the practice became impossible to deny. The damage came in the form of the details these narrators related. Readers could sympathize with the struggles of the victims of slavery. No longer were they mere numbers—they became fellow humans who were suffering needlessly.

Question 1	Interpreting the Theme and Main Idea
Question 2	Analyzing Diction
Question 3	Analyzing Cause and Effect
Question 4	Making Inferences
Question 5	Distinguishing Fact and Opinion
Question 6	Analyzing Diction: Connotation and Denotation
Question 7	Analyzing Predictions
Question 8	Drawing Conclusions
Question 9	Analyzing Development of Tone and Mood
Question 10	Making Generalizations
Question 11	Analyzing the Author's Purpose
Question 12	Analyzing Text Structure and Organization
Question 13	Evaluating Author's Craft
Question 14	Evaluating Author's Style
Question 15	Examining Cultures and Historical Periods in Literature

"I HEAR AMERICA SINGING"
FROM *LEAVES OF GRASS*
by Walt Whitman

I hear America singing, the varied carols I hear;
Those of mechanics—each one singing his, as it should be, blithe and strong;
The carpenter singing his, as he measures his plank or beam,
The mason singing his, as he makes ready for work, or leaves off work;
The boatman singing what belongs to him in his boat—the deckhand singing on the
    steamboat deck;
The shoemaker singing as he sits on his bench—the hatter singing as he stands;
The wood-cutter's song—the ploughboy's, on his way in the morning, or at the noon
    intermission, or at sundown;
The delicious singing of the mother—or of the young wife at work—or of the girl
    sewing or washing—Each singing what belongs to her, and to none else;
The day what belongs to the day—At night, the party of young fellows, robust,
    friendly,
Singing, with open mouths, their strong melodious songs.

1. The songs of these working people are revealed from the perspective of

   a. their bosses.
   b. other workers.
   c. an outsider.
   d. a consumer.

2. In line 2, the word, "blithe," probably means

   a. cheerful.
   b. industrious.
   c. long.
   d. greasy.

3. What kind of place is the America in the poem?

   a. industrious
   b. careful
   c. scholarly
   d. indolent

4. Why does the boatman sing?

   a. to ask help from others
   b. to celebrate personal ownership
   c. to warn the deckhand
   d. in reverence to the water's ebb and flow

257

5. Whose singing does the speaker most enjoy?

    a. the mason
    b. the boatman
    c.   the women
    d. the party

6. What word does the author use the most in repetition?

    a. "hear"
    b.   "singing"
    c. "songs"
    d. "carols"

7. How does the author add a musical quality to his poem?

    a. rhyme scheme
    b. personification
    c.   parallelism
    d. internal rhyme

8. In what line can the shift from day to night **best** be seen?

    a. line 6
    b. line 8
    c.   line 9
    d. line 10

9. Lines 9–10 possess elements of all of the following **except**

    a. celebration.
    b. unity.
    c.   individuality.
    d. friendship.

10. What is the genre of this poem?

    a. elegiac
    b. instructive
    c. discursive
    d.   lyrical

11. In this poem, the workers can be seen as all of the following **except**

    a.   economical.
    b. hardworking.
    c. jolly.
    d. content.

12. What is the tone and mood of this poem? What devices does the poet employ to convey this mood and tone?

The tone of this poem is both happy and industrious. The poet's evocation of personally hearing these songs imparts a musical tone as well as an atmospheric tone. The songs of these workers rise up together in chorus or "carol," as he says. The feeling of a group sing-a-long attitude keeps the mood optimistic and breathes togetherness. The concept of each worker having a song echoes the contribution each makes to the work force. The song of the hat maker is the hat he or she produces as well as the overall worth each effort adds to the idea of a nation coming together to make a new world. Whitman mimics the verses and choruses of songs as well as the repetition and parallelism of classic song canons.

13. What is the speaker of this poem doing? How is the speaker involved in these songs through observation?

The speaker of this poem is observing various men and women in different occupations and reporting on what he sees and hears. The speaker is also the recipient of the song and of the labors expended to make his world better. By "hearing" the song, he acknowledges each of these professions as vital and unique. To him, his fellow man and woman are not just a work force churning out a blur of product. The speaker is also commenting on these songs and making judgements. He says in line 2, "each one singing his, as it should be" verifying that there is an order and sense in how these songs are produced. The speaker celebrates each song, each contribution, by reacting to them one by one. His description is his song, his comment on what he is hearing. Another speaker or listener may hear these songs differently. The adjectives chosen, "strong . . . robust . . . friendly . . . delicious" show him editorializing about what he hears.

14. In lines 1–8, is the "singing" literal or figurative? Why? How could this "singing" be seen as both literal and figurative in other parts of the poem?

The singing in lines 1–8 is figurative. The speaker likens working to the self-expression of song. Each song is different, as each form of work is different. One can imagine that each worker sings a slightly different song as even workers performing the same task do. The songs of the workers are their unique contributions and styles. Whitman's singing is also literal in that workers often did sing as they worked, not only to pass the time, but also because group tasks required co-ordination; railroad gangs or sailors, as examples, kept pace and time in repetitive tasks by singing songs that later became famous.

15. Do you find Whitman's view of the American working man and woman to be accurate and effective? Has he celebrated the labor of the common man or has he perhaps trivialized it?

One possible answer:

I think Whitman reduces the hard labors of these workers to a jolly tune that insults the contributions and sacrifices they have made. People in his era worked long hours under often grueling conditions in unsafe environments and many died early deaths as a result. I realize he is a poet trying to glorify their tireless efforts but poets don't sweat and break their bodies down doing repetitive tasks that require extreme skills. The whole poem seems to be a lazy man's view of what a day of hard work is really all about.

Question 1	Analyzing Point of View
Question 2	Analyzing Diction: Connotation and Denotation
Question 3	Making Inferences
Question 4	Analyzing Character
Question 5	Recognizing the Author's Bias and Beliefs
Question 6	Analyzing Sound Devices and Rhythm
Question 7	Evaluating Author's Craft
Question 8	Analyzing Text Structure and Organization
Question 9	Drawing Conclusions
Question 10	Distinguishing Among Different Genres of Poetry
Question 11	Interpreting the Theme and Main Idea
Question 12	Analyzing Development of Tone and Mood
Question 13	Analyzing the Author's Purpose
Question 14	Analyzing Figurative Language
Question 15	Evaluating the Quality of the Literature

THE METAMORPHOSIS

by Franz Kafka

One morning, when Gregor Samsa woke from troubled dreams, he found himself transformed in his bed into a horrible vermin. He lay on his armor-like back, and if he lifted his head a little he could see his brown belly, slightly domed and divided by arches into stiff sections. The bedding was hardly able to cover it and seemed ready to slide off any moment. His many legs, pitifully thin compared with the size of the rest of him, waved about helplessly as he looked.

"What's happened to me?" he thought. It wasn't a dream. His room, a proper human room although a little too small, lay peacefully between its four familiar walls. A collection of textile samples lay spread out on the table—Samsa was a travelling salesman—and above it there hung a picture that he had recently cut out of an illustrated magazine and housed in a nice, gilded frame. It showed a lady fitted out with a fur hat and fur boa who sat upright, raising a heavy fur muff that covered the whole of her lower arm towards the viewer.

Gregor then turned to look out the window at the dull weather. Drops of rain could be heard hitting the pane, which made him feel quite sad. "How about if I sleep a little bit longer and forget all this nonsense", he thought, but that was something he was unable to do because he was used to sleeping on his right, and in his present state couldn't get into that position. However hard he threw himself onto his right, he always rolled back to where he was. He must have tried it a hundred times, shut his eyes so that he wouldn't have to look at the floundering legs, and only stopped when he began to feel a mild, dull pain there that he had never felt before.

"Oh, God", he thought, "what a strenuous career it is that I've chosen! Travelling day in and day out. Doing business like this takes much more effort than doing your own business at home, and on top of that there's the curse of travelling, worries about making train connections, bad and irregular food, contact with different people all the time so that you can never get to know anyone or become friendly with them. It can all go to Hell!" He felt a slight itch up on his belly; pushed himself slowly up on his back towards the headboard so that he could lift his head better; found where the itch was, and saw that it was covered with lots of little white spots which he didn't know what to make of; and when he tried to feel the place with one of his legs he drew it quickly back because as soon as he touched it he was overcome by a cold shudder.

He slid back into his former position. "Getting up early all the time", he thought, "it makes you stupid. You've got to get enough sleep. Other travelling salesmen live a life of luxury. For instance, whenever I go back to the guest house during the morning to copy out the contract, these gentlemen are always still sitting there eating their breakfasts. I ought to just try that with my boss; I'd get kicked out on the spot. But who knows, maybe that would be the best thing for me. If I didn't have my parents to think about I'd have given in my notice a long time ago, I'd have gone up to the boss and told him just what I think, tell him everything I would, let him know just what I feel. He'd fall right off his desk! And it's a funny sort of business to be sitting up there at your desk, talking down at your subordinates from up there, especially when you have to go right up close because the boss is hard of hearing. Well, there's still some hope; once I've got the money together to pay off my parents' debt to him – another five or six years I suppose – that's definitely what I'll do. That's when I'll make the big change. First of all though, I've got to get up, my train leaves at five."

And he looked over at the alarm clock, ticking on the chest of drawers. "God in Heaven!" he thought. It was half past six and the hands were quietly moving forwards, it was even later than half past, more like quarter to seven. Had the alarm clock not rung? He could see from the bed that it had been set for four o'clock as it should have been; it certainly must have rung. Yes, but was it possible to quietly sleep through that furniture-rattling noise? True, he had not slept peacefully, but probably all the more deeply because of that. What should he do now? The next train went at seven; if he were to catch that he would have to rush like mad and the collection of samples was still not packed, and he did not at all feel particularly fresh and lively. And even if he did catch the train he would not avoid his boss's anger as the office assistant would have been there to see the five o'clock train go, he would have put in his report about Gregor's not being there a long time ago. The office assistant was the boss's man, spineless, and with no understanding. What about if he reported sick? But that would be extremely strained and suspicious as in fifteen years of service Gregor had never once yet been ill. His boss would certainly come round with the doctor from the medical insurance company, accuse his parents of having a lazy son, and accept the doctor's recommendation not to make any claim as the doctor believed that no-one was ever ill but that many were workshy. And what's more, would he have been entirely wrong in this case? Gregor did in fact, apart from excessive sleepiness after sleeping for so long, feel completely well and even felt much hungrier than usual.

He was still hurriedly thinking all this through, unable to decide to get out of the bed, when the clock struck quarter to seven. There was a cautious knock at the door near his head. "Gregor", somebody called—it was his mother—"it's quarter to seven. Didn't you want to go somewhere?" That gentle voice! Gregor was shocked when he heard his own voice answering, it could hardly be recognised as the voice he had had before. As if from deep inside him, there was a painful and uncontrollable squeaking mixed in with it, the words could be made out at first but then there was a sort of echo which made them unclear, leaving the hearer unsure whether he had heard properly or not. Gregor had wanted to give a full answer and explain everything, but in the circumstances contented himself with saying: "Yes, mother, yes, thank-you, I'm getting up now." The change in Gregor's voice probably could not be noticed outside through the wooden door, as his mother was satisfied with this explanation and shuffled away. But this short conversation made the other members of the family aware that Gregor, against their expectations was still at home, and soon his father came knocking at one of the side doors, gently, but with his fist. "Gregor, Gregor", he called, "what's wrong?" And after a short while he called again with a warning deepness in his voice: "Gregor! Gregor!" At the other side door his sister came plaintively: "Gregor? Aren't you well? Do you need anything?"

Gregor answered to both sides: "I'm ready, now", making an effort to remove all the strangeness from his voice by enunciating very carefully and putting long pauses between each, individual word. His father went back to his breakfast, but his sister whispered: "Gregor, open the door, I beg of you." Gregor, however, had no thought of opening the door, and instead congratulated himself for his cautious habit, acquired from his travelling, of locking all doors at night even when he was at home.

The first thing he wanted to do was to get up in peace without being disturbed, to get dressed, and most of all to have his breakfast. Only then would he consider what to do next, as he was well aware that he would not bring his thoughts to any sensible conclusions by lying in bed. He remembered that he had often felt a slight pain in bed, perhaps caused by lying awkwardly, but that had always turned out to be pure imagination and he wondered how his imaginings would slowly resolve themselves today. He did not have the slightest doubt that the change in his voice was nothing more than the first sign of a serious cold, which was an occupational hazard for travelling salesmen.

1. What is the point of view of this story?

    a. first person
    b. second person
    c. third person limited
    d. third person omniscient

2. What is the tone of the story?

    a. horrific and ironic
    b. mock-heroic and brave
    c. learned and colloquial
    d. angry and disdainful

3. What is Gregor's major conflict?

    a. his relationship with his boss
    b. the fact that he is now a bug
    c. his relationship with his family
    d. his inability to get out of bed

4. What is the setting of the story?

    a. an office building
    b. a family apartment
    c. a train station
    d. a guest house

5. What drives the plot?

    a. flashbacks
    b. setting description
    c. character interaction
    d. character development

6. What does Gregor resemble?

   a. *beetle*
   b. bee
   c. slug
   d. caterpillar

7. According to the passage, what can we infer that Gregor sells?

   a. houses
   b. *small goods*
   c. samples
   d. heavy machinery

8. According to the text in paragraph 3, why can't Gregor sleep?

   a. *He could not move onto his side.*
   b. He was worried about his condition.
   c. His sister kept knocking at his door.
   d. He needed to get to work on time.

9. In paragraph 4, which of the following is seen as an alternative to the negative aspects of Gregor's work?

   a. travel stresses
   b. *doing business at home*
   c. horrible food
   d. inability to socialize

10. In paragraph 5, for what reason does the narrator say that Gregor can't quit his job?

    a. He wishes to get married.
    b. He is not trained for anything else.
    c. *His parents are in debt.*
    d. His sister needs violin lessons.

11. Regarding work, what do we know about Gregor?

    a. He enjoys life as a travelling salesman.
    b. *He has not missed work in fifteen years.*
    c. He intends to quit on this very day.
    d. He is studying nights for another career.

12. In paragraph 7, what does Gregor realize?

    a. *His voice has been altered.*
    b. He will be late for work.
    c. He will lose his job.
    d. His parents will be terrified.

13. In paragraph 9, what does Gregor attribute to the changes in his current state?

    a. a pain in his side
    b. a cold forming
    c. his imagination
    d. stress from work

14. What are Gregor's internal and external conflicts? How does the author reveal these torments in the main character?

Internally, Gregor refuses to deal with his transformation into a bug, discussing all his other problems in life without facing the overwhelming reality of this hideous transformation. Externally, he concerns himself with getting to work, appeasing his boss, and supporting his family. The author uses Gregor's common complaints about work to wrap a horrible, undeniable absurdity into the banal everyday worries of life. He mocks the workaholic mentality of lesser men like Gregor who cannot face reality even when it has moved into the realm of the macabre.

15. What is ironic about Gregor's transformation into a bug?

It is ironic that Gregor does not seem to be too troubled about his dilemma and instead chooses to think of the consequences of this change as if it were just a minor delay in going about his ordinary business. The author uses irony here to portray Gregor as a common travelling salesmen, which he clearly is not. The irony goes deeper in that this is a man so accustomed to being browbeaten by others that an alteration in his very existence only causes him to fret about outside appearances and minor inconveniences. Gregor cannot even accept the fact that he is unable to work, noting instead that he does not even feel sick.

16. What effect will not going to work have on Gregor and his family?

Gregor's family will suffer because his family is in debt to Gregor's boss. The text states that Gregor will have to work for at least five or six years before his parents can emerge from their debt. Clearly, Gregor cannot imagine a world without his work and this is part of why he cannot fathom avoiding work even though he is now a bug and cannot possibly carry on normally. He so denies his slavery to his work that even a complete metamorphosis cannot turn this caterpillar into a free butterfly. Gregor might have seen this escape from his very body and soul as a new lease on life, but all he can do is fret about getting to work.

17. Kafka is cited as a precursor to the magical realism of Borges and Marquez. In what way does this work fit the genre of magical realism?

One possible answer:
The effect of magical realism on the reader allows a complete escape from reality while still being grounded in the here and now. What seems impossible and artificial is still tied to ordinary life. Gregor, like characters in magical realism, accepts the incredible as possible and almost ordinary. The extraordinary is accepted and real-life characters trudge on through their lives despite these fantastical events. Kafka uses a mundane character and situation to make social commentary and awaken in the reader almost unthinkable perspectives on both the typical and the extreme.

Question 1   Analyzing Point of View
Question 2   Analyzing Development of Tone and Mood
Question 3   Analyzing Conflict
Question 4   Analyzing Setting
Question 5   Analyzing Plot
Question 6   Evaluating Validity, Credibility, and Reliability of Text
Question 7   Making Inferences
Question 8   Analyzing Problem and Solution
Question 9   Comparing and Contrasting
Question 10   Summarizing and Paraphrasing Information
Question 11   Making Generalizations
Question 12   Analyzing Character
Question 13   Analyzing Cause and Effect
Question 14   Drawing Conclusions
Question 15   Analyzing Irony
Question 16   Analyzing Predictions
Question 17   Distinguishing Among Different Genres of Fiction

OF REGIMENT OF HEALTH

by Sir Francis Bacon

There is a wisdom in this; beyond the rules of physic: a man's own observation, what he finds good of, and what he finds hurt of, is the best physic to preserve health. But it is a safer conclusion to say, This agreeth not well with me, therefore, I will not continue it; than this, I find no offence of this, therefore I may use it. For strength of nature in youth, passeth over many excesses, which are owing a man till his age. Discern of the coming on of years, and think not to do the same things still; for age will not be defied. Beware of sudden change, in any great point of diet, and, if necessity enforce it, fit the rest to it. For it is a secret both in nature and state, that it is safer to change many things, than one. Examine thy customs of diet, sleep, exercise, apparel, and the like; and try, in any thing thou shalt judge hurtful, to discontinue it, by little and little; but so, as if thou dost find any inconvenience by the change, thou come back to it again: for it is hard to distinguish that which is generally held good and wholesome, from that which is good particularly, and fit for thine own body. To be free-minded and cheerfully disposed, at hours of meat, and of sleep, and of exercise, is one of the best precepts of long lasting. As for the passions, and studies of the mind; avoid envy, anxious fears; anger fretting inwards; subtle and knotty inquisitions; joys and exhilarations in excess; sadness not communicated. Entertain hopes; mirth rather than joy; variety of delights, rather than surfeit of them; wonder and admiration, and therefore novelties; studies that fill the mind with splendid and illustrious objects, as histories, fables, and contemplations of nature. If you fly physic in health altogether, it will be too strange for your body, when you shall need it. If you make it too familiar, it will work no extraordinary effect, when sickness cometh. I commend rather some diet for certain seasons, than frequent use of physic, except it be grown into a custom. For those diets alter the body more, and trouble it less. Despise no new accident in your body, but ask opinion of it. In sickness, respect health principally; and in health, action. For those that put their bodies to endure in health, may in most sicknesses, which are not very sharp, be cured only with diet, and tendering. Celsus could never have spoken it as a physician, had he not been a wise man withal, when he giveth it for one of the great precepts of health and lasting, that a man do vary, and interchange contraries, but with an inclination to the more benign extreme: use fasting and full eating, but rather full eating; watching and sleep, but rather sleep; sitting and exercise, but rather exercise; and the like. So shall nature be cherished, and yet taught masteries. Physicians are, some of them, so pleasing and conformable to the humor of the patient, as they press not the true cure of the disease; and some other are so regular, in proceeding according to art for the disease, as they respect not sufficiently the condition of the patient. Take one of a middle temper; or if it may not be found in one man, combine two of either sort; and forget not to call as well, the best acquainted with your body, as the best reputed of for his faculty.

1. What type of essay is this?

   a. instructive
   b. descriptive
   c. persuasive
   d. biographical

2. In lines 1–6, what aspect of life does the speaker say cannot be overcome by man?

   a. excesses
   b. youth
   c. time
   d. revenge

3. What is the purpose of this essay?

   a. to define what are good health habits
   b. to define good and bad health habits
   c. to explain how to live moderately
   d. to explain how the author lives

4. In line 9, of the areas the author suggests to regulate in maintaining health, which seems the least appropriate?

   a. diet
   b. sleep
   c. exercise
   d. apparel

5. In the sentence that begins in line 9, what is the author's argument as to why it is better to change one's habits slowly?

   a. Something done with speed almost never benefits one's body and mind.
   b. Something might be good in parts, but poor in excess or in absence.
   c. Done slowly, one continues to reward oneself for changing one's habits.
   d. Doing things slowly will mirror the pace which humans tend to develop.

6. In lines 14–17, all of the following are passions to be avoided **except**

   a. anxiety.
   b. excess joys and excitement.
   c. love.
   d. unexpressed anger.

7. In line 18, the word, "surfeit," probably means

   a. abundance.
   b. assortment.
   c. supply.
   d. diversity.

8. What is the advice given in lines 19–22?

    a. Medicine should be administered as needed rather than regularly.
    b. If one uses medicine regularly it will be foreign to one's body when needed.
    c. If one uses medicine irregularly it will be too difficult to gauge its effects.
    d. Taking medicine should be discouraged at all times and in all situations.

9. In the opening sentence what does the author argue is the "best physic to preserve health"?

    a. One should only take of the good and never of anything that is bad
    b. One should observe how the body responds to different stimuli.
    c. One should always maintain a balance of the good and the bad.
    d. One should guard against habits that encourage sloth and gluttony.

10. Summarize the author's opinion in this selection.

One possible answer:

The author believes that one should observe how the body responds to different stimuli. In changing a person's diet, one should do it slowly so that one can observe how the changes affect the body. One of the best ways to live a long life is to be carefree and happy when eating, sleeping, and exercising. Proper, seasonal dieting can have a great effect on the body and help it endure, but always remember when seeking variety in foods to consume more of that which is best. In terms of physicians, choose one who considers the most aggressive approach without causing too much distress to the patient.

269

11. In line 27, who is Celsus, why does the author reference him, and what does Celsus say?

One possible answer:

Celsus was a physician whom the author thought very wise. The author uses Celsus in his essay because he considers him an expert in the field of health. In writing, it is important to always try to report what experts have to say on a given topic because it adds weight to an argument. Celsus says that one can take things that are good and bad, but always take more of the good. The author considers this very practical advice that compliments his own argument.

12. Beginning in line 32, the author says that there are two extremes when classifying physicians. What are the two extremes and what kinds of problems could they cause?

One possible answer:

Some physicians are too kind to their patients and not serious about treating the disease. The problem with this approach to medicine is that the physicians are not working actively enough to treat whatever is ailing the patient. Because the approach is not aggressive enough, the patient will not get better. The other kind of physician is too serious about treating the disease and inconsiderate of the patient. The problem with this approach is just the opposite; these physicians are too aggressive and thus do more damage than good to their patients.

13. In what time period was this passage written and what clues from the text help us to determine this?

The language the author uses comes from another era with vastly different constructions than those in modern speech today. He uses words like "agreeth" and "passeth" which are archaic ways to say "agrees" and "passes." He also uses words like "physics" which are what we call "drugs" today, or "shalt" instead of "shall." Instead of using the pronoun "your"; he uses "thine." In addition to word choice, some students might say that some of the author's sentences are structured in an older fashion and can easily be paraphrased into a more modern structure. When this is the case, a reader can usually infer that the text had been written at an earlier period. For example, when the author says: "To be free-minded and cheerfully disposed, at hours of meat, and of sleep, and of exercise, is one of the best precepts of long lasting" the reader can paraphrase this saying "One of the best ways to live a long life is to be carefree and happy when eating, sleeping, and exercising."

14. Does the author back up his arguments with scientific facts? What effect does this have on his argument?

No, in his essay on general health, the author only states his opinions and does not use scientific facts to defend anything he says. He does cite Celsus, a physician whom the author respects, but he does not report Celsus's data on his studies on diet, only giving Celsus's opinion. Science must be practical; demanding that one not only experiment and record results, but do so in the language of science: mathematics. Because this text does not publish the results of the scientific studies, it is not very reliable text from a medical standpoint.

From "Small-boat Sailing"

by Jack London

A sailor is born, not made. And by "sailor" is meant, not the average efficient and hopeless creature who is found to-day in the forecastle of deepwater ships, but the man who will take a fabric compounded of wood and iron and rope and canvas and compel it to obey his will on the surface of the sea. Barring captains and mates of big ships, the small-boat sailor is the real sailor. He knows—he must know—how to make the wind carry his craft from one given point to another given point. He must know about tides and rips and eddies, bar and channel markings, and day and night signals; he must be wise in weather-lore; and he must be sympathetically familiar with the peculiar qualities of his boat which differentiate it from every other boat that was ever built and rigged. He must know how to gentle her about, as one instance of a myriad, and to fill her on the other tack without deadening her way or allowing her to fall off too far.

The deepwater sailor of today needs know none of these things. And he doesn't. He pulls and hauls as he is ordered, swabs decks, washes paint, and chips iron-rust. He knows nothing, and cares less. Put him in a small boat and he is helpless. He will cut an even better figure on the hurricane deck of a horse.

I shall never forget my child-astonishment when I first encountered one of these strange beings. He was a runaway English sailor. I was a lad of twelve, with a decked-over, fourteen-foot, centre-board skiff which I had taught myself to sail. I sat at his feet as at the feet of a god, while he discoursed of strange lands and peoples, deeds of violence, and hair-raising gales at sea. Then, one day, I took him for a sail. With all the trepidation of the veriest little amateur, I hoisted sail and got under way. Here was a man, looking on critically, I was sure, who knew more in one second about boats and the water than I could ever know. After an interval, in which I exceeded myself, he took the tiller and the sheet. I sat on the little thwart amidships, open-mouthed, prepared to learn what real sailing was. My mouth remained open, for I learned what a real sailor was in a small boat. He couldn't trim the sheet to save himself, he nearly capsized several times in squalls, and, once again, by blunderingly jibing over; he didn't know what a centre-board was for, nor did he know that in running a boat before the wind one must sit in the middle instead of on the side; and finally, when we came back to the wharf, he ran the skiff in full tilt, shattering her nose and carrying away the mast-step. And yet he was a really truly sailor fresh from the vast deep.

Which points my moral. A man can sail in the forecastles of big ships all his life and never know what real sailing is. From the time I was twelve, I listened to the lure of the sea. When I was fifteen I was captain and owner of an oyster-pirate sloop. By the time I was sixteen I was sailing in scow-schooners, fishing salmon with the Greeks up the Sacramento River, and serving as sailor on the Fish Patrol. And I was a good sailor, too, though all my cruising had been on San Francisco Bay and the rivers tributary to it. I had never been on the ocean in my life.

Then, the month I was seventeen, I signed before the mast as an able seaman on a three-top-mast schooner bound on a seven-months' cruise across the Pacific and back again. As my shipmates promptly informed me, I had had my nerve with me to sign on as able seaman. Yet behold, I *was* an able seaman. I had graduated from the right school. It took no more than minutes to learn the names and uses of the

273

few new ropes. It was simple. I did not do things blindly. As a small-boat sailor I had learned to reason out and know the *why* of everything. It is true, I had to learn how to steer by compass, which took maybe half a minute; but when it came to steering "full-and-by" and "close-and-by," I could beat the average of my shipmates, because that was the very way I had always sailed. Inside fifteen minutes I could box the compass around and back again. And there was little else to learn during that seven-months' cruise, except fancy rope-sailorising, such as the more complicated lanyard knots and the making of various kinds of sennit and rope-mats. The point of all of which is that it is by means of small-boat sailing that the real sailor is best schooled.

And if a man is a born sailor, and has gone to the school of the sea, never in all his life can he get away from the sea again. The salt of it is in his bones as well as his nostrils, and the sea will call to him until he dies. Of late years, I have found easier ways of earning a living. I have quit the forecastle for keeps, but always I come back to the sea. In my case it is usually San Francisco Bay, than which no lustier, tougher, sheet of water can be found for small-boat sailing.

It really blows on San Francisco Bay. During the winter, which is the best cruising season, we have southeasters, southwesters, and occasional howling northers. Throughout the summer we have what we call the "sea-breeze," an unfailing wind off the Pacific that on most afternoons in the week blows what the Atlantic Coast yachtsmen would name a gale. They are always surprised by the small spread of canvas our yachts carry. Some of them, with schooners they have sailed around the Horn, have looked proudly at their own lofty sticks and huge spreads, then patronizingly and even pityingly at ours. Then, perchance, they have joined in a club cruise from San Francisco to Mare Island. They found the morning run up the Bay delightful. In the afternoon, when the brave west wind ramped across San Pablo Bay and they faced it on the long beat home, things were somewhat different. One by one, like a flight of swallows, our more meagerly sparred and canvassed yachts went by, leaving them wallowing and dead and shortening down in what they called a gale but which we called a dandy sailing breeze. The next time they came out, we would notice their sticks cut down, their booms shortened, and their after-leeches nearer the luffs by whole cloths.

As for excitement, there is all the difference in the world between a ship in trouble at sea, and a small boat in trouble on land-locked water. Yet for genuine excitement and thrill, give me the small boat. Things happen so quickly, and there are always so few to do the work—and hard work, too, as the small-boat sailor knows. I have toiled all night, both watches on deck, in a typhoon off the coast of Japan, and been less exhausted than by two hours' work at reefing down a thirty-foot sloop and heaving up two anchors on a lee shore in a screaming southeaster.

Hard work and excitement? Let the wind baffle and drop in a heavy tide-way just as you are sailing your little sloop through a narrow draw-bridge. Behold your sails, upon which you are depending, flap with sudden emptiness, and then see the impish wind, with a haul of eight points, fill your jib aback with a gusty puff. Around she goes, and sweeps, not through the open draw, but broadside on against the solid piles. Hear the roar of the tide, sucking through the trestle. And hear and see your pretty, fresh-painted boat crash against the piles. Feel her stout little hull give to the impact. See the rail actually pinch in. Hear your canvas tearing, and see the black, square-ended timbers thrusting holes through it. Smash! There goes your topmast stay, and the topmast reels over drunkenly above you. There is a ripping and crunching. If it continues, your starboard shrouds will be torn out. Grab a rope—any rope—and take a turn around a pile. But the free end of the rope is too short. You can't make it fast, and you hold on and wildly yell for your one companion to get a turn with another and longer rope. Hold on! You hold on till you are purple in the face, till it seems your arms are dragging out of their sockets, till the blood bursts from the ends of your fingers. But you hold, and your partner gets the longer rope and makes it fast. You straighten up and look at your hands. They are ruined. You can scarcely relax the crooks of the fingers. The pain is sickening. But there is no time. The skiff, which is always perverse, is pounding against the barnacles on the piles which threaten to scrape its gunwale off. It's drop the peak! Down jib! Then you run lines, and pull and haul and heave, and exchange unpleasant remarks with the bridge-tender who is always willing to meet you more than half way in such repartee. And finally, at the end of an hour, with aching back, sweat-soaked shirt, and slaughtered hands, you are through and swinging along on the placid, beneficent tide between narrow banks where the cattle stand knee-deep and gaze wonderingly at you. Excitement! Work! Can you beat it in a calm day on the deep sea?

I've tried it both ways. I remember laboring in a fourteen days' gale off the coast of New Zealand. We were a tramp collier, rusty and battered, with six thousand tons of coal in our hold. Life lines were stretched fore and aft; and on our weather side, attached to smokestack guys and rigging, were huge rope-nettings, hung there for the purpose of breaking the force of the seas and so saving our mess-room doors. But the doors were smashed and the mess-rooms washed out just the same. And yet, out of it all, arose but the one feeling, namely, of monotony.

1.   What is the purpose of this essay?

   a.   to persuade the reader to consider learning how to sail a small boat
   b.   to inform the reader about different types of sailing and sailors
   c.   ***to persuade the reader that small boats demand the greatest sailing skill***
   d.   to explain the author's history as a sailor since he was the age of eleven

2.   In paragraph 1, the author says that a real sailor must know all of the following **except**

   a.   how to get from A to B on a boat.
   b.   the tides, rips, eddies, and bars.
   c.   ***how to work on a deepwater ship.***
   d.   how to be gentle, and to give the sailor's touch.

275

3. In paragraph 1, why does the author say that only the captains and mates of big ships are real sailors on deepwater ships?

   a. He does not want to offend captains and mates whom he knows.
   b. They need much of the same knowledge that a small-boat sailor has.
   c. He says that he was formerly a mate on a deepwater vessel.
   d. He believes chiefly that the mates and captains are not real sailors.

4. In paragraph 3, the author's attitude towards the sailor changes from

   a. friendly to appreciative.
   b. disappointed to reconciled.
   c. impressed to resentful.
   d. reverent to disgusted.

5. In paragraph 5, what does the author attribute to his quick learning on a deepwater vessel?

   a. his friend's wise advice
   b. small-boat experience
   c. the mate's good teaching
   d. his skill with a compass

6. In paragraph 6, which of the following does **not** express the author's opinion?

   a. A born sailor, schooled by the sea, can never leave the sea.
   b. San Francisco Bay has the toughest conditions for a small boat.
   c. The author says he is no longer employed as a sailor.
   d. The sea calls to a born sailor until he departs from the earth.

7. What is the purpose of paragraph 7?

   a. to prove that small-boat sailing is difficult in the San Francisco Bay
   b. to show how enjoyable it can be to sail a day on the San Francisco Bay
   c. to explain the techniques of Atlantic Coast sailors in San Francisco Bay
   d. to explain that the Atlantic Coast sailors had to cut down their sail area

8. In paragraph 9, what is the overall tone?

   a. tiring and slow
   b. disappointing and angry
   c. exciting and adventurous
   d. violent and uncontrollable

9. Paragraph 9 and 10 compare

   a. a peaceful Pacific sea with a stormy Atlantic sea.
   b. the small boat sailors from the East and West coasts.
   c. dangers on a small boat and dangers on a big boat.
   d. the various trials that one encounters while at sea.

10. What is the genre of this nonfiction work?
    a. biography
    b. interview
    c. persuasive essay
    d. letter

11. Is any information provided about the author's qualifications for writing the article?

The author says he has had years of experience on both small boats and deepwater vessels. He says that when he was twelve years old he was sailing a small fourteen-foot skiff. At fifteen, he was captain and owner of an oyster-pirate sloop. At sixteen he was sailing in scow-schooners on the Sacramento River. At seventeen he first experienced sailing on a deepwater vessel, a three-top-mast schooner, for seven-months in the Pacific. He also says that he sailed a tramp collier, a deepwater vessel for hauling coal. At the point when the author writes this essay, he is again sailing small boats on the San Francisco Bay. The author gives many examples of sailing in all types of conditions on many types of boats; this gives him license to write this story.

12. What claims does the author make in this passage, and how does he support these claims?

Throughout his text, the author makes claims and defends them through example. In paragraph 2, the author claims that deepwater sailors would be lost in a small boat. To support this claim, in paragraph 3 the author tells the story of when he took a supposedly experienced British sailor out on a little skiff and found that the British sailor really did not know how to sail. In paragraph 6, the author claims that of San Francisco Bay, ". . . no lustier, tougher, sheet of water can be found for small-boat sailing." In paragraph 7, the author defends this claim by telling the anecdote of the Atlantic coast sailors who were schooled by the Bay's west wind. In paragraph 8, the author claims that small boats are far more exhausting than deepwater vessels. To support this he says that he has been up for two shifts on a big boat in a typhoon and had "been less exhausted than by two hours' work at reefing down a thirty-foot sloop and heaving up two anchors on a lee shore in a screaming southeaster." The purpose of the whole of paragraph 9 is to further the idea that small boats are exciting and hard work. Paragraph 10, still building on this claim, concludes that being in peril on a deepwater vessel is "monotony."

13. In looking at the author's word choice, which words in the text can be considered sailing jargon? What effect does the jargon have on the text and its audience?

The author uses many sailing terms that the average reader will not understand. Among them are "tack," "falling off," "deadening away," "jibing," "centerboard," "skiff," "capsize," "sloop," "scow-schooner," "gunwale," "jib," and "boom." These words add a sense of authenticity to the text and back the claims of its author. Some students will say that the author's use of jargon in the essay makes them feel like they are conversing with a sailor. Other students will say that the jargon puts too much distance between the reader and his audience, making it harder for the reader to understand. This also reduces the pleasure of reading, forcing the layman to work harder to understand the author's meaning.

14. Paragraph 9, discuss the point of view and what effect it has on the reader. Contrast this point of view with the one used by the author in paragraph 3.

In paragraph 9, the point of view is in the second person. Here the author is using the pronoun "you" to connect directly with his reader. The purpose of this technique is to make readers feel as if they are the ones having the experience mentioned in the text. In this case, the author wants his reader to know the excitement of sailing a small boat. When the author says, "Behold your sails, upon which you are depending, flap with sudden emptiness, and then see the impish wind, with a haul of eight points, fill your jib aback with a gusty puff," the author wants his reader to visualize the empty sails suddenly being hit by a rush of wind that fills them with force. Here the use of "your" brings the reader into the boat with the author. In paragraph 3, the author uses first person to relate a personal moment of awareness after he had encountered someone whom he thought he admired and then found out that this person was not what he seemed. Readers could not relate to this disappointment without the author guiding them through the transformation he endured.

Question 1	Analyzing the Author's Purpose
Question 2	Making Generalizations
Question 3	Making Inferences
Question 4	Recognizing the Author's Bias and Beliefs
Question 5	Analyzing Cause and Effect
Question 6	Distinguishing Fact and Opinion
Question 7	Drawing Conclusions
Question 8	Analyzing Development of Tone and Mood
Question 9	Comparing and Contrasting
Question 10	Distinguishing Among Different Genres of Nonfiction
Question 11	Evaluating Validity, Credibility, and Reliability of Text
Question 12	Analyzing Persuasion and Propaganda Techniques
Question 13	Evaluating Author's Style
Question 14	Analyzing Point of View

THE DIAMOND NECKLACE

by Guy de Maupassant

The girl was one of those pretty and charming young creatures who sometimes are born, as if by a slip of fate, into a family of clerks. She had no dowry, no expectations, no way of being known, understood, loved, married by any rich and distinguished man; so she let herself be married to a little clerk of the Ministry of Public Instruction.

She dressed plainly because she could not dress well, but she was unhappy as if she had really fallen from a higher station; since with women there is neither caste nor rank, for beauty, grace and charm take the place of family and birth. Natural ingenuity, instinct for what is elegant, a supple mind are their sole hierarchy, and often make of women of the people the equals of the very greatest ladies.

Mathilde suffered ceaselessly, feeling herself born to enjoy all delicacies and all luxuries. She was distressed at the poverty of her dwelling, at the bareness of the walls, at the shabby chairs, the ugliness of the curtains. All those things, of which another woman of her rank would never even have been conscious, tortured her and made her angry. The sight of the little Breton peasant who did her humble housework aroused in her despairing regrets and bewildering dreams. She thought of silent antechambers hung with Oriental tapestry, illumined by tall bronze candelabra, and of two great footmen in knee breeches who sleep in the big armchairs, made drowsy by the oppressive heat of the stove. She thought of long reception halls hung with ancient silk, of the dainty cabinets containing priceless curiosities and of the little coquettish perfumed reception rooms made for chatting at five o'clock with intimate friends, with men famous and sought after, whom all women envy and whose attention they all desire.

When she sat down to dinner, before the round table covered with a tablecloth in use three days, opposite her husband, who uncovered the soup tureen and declared with a delighted air, "Ah, the good soup! I don't know anything better than that," she thought of dainty dinners, of shining silverware, of tapestry that peopled the walls with ancient personages and with strange birds flying in the midst of a fairy forest; and she thought of delicious dishes served on marvellous plates and of the whispered gallantries to which you listen with a sphinxlike smile while you are eating the pink meat of a trout or the wings of a quail.

She had no gowns, no jewels, nothing. And she loved nothing but that. She felt made for that. She would have liked so much to please, to be envied, to be charming, to be sought after.

She had a friend, a former schoolmate at the convent, who was rich, and whom she did not like to go to see any more because she felt so sad when she came home.

But one evening her husband reached home with a triumphant air and holding a large envelope in his hand.

"There," said he, "there is something for you."

She tore the paper quickly and drew out a printed card which bore these words:

The Minister of Public Instruction and Madame Georges Ramponneau request the honor of M. and Madame Loisel's company at the palace of the Ministry on Monday evening, January 18th.

Instead of being delighted, as her husband had hoped, she threw the invitation on the table crossly, muttering:

"What do you wish me to do with that?"

"Why, my dear, I thought you would be glad. You never go out, and this is such a fine opportunity. I had great trouble to get it. Every one wants to go; it is very select, and they are not giving many invitations to clerks. The whole official world will be there."

She looked at him with an irritated glance and said impatiently:

"And what do you wish me to put on my back?"

He had not thought of that. He stammered:

"Why, the gown you go to the theatre in. It looks very well to me."

He stopped, distracted, seeing that his wife was weeping. Two great tears ran slowly from the corners of her eyes toward the corners of her mouth.

"What's the matter? What's the matter?" he answered.

By a violent effort she conquered her grief and replied in a calm voice, while she wiped her wet cheeks:

"Nothing. Only I have no gown, and, therefore, I can't go to this ball. Give your card to some colleague whose wife is better equipped than I am."

He was in despair. He resumed:

"Come, let us see, Mathilde. How much would it cost, a suitable gown, which you could use on other occasions—something very simple?"

She reflected several seconds, making her calculations and wondering also what sum she could ask without drawing on herself an immediate refusal and a frightened exclamation from the economical clerk.

Finally she replied hesitating:

"I don't know exactly, but I think I could manage it with four hundred francs."

He grew a little pale, because he was laying aside just that amount to buy a gun and treat himself to a little shooting next summer on the plain of Nanterre, with several friends who went to shoot larks there of a Sunday.

But he said:

"Very well. I will give you four hundred francs. And try to have a pretty gown."

The day of the ball drew near and Madame Loisel seemed sad, uneasy, anxious. Her frock was ready, however. Her husband said to her one evening:

"What is the matter? Come, you have seemed very queer these last three days."

And she answered:

"It annoys me not to have a single piece of jewelry, not a single ornament, nothing to put on. I shall look poverty-stricken. I would almost rather not go at all."

"You might wear natural flowers," said her husband. "They're very stylish at this time of year. For ten francs you can get two or three magnificent roses."

She was not convinced.

"No; there's nothing more humiliating than to look poor among other women who are rich."

"How stupid you are!" her husband cried. "Go look up your friend, Madame Forestier, and ask her to lend you some jewels. You're intimate enough with her to do that."

She uttered a cry of joy:

"True! I never thought of it."

The next day she went to her friend and told her of her distress.

Madame Forestier went to a wardrobe with a mirror, took out a large jewel box, brought it back, opened it and said to Madame Loisel:

"Choose, my dear."

She saw first some bracelets, then a pearl necklace, then a Venetian gold cross set with precious stones, of admirable workmanship. She tried on the ornaments before the mirror, hesitated and could not make up her mind to part with them, to give them back. She kept asking:

"Haven't you any more?"

"Why, yes. Look further; I don't know what you like."

Suddenly she discovered, in a black satin box, a superb diamond necklace, and her heart throbbed with an immoderate desire. Her hands trembled as she took it. She fastened it round her throat, outside her high-necked waist, and was lost in ecstasy at her reflection in the mirror.

Then she asked, hesitating, filled with anxious doubt:

"Will you lend me this, only this?"

"Why, yes, certainly."

She threw her arms round her friend's neck, kissed her passionately, then fled with her treasure.

The night of the ball arrived. Madame Loisel was a great success. She was prettier than any other woman present, elegant, graceful, smiling and wild with joy. All the men looked at her, asked her name, sought to be introduced. All the attaches of the Cabinet wished to waltz with her. She was remarked by the minister himself.

She danced with rapture, with passion, intoxicated by pleasure, forgetting all in the triumph of her beauty, in the glory of her success, in a sort of cloud of happiness comprised of all this homage, admiration, these awakened desires and of that sense of triumph which is so sweet to woman's heart.

She left the ball about four o'clock in the morning. Her husband had been sleeping since midnight in a little deserted anteroom with three other gentlemen whose wives were enjoying the ball.

He threw over her shoulders the wraps he had brought, the modest wraps of common life, the poverty of which contrasted with the elegance of the ball dress. She felt this and wished to escape so as not to be remarked by the other women, who were enveloping themselves in costly furs.

Loisel held her back, saying: "Wait a bit. You will catch cold outside. I will call a cab."

But she did not listen to him and rapidly descended the stairs. When they reached the street they could not find a carriage and began to look for one, shouting after the cabmen passing at a distance.

They went toward the Seine in despair, shivering with cold. At last they found on the quay one of those ancient night cabs which, as though they were ashamed to show their shabbiness during the day, are never seen round Paris until after dark.

It took them to their dwelling in the Rue des Martyrs, and sadly they mounted the stairs to their flat. All was ended for her. As to him, he reflected that he must be at the ministry at ten o'clock that morning.

She removed her wraps before the glass so as to see herself once more in all her glory. But suddenly she uttered a cry. She no longer had the necklace around her neck!

"What is the matter with you?" demanded her husband, already half undressed.

She turned distractedly toward him.

"I have—I have—I've lost Madame Forestier's necklace," she cried.

He stood up, bewildered.

"What!—how? Impossible!"

They looked among the folds of her skirt, of her cloak, in her pockets, everywhere, but did not find it.

"You're sure you had it on when you left the ball?" he asked.

"Yes, I felt it in the vestibule of the minister's house."

"But if you had lost it in the street we should have heard it fall. It must be in the cab."

"Yes, probably. Did you take his number?"

"No. And you--didn't you notice it?"

"No."

They looked, thunderstruck, at each other. At last Loisel put on his clothes.

"I shall go back on foot," said he, "over the whole route, to see whether I can find it."

He went out. She sat waiting on a chair in her ball dress, without strength to go to bed, overwhelmed, without any fire, without a thought.

Her husband returned about seven o'clock. He had found nothing.

He went to police headquarters, to the newspaper offices to offer a reward; he went to the cab companies—everywhere, in fact, whither he was urged by the least spark of hope.

She waited all day, in the same condition of mad fear before this terrible calamity.

Loisel returned at night with a hollow, pale face. He had discovered nothing.

"You must write to your friend," said he, "that you have broken the clasp of her necklace and that you are having it mended. That will give us time to turn round."

She wrote at his dictation.

At the end of a week they had lost all hope. Loisel, who had aged five years, declared:

"We must consider how to replace that ornament."

The next day they took the box that had contained it and went to the jeweler whose name was found within. He consulted his books.

"It was not I, madame, who sold that necklace; I must simply have furnished the case."

Then they went from jeweler to jeweler, searching for a necklace like the other, trying to recall it, both sick with chagrin and grief.

They found, in a shop at the Palais Royal, a string of diamonds that seemed to them exactly like the one they had lost. It was worth forty thousand francs. They could have it for thirty-six.

So they begged the jeweler not to sell it for three days yet. And they made a bargain that he should buy it back for thirty-four thousand francs, in case they should find the lost necklace before the end of February.

Loisel possessed eighteen thousand francs which his father had left him. He would borrow the rest.

He did borrow, asking a thousand francs of one, five hundred of another, five louis here, three louis there. He gave notes, took up ruinous obligations, dealt with usurers and all the race of lenders. He compromised all the rest of his life, risked signing a note without even knowing whether he could meet it; and, frightened by the trouble yet to come, by the black misery that was about to fall upon him, by the prospect of all the physical privations and moral tortures that he was to suffer, he went to get the new necklace, laying upon the jeweler's counter thirty-six thousand francs.

When Madame Loisel took back the necklace Madame Forestier said to her with a chilly manner:

"You should have returned it sooner; I might have needed it."

She did not open the case, as her friend had so much feared. If she had detected the substitution, what would she have thought, what would she have said? Would she not have taken Madame Loisel for a thief?

Thereafter Madame Loisel knew the horrible existence of the needy. She bore her part, however, with sudden heroism. That dreadful debt must be paid. She would pay it. They dismissed their servant; they changed their lodgings; they rented a garret under the roof.

She came to know what heavy housework meant and the odious cares of the kitchen. She washed the dishes, using her dainty fingers and rosy nails on greasy pots and pans. She washed the soiled linen, the shirts and the dishcloths, which she dried upon a line; she carried the slops down to the street every morning and carried up the water, stopping for breath at every landing. And dressed like a woman of the people, she went to the fruiterer, the grocer, the butcher, a basket on her arm, bargaining, meeting with impertinence, defending her miserable money, sou by sou.

Every month they had to meet some notes, renew others, obtain more time.

Her husband worked evenings, making up a tradesman's accounts, and late at night he often copied manuscript for five sous a page.

This life lasted ten years.

At the end of ten years they had paid everything, everything, with the rates of usury and the accumulations of the compound interest.

Madame Loisel looked old now. She had become the woman of impoverished households—strong and hard and rough. With frowsy hair, skirts askew and red hands, she talked loud while washing the floor with great swishes of water. But sometimes, when her husband was at the office, she sat down near the window and she thought of that gay evening of long ago, of that ball where she had been so beautiful and so admired.

What would have happened if she had not lost that necklace? Who knows? who knows? How strange and changeful is life! How small a thing is needed to make or ruin us! But one Sunday, having gone to take a walk in the Champs Elysees to refresh herself after the labors of the week, she suddenly perceived a woman who was leading a child. It was Madame Forestier, still young, still beautiful, still charming.

Madame Loisel felt moved. Should she speak to her? Yes, certainly. And now that she had paid, she would tell her all about it. Why not?

She went up.

"Good-day, Jeanne."

The other, astonished to be familiarly addressed by this plain good-wife, did not recognize her at all and stammered:

"But—madame!—I do not know—You must have mistaken."

"No. I am Mathilde Loisel."

Her friend uttered a cry.

"Oh, my poor Mathilde! How you are changed!"

"Yes, I have had a pretty hard life, since I last saw you, and great poverty--and that because of you!"

"Of me! How so?"

"Do you remember that diamond necklace you lent me to wear at the ministerial ball?"

"Yes. Well?"

"Well, I lost it."

"What do you mean? You brought it back."

"I brought you back another exactly like it. And it has taken us ten years to pay for it. You can understand that it was not easy for us, for us who had nothing. At last it is ended, and I am very glad."

Madame Forestier had stopped.

"You say that you bought a necklace of diamonds to replace mine?"

"Yes. You never noticed it, then! They were very similar."

And she smiled with a joy that was at once proud and ingenuous.

Madame Forestier, deeply moved, took her hands.

"Oh, my poor Mathilde! Why, my necklace was paste! It was worth at most only five hundred francs!"

1. What is the tone of the opening paragraph?

   a. chaotic
   b. curious
   c. forlorn
   d. thoughtful

2. What is the author assuming in the following sentence?

   "The girl was one of those pretty and charming young creatures who sometimes are born, as if by a slip of fate, into a family of clerks."

   a. Pretty girls should only live with clerks.
   b. Attractive, charming women should be born into wealthy families.
   c. Being a clerk's daughter is very lucky.
   d. Clerks are often affected by fate and are usually well known.

3. What can the reader tell about the author from the second paragraph?

   a. He thinks that women aren't as intelligent as men.
   b. He thinks that women should always be happy with their station in life.
   c. He thinks that the greatest ladies are plain and were once of high social status.
   d. He thinks that ordinary women need only to act a certain way to be considered ladies.

4. How does Mathilde feel about the people who have things she doesn't?

   a. anxious
   b. delighted
   c. content
   d. jealous

5. Early in the story, which of the following items most likely serves as a metaphor for Mathilde's day-to-day life?

   a. strange birds
   b. three-day-old tablecloth
   c. pink meat of a trout
   d. Oriental tapestries

6. What effect does the invitation have on Mathilde?

   a. She immediately starts thinking of ways to get a new dress.
   b. She thanks her husband for the lovely sentiment.
   c. She realizes that things weren't as bad as she thought.
   d. She becomes agitated and begins to cry.

7. Why did Mathilde choose the diamond necklace?

   a. It was the most noticeable.
   b. It was the only jewelry her friend would lend her.
   c. She knew her husband would like it.
   d. She thought it would look best with her dress.

8. How was Mathilde first reminded of the contrast between her real life and her place at the ball?

   a. Her husband was asleep in an adjoining room.
   b. Her friend deserted her.
   c. Her husband helped her to put her ordinary wrap on.
   d. Her friend offered to call a cab.

9. What does the author mean when he says that Loisel had "aged five years"?

   a. He was frightened and angry.
   b. He was nervous and overly tired.
   c. He had many more wrinkles.
   d. He had just had a birthday.

10. What is the author's purpose in this story?

    a. *to teach readers a lesson*
    b. to inform readers of a time in history
    c. to show readers how to solve problems
    d. to persuade readers to buy expensive jewelry

11. M. Loisel is a

    a. *flat, static character.*
    b. flat, dynamic character.
    c. round, static character.
    d. round, dynamic character.

12. Using examples of direct and indirect characterization to support your point, describe Mme. Loisel before she goes to the party.

One possible answer:

Mme Loisel could be described as selfish and obsessed with the material things that define social status. This is directly referred to when the narrator mentions that she was "unhappy as though kept out of her own class," "born by a blunder of destiny in a family of employees," and wanting expensive, flashy jewelry and dresses. Instead of being thankful for what she has, she continually "suffers" and thinks about such things as the fancy parlors with delicate furniture that she does not have. Her thoughts indirectly develop her character. This is further emphasized indirectly through her actions; Mme. Loisel does not want to go to the party because she does not have the right dress.

13. Why does the author say that the sight of "the little Breton peasant" aroused Mathilde's regrets and dreams?

One possible answer:

Mathilde is not poverty-stricken. She has a servant. Oddly enough, it is the presence of this servant that makes her wish for more servants and a grander life. Perhaps it is because, in feeling superior to one, she wishes she could feel superior to others. A little feeling of grandeur arouses the desire for even more. Or perhaps she feels that her own life is not that different from the servant's.

A second possible answer:

Mathilde feels "tortured and angry" when she thinks of all the things she wants but does not have. In her mind, she compares the peasant, who is probably shabbily dressed, to the servants wealthy women have in their homes: "two great footmen in knee breeches." While her servant must do their meager housework, she imagines these footmen lounging about on great armchairs. The peasant reminds her of all she longs for and, because of her social status, cannot have—Oriental rugs, bronze candelabra, and parlors in which to entertain fancy guests. Mme. Loisel feels that she should have been "born to enjoy all delicacies and luxuries." Nevertheless, she looks around her and sees the symbols of modest living: "the bareness of the walls, . . . the shabby chairs, the ugliness of the curtains." While, as the author points out, another woman in her position might not even bother about these trivial things, Mathilde is "distressed" and suffers for lack of having them.

14. When she thinks she has lost the diamond necklace, Mathilde panics. However, she does not at first go out to look for it with her husband. Neither does she go to look for it by herself. Why do you think this is?

One possible answer:

Mathilde is a very selfish person. She has always thought only of herself and her own needs and desires. She has always been envious of others and thought nothing of her husband's struggle to keep them from being completely impoverished. She doesn't even consider what an honor it was for him — as a clerk — to have been invited to the ball. Mathilde, who has grown used to having her husband take care of her, despite her endless dissatisfaction, doesn't even seem to consider making an effort to help Loisel. (One might notice, however, that she hurried to her friend's house to obtain the necklace in the first place.) Loisel even sticks his neck out to borrow the money to buy a new necklace, even though it was Mathilde's fault that it had been lost.

In answering this question, students should discuss Mathilde's character and personality. They should also show an understanding both of the facts in the story and the attitudes of the couple toward one another. Their answers should be clearly expressed and well written.

15. Why do you think M. and Mme. Loisel felt compelled to replace the necklace? What does this say about them?

It is clear that M. Loisel is an honorable, honest man. Until they lose the necklace, Mathilde has seemed dreamy, dissatisfied, and perhaps even selfish. However, she is willing to follow her husband's lead and accept responsibility for replacing the necklace. Students may differ about whether or not this is a new development in her character or if it was inherent all along.

16. Predict what will happen next. How will Mathilde be the same and how will she be different? Also, tell whether or not you feel Mathilde is a "dynamic character" or a "static character." Use specific details from the passage to support your answer.

One possible answer:

One could argue that until the loss of the necklace, Mathilde is concerned mainly with herself and her needs. Unfortunately for her, she could not exchange these feelings for, as the author says in the second paragraph, "grace and charm [which would] take the place of family and birth." Instead, she feels herself to be cheated and unlucky. She envies wealthy women for their material possessions and for their roles in society.

Near the end of the story, however, Mathilde has lost any grace, charm, or beauty she once had. Her social status is lower than before. She has had to give up even the meager home and servant. She has learned to take care of herself and her husband alone. She reminisces about the ball and wonders how "such a small thing" could "ruin" them. She has become mindful of the possibility of everything changing. By the end of the story, Mathilde is seen to be a dynamic character who has changed from being selfish and materialistic to being hardworking and frank.

The unexpected twist at the end of this story greatly affects the outcome of the couple's future. It is possible that Mme. Forestier will think nothing of Mathilde having paid nearly full price for an actual diamond necklace. However, she does not seem cold-hearted. It is perhaps even possible that she will return the necklace to M. and Mme. Loisel. If that were to happen, Mathilde would then be in a position to sell the necklace, and perhaps to reimburse her friend for the 500 francs she had paid for the fake necklace, and go on to live a wealthy, fortunate life. Mathilde will not be able to restore her youth or beauty, but she may be able to restore her spirit. After having been taught a lesson for having succumbed to being envious of others and living in miserable conditions, it could be that fate would grant her wish after all.

The surprise twist at the end of this story should make students' answers to this question quite interesting. They should show an understanding of the basic plot, and support their answers with details. A thorough answer will provide some explanation of Mathilde's progression as a character, and perhaps offer reasons why she suffered for her behavior.

17. Evaluate "The Diamond Necklace." What qualities does it have that make it effective or ineffective for you as a reader? Give specific examples from the story to support your reasons for your evaluation.

Students who favorably evaluate the story might, for example, point out that the characters are believable for their real emotions and desires; the conflict is intriguing; the themes are appropriate to the setting and historical period; and the mood and tone are consistent throughout. Also, the author is unwavering in his bias and beliefs throughout, as indicated by his statements that a certain kind of woman—while able to raise herself above social classes through good manners, grace, and beauty—still remain dissatisfied with her station in life. The lesson in this story will most likely lead students to say that it is an honest tale of greed, ingratitude, and conflict.

PLATO'S "THE APOLOGY" FROM *THE DIALOGUES OF SOCRATES*

translated by Benjamen Jowett

Socrates: How you, O Athenians, have been affected by my accusers, I cannot tell; butI know that they almost made me forget who I was—so persuasively did they speak; and yet they have hardly uttered a word of truth. But of the many falsehoods told by them, there was one which quite amazed me;—I mean when they said that you should be upon your guard and not allow yourselves to be deceived by the force of my eloquence. To say this, when they were certain to be detected as soon as I opened my lips and proved myself to be anything but a great speaker, did indeed appear to me most shameless—unless by the force of eloquence they mean the force of truth; for is such is their meaning, I admit that I am eloquent. But in how different a way from theirs! Well, as I was saying, they have scarcely spoken the truth at all; but from me you shall hear the whole truth: not, however, delivered after their manner in a set oration duly ornamented with words and phrases. No, by heaven! but I shall use the words and arguments which occur to me at the moment; for I am confident in the justice of my cause (Or, I am certain that I am right in taking this course.): at my time of life I ought not to be appearing before you, O men of Athens, in the character of a juvenile orator—let no one expect it of me. And I must beg of you to grant me a favor:—If I defend myself in my accustomed manner, and you hear me using the words which I have been in the habit of using in the agora, at the tables of the money-changers, or anywhere else, I would ask you not to be surprised, and not to interrupt me on this account. For I am more than seventy years of age, and appearing now for the first time in a court of law, I am quite a stranger to the language of the place; and therefore I would have you regard me as if I were really a stranger, whom you would excuse if he spoke in his native tongue, and after the fashion of his country:—Am I making an unfair request of you? Never mind the manner, which may or may not be good; but think only of the truth of my words, and give heed to that: let the speaker speak truly and the judge decide justly.

And first, I have to reply to the older charges and to my first accusers, and then I will go on to the later ones. For of old I have had many accusers, who have accused me falsely to you during many years; and I am more afraid of them than of Anytus and his associates, who are dangerous, too, in their own way. But far more dangerous are the others, who began when you were children, and took possession of your minds with their falsehoods, telling of one Socrates, a wise man, who speculated about the heaven above, and searched into the earth beneath, and made the worse appear the better cause. The disseminators of this tale are the accusers whom I dread; for their hearers are apt to fancy that such enquirers do not believe in the existence of the gods. And they are many, and their charges against me are of ancient date, and they were made by them in the days when you were more impressible than you are now—in childhood, or it may have been in youth—and the cause when heard went by default, for there was none to answer. And hardest of all, I do not know and cannot tell the names of my accusers; unless in the chance case of a Comic poet. All who from envy and malice have persuaded you—some of them having first convinced themselves—all this class of men are most difficult to deal with; for I cannot have them up here, and cross-examine them, and therefore I must simply fight with shadows in my own defense, and argue when there is no one who answers. I will ask you then to assume with me, as I was saying, that my opponents are of two

293

kinds; one recent, the other ancient: and I hope that you will see the propriety of my answering the latter first, for these accusations you heard long before the others, and much oftener.

Well, then, I must make my defense, and endeavor to clear away in a short time, a slander which has lasted a long time. May I succeed, if to succeed be for my good and yours, or likely to avail me in my cause! The task is not an easy one; I quite understand the nature of it. And so leaving the event with God, in obedience to the law I will now make my defense.

1. What is Socrates purpose in speaking to the Athenians?

   a. to persuade them that he is innocent
   b. to inform them of his plans for the future
   c. to entertain them with his dramatic humor.
   d. to apologize for his past behavior

2. In what way can you be sure that Socrates is telling the truth?

   a. He is a famous Greek philosopher and would never tell a lie.
   b. It is not possible to know whether or not he is telling the truth.
   c. It is possible to tell by reading his words very carefully.
   d. Socrates is honest because Socrates has included this in his dialogues.

3. Which was the falsehood that particularly amazed Socrates?

   a. His listeners should listen very carefully to him to understand what he says.
   b. His listeners should listen very carefully to him to spot the lies he tells.
   c. His listeners should listen very carefully and not be swayed by his eloquence.
   d. His listeners should listen very carefully and trust everything he says.

4. Socrates equates the "force of eloquence" to

   a. meaning.
   b. his accusers.
   c. a lie.
   d. the truth.

5. How does Socrates compare his eloquence with that of his accusers?

   a. He says that they have spoken very unpersuasively and were not prepared.
   b. He says that they have read their words while he will speak spontaneously.
   c. He says that he alone is convinced that his cause is right and just.
   d. He says that they have made up their arguments and he will not.

6. What is the tone of Socrates's speech?

    a. dull and sleepy
    b. lighthearted and humorous
    c. ***forceful and direct***
    d. angry and bitter

7. Socrates asks the court to treat him as if he "were really a stranger" because he

    a. ***has never been in court and does not know the language of the court.***
    b. has recently come to Athens from another country far away.
    c. does not know any of the Athenians present at the court.
    d. is well known because he has been in court many times before.

8. Plato has Socrates clearly state his bias when Socrates says that

    a. he should be treated like a stranger.
    b. he is unable to face his accusers.
    c. ***his accusers speak nothing but lies.***
    d. he will only speak the truth.

9. For what reason does Socrates greatly fear his older accusers?

    a. He says that the Athenians heard the arguments of his older accusers when young and sure of themselves.
    b. ***He says that the Athenians heard the arguments of his older accusers when young and impressionable.***
    c. He says that his older accusers are more dangerous because they don't believe in the existence of the gods.
    d. He says that his older accusers are more dangerous because they do believe in the existence of the gods

10. Based on reading the text, which of the following generalizations is most accurate?

    a. There are many people who defend Socrates.
    b. The Athenian court is very fair to Socrates.
    c. The court has little power over Socrates.
    d. ***Socrates is at the mercy of the Athenian court.***

11. Socrates says the following:

    "And hardest of all, I do not know and cannot tell the names of my accusers; unless in the chance case of a Comic poet."

    When Socrates mentions "a Comic poet" to what is he most likely referring?

    a. ***a poet or writer of the time who has criticized him in his work***
    b. a joke or a comedy that he has read from a time long in the past
    c. a humorous poet who has by chance decided to support Socrates
    d. the Athenians, whom he is ridiculing by calling them Comic poets

12. Summarize what Socrates has said in his opening remarks to the Athenians. Be sure to include all of his important points.

One possible answer:

Socrates says that he cannot know the effect of his accusers on the Athenians. He says that his accusers spoke very well, but have not spoken a bit of truth. He objects to them warning the Athenians to watch out for Socrates's ability to speak very well. He says that he will only speak the truth and that he will speak without preparation or notes. He says that he will speak in his normal manner as he does not know the special language of the court. He asks them only to listen for the truth, and not to the style of his words. Socrates says that he will first respond to those who have accused him for many years. Then he will respond to those who have recently and are now accusing him. He points out that he does not know who his accusers are, and that he is not allowed to confront them directly. Finally Socrates says that he will make his defense and try to clear away the slander that has lasted a long time.

Students should write concise and detailed summaries of the words of Socrates. They should include all the important points without including any unimportant information. Each student should reveal in her or his answer the knowledge that a summary will be shorter than the original.

13. Socrates says the following:

All who from envy and malice have persuaded you—some of them having first convinced themselves—all this class of men are most difficult to deal with; for I cannot have them up here, and cross-examine them, and therefore I must simply fight with shadows in my own defense, and argue when there is no one who answers. I will ask you then to assume with me, as I was saying, that my opponents are of two kinds; one recent, the other ancient: and I hope that you will see the propriety of my answering the latter first, for these accusations you heard long before the others, and much oftener.

What conclusions can you draw about Socrates from this passage?

One possible answer:

It is reasonable to conclude that Socrates has had enemies for many years. He feels that these people have felt jealous of him, envy him and for this reason wish to do him harm. Socrates must have been a public figure of some kind, or had influence on some of the people of Athens in order to have fostered the anger and malice of others. It is likely that he has been a teacher of some sort. He says: "All who from envy and malice . . ." It also seems that Socrates feels that he is at a disadvantage when he says that he "must simply fight with shadows in my own defense . . ."

Students should draw conclusions and support them with examples from the passage.

14. What main problem is Socrates facing? Of what has he been accused? Why is he speaking in front of the Athenians?

One possible answer:

Socrates has been accused of a crime of some sort. It is not entirely clear from this introduction what the crime is. It seems that it may have something to do with whether or not he believes in the Greek gods. It is also clear that he cannot face his accusers, which is another serious problem. He is speaking in front of the Athenians in order to defend himself.

Students should identify the main problem faced by Socrates. They should describe the problem and explain why he is speaking in front of the Athenians.

15. What paradox does Socrates face as he tries to defend himself in front of the court?

The paradox faced by Socrates is that he cannot face those people who have accused him of crimes. He cannot ask them questions. He must speak in his own defense only through his own words and has no chance to directly confront and argue with the people who are against him.

16. Describe Socrates's main ideas in this speech.

One possible answer:
Socrates says that he will defend himself as best he can even though he cannot face his accusers. He says that he will divide his defense into two parts: the first toward his older accusers and the second to those who are more recent.

Each student should clearly and thoughtfully state the main ideas of the speech. Look for accuracy and completeness.

Question 1	Analyzing Author's Purpose
Question 2	Evaluating Validity, Credibility, and Reliability of Text
Question 3	Interpreting the Theme and Main Idea
Question 4	Analyzing Persuasion and Propaganda Techniques
Question 5	Comparing and Contrasting
Question 6	Analyzing Development of Tone and Mood
Question 7	Analyzing Cause and Effect
Question 8	Recognizing Author's Bias and Beliefs
Question 9	Interpreting Text Features
Question 10	Making Generalizations
Question 11	Interpreting References from Culture and the Past
Question 12	Summarizing and Paraphrasing
Question 13	Drawing Conclusions
Question 14	Analyzing Problem and Solution
Question 15	Analyzing Paradox
Question 16	Interpreting the Theme and Main Idea

THE PLUMBER

by Charles Dudley Warner

Speaking of the philosophical temper, there is no class of men whose society is to be more desired for this quality than that of plumbers! They are the most agreeable men I know; and the boys in the business begin to be agreeable very early. I suspect the secret of it is, that they are *agreeable by the hour*. In the driest days, my fountain became disabled: the pipe was stopped up. A couple of plumbers, with the implements of their craft, came out to view the situation. There was a good deal of difference of opinion about where the stoppage was. I found the plumbers perfectly willing to sit down and talk about it,—*talk by the hour*. Some of their guesses and remarks were exceedingly ingenious; and their general observations on other subjects were excellent in their way, and could hardly have been better if they had been made by the job. The work dragged a little,—as it is apt to do by the hour. The plumbers had occasion to make me several visits. Sometimes they would find, upon arrival, that they had forgotten some indispensable tool; and one would go back to the shop, a mile and a half, after it; and his comrade would await his return with the most exemplary patience, and sit down and talk,—always by the hour. I do not know but it is a habit to have something wanted at the shop. They seemed to me very good workmen, and always willing to stop and talk about the job, or any thing else, when I went near them. Nor had they any of that impetuous hurry that is said to be the bane of our American civilization. To their credit be it said, that I never observed any thing of it in them. *They can afford to wait.* Two of them will sometimes wait nearly half a day while a comrade goes for a tool. They are patient and philosophical. It is a great pleasure to meet such men. One only wishes there was some work he could do for *them* by the hour. There ought to be reciprocity. I think they have very nearly solved the problem of Life: it is to work for other people, never for yourself, and get your pay by the hour. You then have no anxiety, and little work. If you do things by the job, you are perpetually driven: the hours are scourges. If you work by the hour, you gently sail on the stream of Time, which is always bearing you on to the haven of Pay, whether you make any effort or not. Working by the hour tends to make one moral. A plumber working by the job, trying to unscrew a rusty, refractory nut, in a cramped position, where the tongs continually slipped off, would swear; but I never heard one of them swear, or exhibit the least impatience at such a vexation, working by the hour. Nothing can move a man who is paid by the hour. How sweet the flight of time seems to his calm mind!–My Summer in a Garden.

1. What is the purpose of this piece?

   a. to inform
   b. *to give an opinion*
   c. to persuade
   d. to criticize

2. Which genre of nonfiction is this piece?

    a. biography

    b. autobiography

    c. letter

    d. essay

3. The tone of this piece is

    a. lighthearted.

    b. enthusiastic.

    c. foreboding.

    d. clinical.

4. According to the piece, which is **not** an effect of working by the hour?

    a. being very tense about the job

    b. being very agreeable

    c. having the work drag a little

    d. always being willing to stop and talk

5. In the first paragraph, the author says, "I suspect the secret of it is, that they are agreeable by the hour." What is the connotation of the words, "agreeable by the hour"?

    a. These men are agreeable because they keep very close track of the time.

    b. All people who are paid by the hour are unhappy.

    c. All people who are paid by the hour are agreeable.

    d. The workers are very agreeable because they are getting paid by the hour.

6. From this passage, it can be inferred that Warner believes that workers who are paid by the hour

    a. are better off than those who do not work by the hour.

    b. are not as skilled as other workers.

    c. only speak about the job on which they are working.

    d. can become easily agitated when things don't go well.

7. The author says, "If you work by the hour, you gently sail on the stream of Time, which is always bearing you on to the haven of Pay, whether you make any effort or not." This is an example of

    a. simile.

    b. personification.

    c. metaphor.

    d. alliteration.

8. Which of the following **best** states the main idea of the piece?

    a. Being a plumber is the best possible job that anyone could have.

    b. People who are paid by the hour are not necessarily inspired to work hard.

    c. The best way to work is to have someone else be your boss.

    d. Working by the hour is very challenging and makes people tense.

9. What was the problem that the author faced in this piece?

    a. He had a leak in his fountain that needed to be fixed.

    b. He was upset because the plumbers would not stop talking.

    c. He discovered that the plumbers he had hired were not working.

    d. His fountain had become stopped up and it no longer worked.

10. According to the author, what will happen when the workers realize that they have forgotten a tool?

    a. One will go to get the tool while the others wait without working.

    b. They figure out how to keep working in spite of needing the tool.

    c. They usually decide to stop working for the day and go home.

    d. They will all leave the job site and go searching for the tool they need.

11. What does the author mean when he says, "There ought to be reciprocity"?

    a. He thinks that the plumbers should be punished for their work.

    b. He is hoping that he can find a gift that he can offer to the plumbers.

    c. He wishes that he could charge the plumbers by the hour for his time.

    d. He is suggesting that the plumbers should stop working by the hour.

12. How does the author compare the worker who does not work by the hour to one who does when they encounter a problem?

    a. He says that the worker who is not paid by the hour will gently sail on the stream of Time.

    b. He says that there is no difference between the worker who does not work by the hour and the one who does not when they encounter a problem.

    c. The worker who does not work by the hour will never become very upset when he encounters a problem and will never swear; the plumber who works by the hour will easily become agitated or impatient and will probably swear.

    d. The worker who does not work by the hour will become very upset when he encounters a problem and will probably swear; the plumber who works by the hour will never become agitated or impatient.

301

13. Describe the author's style in this piece. How does the author present his ideas? Does he state them directly, or does he use other means to make his points? Use examples from the piece to support your ideas.

The author uses humor and irony to make his point. He writes in a lighthearted style and never actually comes out and directly states his own point of view—it is driving him crazy to watch people work by the hour and not work quickly. Rather, he says that it is such a pleasure to meet men who are so patient that they can wait for two hours without working and still expect to be paid.

Students should cite similar examples, including "Nothing can move a man who is paid by the hour," "I think they have very nearly solved the problem of Life," and "They seemed to me very good workmen, and always willing to stop and talk about the job, or any thing else, when I went near them."

14. In this piece Warner praises plumbers for their agreeable nature. He goes on to explain why he thinks that they are so agreeable. How would you describe his point of view about plumbers? Do you think that he believes everything that he says? Analyze the author's point of view. Give examples from the piece to support your ideas.

One possible answer:
The author seems to be saying that plumbers are wonderful and agreeable people. He says that they make excellent workers. At the same time he gives several examples that do not show this to be true. These include the statement that plumbers are always willing to talk about almost anything as long as they are being paid. They are also likely to forget a tool and have to sit around while one person goes to get it, and expect to be paid for their time. By saying one thing (that plumbers are agreeable and very good workmen) and then using examples to prove his point by showing that they are not the best workmen, the author creates an ironic and humorous tone. By the end of the piece, after he says that there ought to be reciprocity, it is clear that he is really saying that because the plumbers are paid by the hour they are, in fact, lazy and not good workers, even though they are agreeable.

15. The author says at the end of the piece that "Nothing can move a man who is paid by the hour." Analyze what he means by that statement. Be sure to think of the literal meaning of the words in the context of the piece. Note how the sentence is used in contrast to the previous description of a plumber working by the job. Then think about what the author is really trying to say when he makes this statement. Use specific evidence from the text to support your answer.

One possible answer:

The author is literally saying that nothing can move a man who works by the hour in the sense that nothing will upset him. He contrasts this with the previous sentences that describe a man who works by the job becoming very upset when the job goes badly. At the same time, the author is implying with irony that the man who works by the hour will go very slowly and at times will do no work at all. He is stating that there is no pressure to do a job when being paid by the hour; the flight of time to him is very sweet. This man will reach the "haven of Pay whether [he makes] any effort or not."

16. Identify one fact and one opinion from the passage, explaining how you know which is which.

Students may choose facts in the essay, e.g., "In the driest days, my fountain became disabled: the pipe was stopped up"; "A couple of plumbers, with the implements of their craft, came out to view the situation"; and "The plumbers had occasion to make me several visits." Students should recognize that facts tell something that is known to be true. Students may also mention that a fact is something that can be proven with evidence. For example, it would be possible to verify that the author's fountain was broken. Students should then identify opinions, e.g., "I suspect the secret of it is, that they are agreeable by the hour"; "It is a great pleasure to meet such men"; and "There ought to be reciprocity." Students should state that an opinion is someone's belief, thought, or feeling and that not everyone may agree with an opinion. For example, when the author says that it is a great pleasure to meet such men who are willing to wait and wait—supposedly while they are working—it is likely that many people would find this agitating or unpleasant, particularly when they are paying these men. In the end the author says, "Nothing can move a man who is paid by the hour." This is another example of an opinion that another person may not share.

THE SERVANT

by S.T. Semyonov

I.

Gerasim returned to Moscow just at a time when it was hardest to find work, a short while before Christmas, when a man sticks even to a poor job in the expectation of a present. For three weeks the peasant lad had been going about in vain seeking a position.

He stayed with relatives and friends from his village, and although he had not yet suffered great want, it disheartened him that he, a strong young man, should go without work.

Gerasim had lived in Moscow from early boyhood. When still a mere child, he had gone to work in a brewery as bottle-washer, and later as a lower servant in a house. In the last two years he had been in a merchant's employ, and would still have held that position, had he not been summoned back to his village for military duty. However, he had not been drafted. It seemed dull to him in the village, he was not used to the country life, so he decided he would rather count the stones in Moscow than stay there.

Every minute it was getting to be more and more irk-some for him to be tramping the streets in idleness. Not a stone did he leave unturned in his efforts to secure any sort of work. He plagued all of his acquaintances, he even held up people on the street and asked them if they knew of a situation—all in vain.

Finally Gerasim could no longer bear being a burden on his people. Some of them were annoyed by his coming to them; and others had suffered unpleasantness from their masters on his account. He was altogether at a loss what to do. Sometimes he would go a whole day without eating.

II.

One day Gerasim betook himself to a friend from his village, who lived at the extreme outer edge of Moscow, near Sokolnik. The man was coachman to a merchant by the name of Sharov, in whose service he had been for many years. He had ingratiated himself with his master, so that Sharov trusted him absolutely and gave every sign of holding him in high favor. It was the man's glib tongue, chiefly, that had gained him his master's confidence. He told on all the servants, and Sharov valued him for it.

Gerasim approached and greeted him. The coachman gave his guest a proper reception, served him with tea and something to eat, and asked him how he was doing.

"Very badly, Yegor Danilych," said Gerasim. "I've been without a job for weeks."

"Didn't you ask your old employer to take you back?"

"I did."

"He wouldn't take you again?"

"The position was filled already."

"That's it. That's the way you young fellows are. You serve your employers so-so, and when you leave your jobs, you usually have muddied up the way back to them. You ought to serve your masters so that they will think a lot of you, and when you come again, they will not refuse you, but rather dismiss the man who has taken your place."

"How can a man do that? In these days there aren't any employers like that, and we aren't exactly angels, either."

"What's the use of wasting words? I just want to tell you about myself. If for some reason or other I should ever have to leave this place and go home, not only would Mr. Sharov, if I came back, take me on again without a word, but he would be glad to, too."

Gerasim sat there downcast. He saw his friend was boasting, and it occurred to him to gratify him.

"I know it," he said. "But it's hard to find men like you, Yegor Danilych. If you were a poor worker, your master would not have kept you twelve years."

Yegor smiled. He liked the praise.

"That's it," he said. "If you were to live and serve as I do, you wouldn't be out of work for months and months."

Gerasim made no reply.

Yegor was summoned to his master.

"Wait a moment," he said to Gerasim. "I'll be right back."

"Very well."

III.

Yegor came back and reported that inside of half an hour he would have to have the horses harnessed, ready to drive his master to town. He lighted his pipe and took several turns in the room. Then he came to a halt in front of Gerasim.

"Listen, my boy," he said, "if you want, I'll ask my master to take you as a servant here."

"Does he need a man?"

"We have one, but he's not much good. He's getting old, and it's very hard for him to do the work. It's lucky for us that the neighborhood isn't a lively one and the police don't make a fuss about things being kept just so, else the old man couldn't manage to keep the place clean enough for them."

"Oh, if you can, then please do say a word for me, Yegor Danilych. I'll pray for you all my life. I can't stand being without work any longer."

"All right, I'll speak for you. Come again tomorrow, and in the meantime take this ten-kopek piece. It may come in handy."

"Thanks, Yegor Danilych. Then you *will* try for me? Please do me the favor."

"All right. I'll try for you."

Gerasim left, and Yegor harnessed up his horses. Then he put on his coachman's habit, and drove up to the front door. Mr. Sharov stepped out of the house, seated himself in the sleigh, and the horses galloped off. He attended to his business in town and returned home. Yegor, observing that his master was in a good humour, said to him:

"Yegor Fiodorych, I have a favor to ask of you."

"What is it?"

"There's a young man from my village here, a good boy. He's without a job."

"Well?"

"Wouldn't you take him?"

"What do I want him for?"

"Use him as man of all work round the place."

"How about Polikarpych?"

"What good is he? It's about time you dismissed him."

"That wouldn't be fair. He has been with me so many years. I can't let him go just so, without any cause."

"Supposing he *has* worked for you for years. He didn't work for nothing. He got paid for it. He's certainly saved up a few dollars for his old age."

"Saved up! How could he? From what? He's not alone in the world. He has a wife to support, and she has to eat and drink also."

"His wife earns money, too, at day's work as charwoman."

"A lot she could have made! Enough for *kvas*."

"Why should you care about Polikarpych and his wife? To tell you the truth, he's a very poor servant. Why should you throw your money away on him? He never shovels the snow away on time, or does anything right. And when it comes his turn to be night watchman, he slips away at least ten times a night. It's too cold for him. You'll see, some day, because of him, you will have trouble with the police. The quarterly inspector will descend on us, and it won't be so agreeable for you to be responsible for Polikarpych."

"Still, it's pretty rough. He's been with me fifteen years. And to treat him that way in his old age—it would be a sin."

"A sin! Why, what harm would you be doing him? He won't starve. He'll go to the almshouse. It will be better for him, too, to be quiet in his old age."

Sharov reflected.

"All right," he said finally. "Bring your friend here. I'll see what I can do."

"Do take him, sir. I'm so sorry for him. He's a good boy, and he's been without work for such a long time. I know he'll do his work well and serve you faithfully. On account of having to report for military duty, he lost his last position. If it hadn't been for that, his master would never have let him go."

IV.

The next evening Gerasim came again and asked:

"Well, could you do anything for me?"

"Something, I believe. First let's have some tea. Then we'll go see my master."

Even tea had no allurements for Gerasim. He was eager for a decision; but under the compulsion of politeness to his host, he gulped down two glasses of tea, and then they betook themselves to Sharov.

Sharov asked Gerasim where he had lived before and what work he could do. Then he told him he was prepared to engage him as man of all work, and he should come back the next day ready to take the place.

Gerasim was fairly stunned by the great stroke of fortune. So overwhelming was his joy that his legs would scarcely carry him. He went to the coachman's room, and Yegor said to him:

"Well, my lad, see to it that you do your work right, so that I shan't have to be ashamed of you. You know what masters are like. If you go wrong once, they'll be at you forever after with their fault-finding, and never give you peace."

"Don't worry about that, Yegor Danilych."

"Well—well."

Gerasim took leave, crossing the yard to go out by the gate. Polikarpych's rooms gave on the yard, and a broad beam of light from the window fell across Gerasim's way. He was curious as to get a glimpse of his future home, but the panes were all frosted over, and it was impossible to peep through. However, he could hear what the people inside were saying.

"What will we do now?" was said in a woman's voice.

"I don't know, I don't know," a man, undoubtedly Polikarpych, replied. "Go begging, I suppose."

"That's all we can do. There's nothing else left," said the woman. "Oh, we poor people, what a miserable life we lead. We work and work from early morning till late at night, day after day, and when we get old, then it's, 'Away with you!'"

307

"What can we do? Our master is not one of us. It wouldn't be worth the while to say much to him about it. He cares only for his own advantage."

"All the masters are so mean. They don't think of any one but themselves. It doesn't occur to them that we work for them honestly and faithfully for years, and use up our best strength in their service. They're afraid to keep us a year longer, even though we've got all the strength we need to do their work. If we weren't strong enough, we'd go of our own accord."

"The master's not so much to blame as his coachman. Yegor Danilych wants to get a good position for his friend."

"Yes, he's a serpent. He knows how to wag his tongue. You wait, you foul-mouthed beast, I'll get even with you. I'll go straight to the master and tell him how the fellow deceives him, how he steals the hay and fodder. I'll put it down in writing, and he can convince himself how the fellow lies about us all."

"Don't, old woman. Don't sin."

"Sin? Isn't what I said all true? I know to a dot what I'm saying, and I mean to tell it straight out to the master. He should see with his own eyes. Why not? What can we do now anyhow? Where shall we go? He's ruined us, ruined us."

The old woman burst out sobbing.

Gerasim heard all that, and it stabbed him like a dagger. He realized what misfortune he would be bringing the old people, and it made him sick at heart. He stood there a long while, saddened, lost in thought, then he turned and went back into the coachman's room.

"Ah, you forgot something?"

"No, Yegor Danilych." Gerasim stammered out, "I've come—listen—I want to thank you ever and ever so much—for the way you received me—and—and all the trouble you took for me—but—I can't take the place."

"What! What does that mean?"

"Nothing. I don't want the place. I will look for another one for myself."

Yegor flew into a rage.

"Did you mean to make a fool of me, did you, you idiot? You come here so meek—'Try for me, do try for me'—and then you refuse to take the place. You rascal, you have disgraced me!"

Gerasim found nothing to say in reply. He reddened, and lowered his eyes. Yegor turned his back scornfully and said nothing more.

Then Gerasim quietly picked up his cap and left the coachman's room. He crossed the yard rapidly, went out by the gate, and hurried off down the street. He felt happy and lighthearted.

1. Which genre of fiction is this piece?

   a. fantasy
   b. realistic
   c. mystery
   d. action

2. Why does the author include the Roman Numerals in the text?

   a. The author uses them to show when the action is taking place.
   b. The author uses them to indicate where the action is taking place.
   c. The author uses them to show which character is the focus of the text.
   d. The author uses them to indicate that time has passed by.

3. What is S.T. Semyonov's purpose in writing "The Servant"?

   a. to persuade readers that servants are important people
   b. to inform readers about life in Moscow at Christmas time
   c. to communicate a message about treating people well
   d. to entertain readers with a very humorous account

4. After returning to Moscow, the main problem Gerasim faces is that he

   a. is unable to find a job.
   b. doesn't know anyone.
   c. does not know the city.
   d. is homesick for his village.

5. Why had Gerasim left his job working for a merchant?

   a. He was tired of working for his employer.
   b. He had to go home for military service.
   c. He was fired for not being a good worker.
   d. He had to go home to help his parents.

6. The author writes that Gerasim "plagued all of his acquaintances, he even held up people on the street and asked them if they knew of a situation—all in vain." As used in this sentence, the word, "plagued," means

   a. made very ill.
   b. bothered incessantly.
   c. ignored.
   d. yelled at.

7. How did Yegor Danilyich ingratiate himself with his master, Mr. Sharov?

   a. He worked harder than anyone else.
   b. He told on all the other servants.
   c. He was always completely honest.
   d. He had a very good sense of humor.

8. The author writes that Gerasim "saw his friend was boasting, and it occurred to him to gratify him." What is he inferring through Gerasim's reaction?

   a. People who boast like to be flattered.
   b. Boastful people are interested in others.
   c. Gerasim hated to listen to his friend
   d. Gerasim wanted to give a present to Yegov.

9. What conclusion can you draw from the reaction of Polikarpych and his wife to the news that they have been fired?

   a. They have not worked long for Mr. Sharov.
   b. They can choose whether or not to leave.
   c. They are on good terms with Mr. Sharov.
   d. They have no power over their situation.

10. In which point of view is this story written?

   a. first person
   b. third person limited
   c. third person omniscient
   d. objective

11. What is the climax of the story?

   a. Polikarpych and his wife find out that they have been fired.
   b. Mr. Sharov agrees to offer a job to Gerasim.
   c. Gerasim refuses to take the job and walks away feeling happy.
   d. Yegor Danilych tells Gerasim that he has a job.

310

12. What does Mr. Sharov's reaction to Yegor's proposal say to you about the culture in which they were living? Use examples from the story to support your ideas.

One possible answer:

This was a time and place where people who did not have wealth or position had little or no power. Those who had material or other types of power held little regard for those who did not. Sharov was willing to let this couple—who had worked hard for him for many years and now were in their old age—go. They were much less able to take care of themselves than a younger person would have been, and yet Sharov was easily convinced to fire them. Even though he enumerates all the good reasons that he should not fire them and even calls it a sin, he agrees to do it anyway. There is a general sense that people who have little deserve their fate.

Students should clearly state their ideas and support them with examples from the story.

13. Compare and contrast the characters of Gerasim and Yegor Danilych. Include examples from the piece to support your ideas.

One possible answer:

They are both from the same village and must work for other people. However, Gerasim is without a job while Yegor has been working for the same person for many years. Yegor is a mean-spirited person who has little feeling for others. He likes to be praised and, though he is helpful to Gerasim, the feeling is that he will use this favor for power over his friend in the future. He seems to care nothing for the plight of Polikarpych and his wife, even though they will be fired just before Christmas, a time that most people try to be kind to others. Gerasim turns out to be a kind-hearted person. Though he had been desperate for work, when he hears the older couple wondering what they will do, he realizes that he cannot turn them out of their job and home. He turns down the job and feels far better than he had during the past weeks.

Students should describe details about both characters and then use this information to compare and contrast them.

14. How does the author let the reader know what the different characters are feeling? Show how he does this for each character and give an example for each.

One possible answer:

The author tells the reader directly what Gerasim is thinking and feeling. He also uses dialogue to describe Gerasim. Examples:

- *Every minute it was getting to be more and more irk-some for him to be tramping the streets in idleness.*
- *"Very badly, Yegor Danilych," said Gerasim. "I've been without a job for weeks."*

The author uses direct description and dialogue to show what Yegov is feeling and thinking. Examples:

- *"That's it. That's the way you young fellows are. You serve your employers so-so, and when you leave your jobs, you usually have muddied up the way back to them."*
- *Yegor smiled. He liked the praise.*

The author uses dialogue to tell about the other characters.

- *Mr. Sharov: "That wouldn't be fair. He has been with me so many years. I can't let him go just so, without any cause."*
- *Polikarpych: "I don't know, I don't know," a man, undoubtedly Polikarpych, replied. "Go begging, I suppose."*
- *Polikapyrch's wife: "All the masters are so mean. They don't think of any one but themselves. It doesn't occur to them that we work for them honestly and faithfully for years, and use up our best strength in their service. They're afraid to keep us a year longer, even though we've got all the strength we need to do their work."*

Each student should describe how the author communicates the thoughts and feelings of the characters and write at least one example for each.

15. Evaluate "The Servant." What qualities does it have that make it an effective or ineffective story? Use specific examples from the story to support your ideas.

Students who appreciate this story may value the realistic nature of its characters and the setting. They may also appreciate the ending of the story, when Gerasim feels far better than he did in the beginning because he has helped other people when they needed it. Also, the character of Yegor Danilych at first appears to be helpful and goodhearted but, as events unfold, it becomes clear that he is a vain person who is only really out for himself. There is satisfaction in the end when Gerasim refuses the job and walks away. Whatever the response, each student should use examples from the story to support his or her ideas.

FROM *WAR OF THE WORLDS*

by H.G. Wells

Then came the night of the first falling star. It was seen early in the morning, rushing over Winchester eastward, a line of flame high in the atmosphere. Hundreds must have seen it, and taken it for an ordinary falling star. Albin described it as leaving a greenish streak behind it that glowed for some seconds. Denning, our greatest authority on meteorites, stated that the height of its first appearance was about ninety or one hundred miles. It seemed to him that it fell to earth about one hundred miles east of him.

I was at home at that hour and writing in my study; and although my French windows face towards Ottershaw and the blind was up (for I loved in those days to look up at the night sky), I saw nothing of it. Yet this strangest of all things that ever came to earth from outer space must have fallen while I was sitting there, visible to me had I only looked up as it passed. Some of those who saw its flight say it traveled with a hissing sound. I myself heard nothing of that. Many people in Berkshire, Surrey, and Middlesex must have seen the fall of it, and, at most, have thought that another meteorite had descended. No one seems to have troubled to look for the fallen mass that night.

But very early in the morning poor Ogilvy, who had seen the shooting star and who was persuaded that a meteorite lay somewhere on the common between Horsell, Ottershaw, and Woking, rose early with the idea of finding it. Find it he did, soon after dawn, and not far from the sand pits. An enormous hole had been made by the impact of the projectile, and the sand and gravel had been flung violently in every direction over the heath, forming heaps visible a mile and a half away. The heather was on fire eastward, and a thin blue smoke rose against the dawn.

The Thing itself lay almost entirely buried in sand, amidst the scattered splinters of a fir tree it had shivered to fragments in its descent. The uncovered part had the appearance of a huge cylinder, caked over and its outline softened by a thick scaly dun-colored incrustation. It had a diameter of about thirty yards. He approached the mass, surprised at the size and more so at the shape, since most meteorites are rounded more or less completely. It was, however, still so hot from its flight through the air as to forbid his near approach. A stirring noise within its cylinder he ascribed to the unequal cooling of its surface; for at that time it had not occurred to him that it might be hollow.

He remained standing at the edge of the pit that the Thing had made for itself, staring at its strange appearance, astonished chiefly at its unusual shape and color, and dimly perceiving even then some evidence of design in its arrival. The early morning was wonderfully still, and the sun, just clearing the pine trees towards Weybridge, was already warm. He did not remember hearing any birds that morning, there was certainly no breeze stirring, and the only sounds were the faint movements from within the cindery cylinder. He was all alone on the common.

Then suddenly he noticed with a start that some of the grey clinker, the ashy incrustation that covered the meteorite, was falling off the circular edge of the end. It was dropping off in flakes and raining down upon the sand. A large piece suddenly came off and fell with a sharp noise that brought his heart into his mouth.

For a minute he scarcely realized what this meant, and, although the heat was excessive, he clambered down into the pit close to the bulk to see the Thing more clearly. He fancied even then that the cooling of the body might account for this, but what disturbed that idea was the fact that the ash was falling only from the end of the cylinder.

And then he perceived that, very slowly, the circular top of the cylinder was rotating on its body. It was such a gradual movement that he discovered it only through noticing that a black mark that had been near him five minutes ago was now at the other side of the circumference. Even then he scarcely understood what this indicated, until he heard a muffled grating sound and saw the black mark jerk forward an inch or so. Then the thing came upon him in a flash. The cylinder was artificial—hollow—with an end that screwed out! Something within the cylinder was unscrewing the top!

"Good heavens!" said Ogilvy. "There's a man in it—men in it! Half roasted to death! Trying to escape!"

At once, with a quick mental leap, he linked the Thing with the flash upon Mars.

The thought of the confined creature was so dreadful to him that he forgot the heat and went forward to the cylinder to help turn. But luckily the dull radiation arrested him before he could burn his hands on the still-glowing metal. At that he stood irresolute for a moment, then turned, scrambled out of the pit, and set off running wildly into Woking. The time then must have been somewhere about six o'clock. He met a waggoner and tried to make him understand, but the tale he told and his appearance were so wild—his hat had fallen off in the pit—that the man simply drove on. He was equally unsuccessful with the potman who was just unlocking the doors of the public-house by Horsell Bridge. The fellow thought he was a lunatic at large and made an unsuccessful attempt to shut him into the taproom. That sobered him a

little; and when he saw Henderson, the London journalist, in his garden, he called over the palings and made himself understood.

"Henderson," he called, "you saw that shooting star last night?"

"Well?" said Henderson.

"It's out on Horsell Common now."

"Good Lord!" said Henderson. "Fallen meteorite! That's good."

"But it's something more than a meteorite. It's a cylinder—an artificial cylinder, man! And there's something inside."

Henderson stood up with his spade in his hand.

"What's that?" he said. He was deaf in one ear.

Ogilvy told him all that he had seen. Henderson was a minute or so taking it in. Then he dropped his spade, snatched up his jacket, and came out into the road. The two men hurried back at once to the common, and found the cylinder still lying in the same position. But now the sounds inside had ceased, and a thin circle of bright metal showed between the top and the body of the cylinder. Air was either entering or escaping at the rim with a thin, sizzling sound.

They listened, rapped on the scaly burnt metal with a stick, and, meeting with no response, they both concluded the man or men inside must be insensible or dead.

Of course the two were quite unable to do anything. They shouted consolation and promises, and went off back to the town again to get help. One can imagine them, covered with sand, excited and disordered, running up the little street in the bright sunlight just as the shop folks were taking down their shutters and people were opening their bedroom windows. Henderson went into the railway station at once, in order to telegraph the news to London. The newspaper articles had prepared men's minds for the reception of the idea.

By eight o'clock a number of boys and unemployed men had already started for the common to see the "dead men from Mars." That was the form the story took. I heard of it first from my newspaper boy about a quarter to nine when I went out to get my *Daily Chronicle*. I was naturally startled, and lost no time in going out and across the Ottershaw bridge to the sand pits.

1. Which genre of fiction is this piece?

   a. romance
   b. historical
   c. science fiction
   d. mystery

2. In which point of view is this story written?

   a. first person
   b. third person limited
   c. third person omniscient
   d. objective

3. The author writes in the second paragraph, "Yet this strangest of all things that ever came to earth from outer space must have fallen while I was sitting there, visible to me had I only looked up as it passed." This is an example of

   a. hyperbole.
   b. flashback.
   c. alliteration.
   d. foreshadowing.

4. When "poor Ogilvy" walked out on the common to find the meteorite, he

   a. found a large meteorite that had made a big hole.
   b. found a large cylinder about thirty years in diameter.
   c. was not able to find any evidence of the falling star.
   d. encountered the London journalist, Henderson.

5. Which of the following elements does the author most use to communicate the plot of the story?

   a. dialogue
   b. description
   c. thoughts
   d. foreshadowing

6. Which of the following **best** expresses the mood of the story?

   a. mysterious
   b. morose
   c. hilarious
   d. frightening

7. What is the author inferring when he says that Ogilvy "linked the Thing with the flash upon Mars?"

   a. Ogilvy is a very smart person and brilliant scientist.
   b. Ogilvy is convinced that the cylinder is a strange sort of meteorite.
   c. Ogilvy thinks that the launching of the cylinder had caused the flash.
   d. Ogilvy thinks that the flash upon Mars was caused by a meteorite.

8. The narrator states, "He remained standing at the edge of the pit that the Thing had made for itself, staring at its strange appearance, astonished chiefly at its unusual shape and color, and dimly perceiving even then some evidence of design in its arrival." What does this passage imply?

   a. Ogilvy realizes that the Thing could be very dangerous.
   b. Ogilvy has remembered that he is there all by himself.
   c. Ogilvy is surprised that the Thing looks just like a meteorite.
   d. Ogilvy is beginning to suspect that someone made the Thing.

9. Why is the heat excessive around the cylinder and the heather to the east on fire?

   a. The friction from the landing cylinder caused the heat.
   b. The heat was caused by the size of the cylinder.
   c. It is not clear from the story why there is heat and fire.
   d. It is an extremely hot and sunny day and the sand is too hot.

10. What is the significance of the following passage?

    And then he perceived that, very slowly, the circular top of the cylinder was rotating on its body. It was such a gradual movement that he discovered it only through noticing that a black mark that had been near him five minutes ago was now at the other side of the circumference. Even then he scarcely understood what this indicated, until he heard a muffled grating sound and saw the black mark jerk forward an inch or so.

    a. The Thing is cooling very rapidly.
    b. The Thing is actually a meteorite.
    c. There must be someone or something inside.
    d. It seems that the Thing is actually alive.

317

11. The author writes, "But luckily the dull radiation arrested him before he could burn his hands on the still-glowing metal." As used in this sentence, the word, "arrested," means

   a. stopped.
   b. took to jail.
   c. hurt.
   d. frightened.

12. When Ogilvy tries to tell people about what he has found, the first two ignore him or think he is crazy. One tries to lock him up in the taproom. What factors do you think led the two men in the story to assume that Ogilvy was insane and to not take him seriously? What does this tell you about people's perceptions of other people? Answer the questions about the story and include your own experience if appropriate.

One possible answer:

The main factor that led the two men to react badly to Ogilvy was first of all the fantastic nature of his story. Neither of them was likely to believe that there might be an artificial machine that had landed from outer space. The other factor that added to the problem was Ogilvy's appearance. He was disheveled, looked wild, and must have been very excited. The first two men who saw him were persuaded by his outward appearance that his story was not true. This is a familiar scenario, one in which we often make judgments about others based on how they look.

Students should state the factors that led the two men not to take Ogilvy seriously. Each student should declare what he or she thinks this tells them about people's perceptions of others. If students know of examples from their own experience of this type of reaction, they should include references to it as part of their answers.

13. Describe what you have learned about the character of the narrator.

One possible answer:

The narrator states at the beginning that he is interested in the night sky. When he states that he barely missed seeing or hearing the falling star, he implies that he is connected to the event nonetheless. The fact that he has taken the time to relate the story in great detail also shows that he is intimately involved with the event and the characters around it. To have gotten his story he must have taken the time to speak to Ogilvy or others. Finally, at the end of the passage, the narrator says that as soon as he heard about the "dead men from Mars," he immediately went out to see for himself. He is clearly a curious person who wants to know firsthand about what is happening.

Students should use the text to draw conclusions about the narrator's character.

14. What is the reaction of Ogilvy and then later of Henderson to the situation with the Thing? What do they see as their role? Do they ever worry about their own safety? Use examples from the text to support your ideas.

One possible answer:

Ogilvy and Henderson were only thinking of helping out whatever or whoever might be trapped inside the Thing. They saw their role as a helping one. When Ogilvy thought that there might have been a man inside trying to escape, he quickly ran up to the cylinder to try to help turn, but was unable to do so due to the intense heat. When he returned with Henderson, they rapped on the cylinder to determine whether or not there would be a response. Then, when they realized that they couldn't do anything, they "shouted consolation and promises," meaning that they would have done whatever they could to go and get help. Neither of them ever really considered that the occupants of the cylinder could be dangerous to them.

15. Evaluate this excerpt from "War of the Worlds." In what ways does the author keep you interested in the story? Are there elements that you think could be stronger?

Students who appreciate the story may comment that the author uses the plot to keep the reader's interest. He does this by slowly revealing a bit at a time what is taking place. He does this without giving away the whole story, keeps the plot veiled in mystery and, thus, encourages the reader to want to know what is going to happen next. Some students may wish that the story was more exciting, that it moved faster. Also, Wells uses description in great detail to give the reader a clear and vivid picture of the setting of the story and to describe what is taking place.

Question 1	Distinguishing Among Different Genres of Fiction
Question 2	Analyzing Point of View
Question 3	Analyzing Figurative Language
Question 4	Analyzing Conflict, Plot, and Setting
Question 5	Analyzing Author's Craft
Question 6	Analyzing Development of Tone and Mood
Question 7	Making Inferences
Question 8	Drawing Conclusions
Question 9	Analyzing Cause and Effect
Question 10	Analyzing Conflict, Plot, and Setting
Question 11	Analyzing Diction: Connotation/Denotation
Question 12	Analyzing Character
Question 13	Analyzing Character
Question 14	Analyzing Character
Question 15	Evaluating Quality of Literature

Made in the USA
Lexington, KY
27 June 2016